MW01170071

Norman Mailer Revisited

Twayne's United States Authors Series

Warren French, Editor
University College of Swansea, Wales

TUSAS 322

Norman Mailer
©1992 Jerry Bauer

Norman Mailer Revisited

Robert Merrill

University of Nevada, Reno

Twayne Publishers ■ New York

Maxwell Macmillan Canada ■ Toronto

Maxwell Macmillan International ■ New York Oxford Singapore Sydney

Norman Mailer Revisited
Robert Merrill

Twayne Publishers   Maxwell Macmillan Canada, Inc.
Macmillan Publishing Company   1200 Eglinton Avenue East
866 Third Avenue   Suite 200
New York, New York 10022   Don Mills, Ontario M3C 3N1

Macmillan Publishing Company is part of the Maxwell Communications
Group of Companies.

Library of Congress Cataloging-in-Publication Data

Merrill, Robert, 1944-
    Norman Mailer revisited / Robert Merrill.
        p. cm. – (Twayne's United States authors series ; TUSAS 322)
    Includes bibliographical references and index.
    ISBN 0-8057-3967-X (alk. paper)
    1. Mailer, Norman – Criticism and interpretation. I. Title. II. Series.
PS3525.A4152Z774   1992
813'.54 – dc20   92-7282
                                                          CIP

The paper used in this publication meets the minimum requirements of
American National Standard for Information Sciences – Permanence of
Paper for Printed Library Materials, ANSI Z39.48-1984.

10 9 8 7 6 5 4 3 2 1

Printed in the United States of America.

To Dotson and the kitties

Contents

Preface   ix
Acknowledgments   xv
Chronology   xvii

Chapter One
Mailer as Man and Legend   1

Chapter Two
The Naked and the Dead: The Beast and the Seer in Man   11

Chapter Three
The Deer Park: The Rare Tenderness of Tragedy   31

Chapter Four
Mailer as Fabulist: The Novels of the 1960s   61

Chapter Five
Mailer's Miscellanies: The Art of Self-Revelation   83

Chapter Six
The Armies of the Night: The Education of Norman Mailer   105

Chapter Seven
After *Armies:* Mailer's More Recent Nonfiction   129

Chapter Eight
The Executioner's Song: Mailer's Sad Comedy   151

Chapter Nine
Mailer as Storyteller: The Novels of the 1980s   179

Chapter Ten
Mailer's Career: A Brief Review   209

Notes and References   213
Selected Bibliography   231
Index   239

Preface

More than 10 years ago I began this preface by remarking, "It has not been easy to avoid Norman Mailer these last fifteen years." My purpose was to contrast Mailer's notoriety with the lack of consensus about his literary achievement. As I think this contrast still prevails today, I begin this new preface by suggesting that it has not been easy to avoid Norman Mailer these last 25 years. Since 1965 he has published 27 books; dramatized *The Deer Park* off-Broadway; written, directed, and starred in three of his own movies, while writing the script for *The Executioner's Song* (1982) and directing his own adaptation of *Tough Guys Don't Dance* (1987); appeared on every television talk show this side of the Iron Curtain; run for mayor of New York City; taken up three entire issues of *Harper's* with his accounts of the 1967 March on the Pentagon, the 1968 political conventions, and women's liberation, respectively; received the ultimate acknowledgment of a *Playboy* interview; spent a few well-publicized days in jail; testified in behalf of a violent ex-convict; organized the 1986 International PEN Conference; allowed himself to be interviewed by numerous magazines interested in his six marriages and nine children; and aroused discussion in magazines and journals as diverse as *People* and *Partisan Review*. No fewer than 22 books have been published on his life and works. Like one of his own favorites, Muhammad Ali, Mailer has become a household word.

Honors have come Mailer's way in these years: election to the National Institute of Arts and Letters (1967) and the American Academy of Arts and Sciences (1970); the 1969 Pulitzer Prize in general nonfiction and the 1969 National Book Award in arts and letters (both for *The Armies of the Night*); the 1980 Pulitzer Prize in fiction (for *The Executioner's Song*); and the presidency of the American PEN Center in 1986. He is rumored to have been one of four writers considered for the 1969 Nobel Prize in literature (the others: André Malraux, W. H. Auden, and Samuel Beckett, the winner). And there have been more material rewards: Mailer is supposed to have made at least $500,000 with *An American Dream* (1965) and $450,000 with *Of a Fire on the Moon* (1970); his work on *The Executioner's Song* (1979) netted him $500,000; and he received a $1 million contract from Little, Brown for *Ancient Evenings* (1983) and its projected sequels.[1] Mailer's career has taken on the appearance of the American success story he attacks in so many of his own books.

Curiously, however, Mailer's work is still not generally admired. He has won awards, made money, and publicized himself with remarkable success. *The Armies of the Night* (1968) won many converts among his critics, *The Executioner's Song* was one of his best-received books, and even the controversial *Ancient Evenings* was thought by many to be (finally) the major novel Mailer has been promising since the late 1950s. Yet too many of Mailer's friends and foes tend to agree that his achievement is not "literary." Much writing on Mailer concerns the man, his ideas, or his relationship to his period (his "representativeness"). Mailer's critical reputation is therefore suspect, for a writer's work must be respected for its artistic value if it is to enjoy a critical status commensurate with its popular success or notoriety.

To illustrate Mailer's anomalous critical reputation, I would ask who is being described in the following passage: "[He] lacks discipline, intelligence, honesty and a sense of the novel. His rhythms are erratic, his sense of character is nil, and he is as pretentious as a rich whore, as sentimental as a lollypop. Yet I think he has a large talent. His literary energy is enormous, and he had enough of a wild eye to go along with his instincts and so become the first figure for a new generation."[2] It happens that "he" is Jack Kerouac, not Norman Mailer. (The critic is, of course, Mailer himself; how many academic critics would say that a writer is "as pretentious as a rich whore"?) But anyone who has read the published commentary on Mailer's works may be excused for thinking the quotation referred to Mailer. What he says about Kerouac is often said about Mailer himself: that he lacks everything but "talent." Somehow, the argument goes, there is *something* in Mailer, some "power" that he has never really harnessed to an appropriate literary form. It is a pity, but Mailer's example is that of "a great gift squandered."[3]

Three crucial assumptions are at work in many discussions of Mailer: (a) his ideas are more interesting than his art, or in fact dominate his art; (b) his personality is more interesting than anything he has written, especially as he has become so "representative" a figure; and (c) he has squandered his great gift on works that fail precisely because Mailer is too little the conscious artist.

Mailer's ideas surely engage more commentators than the books in which they are expressed. Mailer is often treated as "a literary sociologist,"[4] "a literary terrorist,"[5] even, in one of his phases, a "dotty messiah" ("What Might Have Been," 127); he is treated as almost everything except a major literary artist. Even his much-admired first novel, *The Naked and the Dead* (1948), did not inspire its reviewers or subsequent critics to congratulate him on his artistic success; instead, there was much talk about Mailer's critique of American society in general and the American army in particular. Early criticism on Mailer almost always reflects the belief that his social and political ideas are more interesting than his individual works. Thus, we get Edmund Fuller writing on Mailer's sexual notions, Frederick Hoffman and George Schrader on Mailer's advocacy of hip, and, most impressively, Diana Trilling on Mailer's moral development.[6] Trilling's essay is perhaps the most discouraging of these studies, for it is one thing for an unsympathetic critic like Fuller to have little respect for Mailer's art, and quite another for a sympathetic critic like Trilling to concede that Mailer's role as a writer is "more messianic than creative" and that he is really an "anti-artist." More recent critics avoid such extreme judgments but continue to focus on Mailer's "intellectual career," not his pretensions as an artist.[7]

Critics are just as often fascinated by Mailer's public image. Harvey Swados once deplored the fact that Mailer was cashing in on the current "cult of personality" in American letters, thus receiving more attention than he deserved.[8] There is another side to such popularity, however. Because they receive this *kind* of attention, Mailer's works are seldom judged on their literary merits. It is Mailer the man who interests the media. We have been exposed to Mailer interviews in such publications as *Mademoiselle*[9]; we have been informed of Mailer's domestic problems, his court trials, his testimony in behalf of another man's "pornographic" novel[10]; we have been provided with lengthy accounts in *Life, Look,* and *Esquire* of how Mailer lives now.[11] Mailer the man is so much a part of our culture that it is hardly surprising critics are quick to emphasize the figure behind the books. In doing so, however, they usually fail to illuminate the nature of Mailer's art.

Dissatisfaction with this art often lies behind the detours critics take in discussing Mailer's philosophy and personality. Implicit in all the discussions just cited, for example, is the assumption that Mailer's books will not sustain detailed aesthetic contemplation. This assumption is to be expected of readers who do not really value Mailer's books, but it is disturbing to find sympathetic critics like Richard Foster arguing that Mailer, for all his virtues, "is not the finished and fully responsible writer-as-*artist* that many of his peers are." This is a curious argument from someone who sees Mailer as our most impressive contemporary novelist, for it is finally insufficient to praise Mailer, as Foster does, for "the obstinate vigor of [his] restless creativity," for "his ambitious fluency of expression," and for "his ideas and his humanity"[12] – as if these qualities were divorced from successful art! One must praise Mailer – wherever he deserves it – for exhibiting these qualities in realized works of art. The corollary, of course is that one must also point out those occasions where Mailer fails to achieve anything like these effects. Only by making these aesthetic distinctions will we ever arrive at a just assessment of Mailer's importance as a writer.

It should be clear that my intention is to make just such an assessment. Unlike most other critics, I focus on questions of literary structure rather than theme alone and avoid biographical speculation almost entirely. Robert Solotaroff's book remains the best thematic study, though Richard Poirier, Tony Tanner, and Michael Cowan are still essential early critics and more recent books by Robert Begiebing and Joseph Wenke trace patterns crucial to any serious thematic analysis.[13] Robert Lucid and J. Michael Lennon are the biographical critics who prove that there is much to be learned from the better critics who do not share my formalist bias.[14] Nonetheless, my own interest is in Mailer as what Lennon calls "a connoisseur of narrative forms."[15] In each chapter I engage the generic and structural questions that seem to me most relevant. Whereas others engage such questions sporadically as they pursue their own conclusions, I address them as central to a just assessment of Mailer's achievement.

In the chapters that follow, then, I am largely concerned with the aesthetic structure of Mailer's individual works, both his novels and his works of nonfiction. Necessarily, I often focus on the question of a work's unity or coherence. I am aware that unity and coherence are not synonymous with "success" or "greatness." Indeed, literary structure can be seen as irrelevant to a writer's success or failure, as Poirier seems to suggest in *The Performing Self:* "The literary structures that critics are so happy to locate are not so much equivalent to performance as merely the stage upon which it can take place. For a writer of great energy, structure may even be the element against which he is performing." Poirier argues that literary criticism places far too much emphasis on structure and thus on the "work," "the book or poem," as opposed to "writing as an act," or "performance." It happens that Mailer is one of his favorite examples of a contemporary performer, one whose "writing" is much more interesting than whatever can be made of his "works."[16] It also happens that Poirier is one of Mailer's most perceptive and sympathetic critics. It is therefore a bit embarrassing to suggest that coherence may not *equal* success, but structure is still a great deal more than the mechanical "stage" Poirier invokes. Anyone who admires Mailer does so in part (usually in large part) because his works exhibit the local energy and stylistic resources Poirier is always pointing to. But these local successes are not isolated beauties in a general ruin; the foundations of Mailer's works are solid enough, much sturdier than even Mailer's friendlier critics acknowledge. I assume that the best answer to those who chide Mailer for his structural incoherences is not that such things do not matter but that they do not exist.

My assumption is that the successful design of Mailer's better works gives point to and oversees those local instances of stylistic "energy" which contribute to the design. In any case, I say little about style and much about structure because it is structure that is underexamined and underappreciated in Mailer's books. Poirier to the contrary, I do not see how Mailer can ever achieve the reputation he deserves if this examination and appreciation are not forthcoming. For that matter, we will continue to have a very imperfect understanding of Mailer's failures unless we begin to focus on his literary designs. For better or worse, Mailer's books succeed or fail in just such aesthetic terms.

I should clarify how this second edition differs from the first. I have updated all scholarly references (including the annotated bibliography) and revised all chapters stylistically. I have recast the preface, the first chapter, the conclusion to chapter 6 (on *The Armies of the Night*), and bits and pieces of the other surviving chapters. Chapter 3 now begins with sections on *Barbary Shore* (1951) and the short fiction Mailer wrote in the years leading up to *The Deer Park* (1955). The final chapter, a review of Mailer's career, is substantially new and includes commentary on Mailer's films. The primary additions are chapters 8 and 9, in which I discuss *The Executioner's Song, Ancient Evenings,* and *Tough Guys Don't Dance* (1984). I fear that chapter 4 (on *An American Dream* and *Why Are We in Vietnam?* [1967]) is the least revised of my older chapters. Even friendly reviewers of the first edition questioned my lack of enthusiasm for the novels of the 1960s, but I find that my views are substantially unchanged. Solotaroff and I seem to be the only Mailerians who do not share Mailer's view that *An American Dream* is "perhaps my best book."[17] Should I live to do a third edition of this study, I will no doubt reconsider the matter once again.

Acknowledgments

I want to thank the editors of the following journals for allowing me to use materials that first appeared in their pages: *Western Humanities Review, Illinois Quarterly, Centennial Review, Aegis, Texas Studies in Literature and Language,* and *Critique.*

I also want to thank the following persons who read portions of this book and made useful suggestions: Robert Streeter, James E. Miller, Jr., Robert Harvey, Richard Brown, Bernard Schopen, and, most especially, my wife, Dotson. I am particularly grateful to J. Michael Lennon, whose assistance with this second edition has been indispensable. As before, my debt to Warren French, my editor, is very great. And I would again like to acknowledge the assistance of the late Sheldon Sacks, whose excellent influence is imperfectly embodied in this book.

Chronology

1923   Norman Mailer born 31 January to Isaac Barnett Mailer and Fanny Schneider Mailer in Long Branch, New Jersey.

1939   Enters Harvard as an aeronautical engineering major.

1941   Publishes "The Greatest Thing in the World" in the *Harvard Advocate*. Wins first prize in *Story* magazine's annual college contest.

1943   Graduates from Harvard.

1944   Enters the U.S. Army and serves at Leyte, Luzon, in the Pacific Ocean, and Japan.

1946   Discharged from the army and begins *The Naked and the Dead*.

1948   *The Naked and the Dead*.

1951   *Barbary Shore*.

1955   *The Deer Park*.

1959   *Advertisements for Myself*.

1963   *The Presidential Papers*.

1965   *An American Dream*.

1967   *Why Are We in Vietnam?* First performance of *The Deer Park: A Play* at the Theatre de Lys, New York City, on 31 January. Films first and second movies, *Wild 90* and *Beyond the Law*. Elected to the National Institute of Arts and Letters.

1968   *The Armies of the Night, Miami and the Siege of Chicago*. Films third movie, *Maidstone*.

1969   Wins the Pulitzer Prize and the National Book Award for *The Armies of the Night*. Awarded the honorary degree of Doctor of Letters by Rutgers University. Runs for mayor of

New York City in the Democratic primary and finishes fourth in a field of five.

1970   *Of a Fire on the Moon.* Elected to the American Academy of Arts and Sciences.

1971   *The Prisoner of Sex.*

1972   *Existential Errands. St. George and the Godfather.*

1973   *Marilyn: A Biography.*

1975   *The Fight.*

1976   *Genius and Lust: A Journey through the Major Writings of Henry Miller.*

1978   *A Transit to Narcissus.*

1979   *The Executioner's Song.*

1980   *Of Women and Their Elegance.* Wins the Pulitzer Prize in fiction for *The Executioner's Song.*

1982   *Pieces. Pontifications.* Appears in Milos Forman's *Ragtime.* Writes the script for Lawrence Schiller's film adaptation of *The Executioner's Song.*

1983   *Ancient Evenings.*

1984   *Tough Guys Don't Dance.*

1986   Organizes the International PEN Conference in New York City as president of the American PEN Center. Writes the play *Strawhead,* produced at the Actors' Studio in New York City.

1987   Writes and directs the film version of *Tough Guys Don't Dance.*

1991   *Harlot's Ghost.*

Chapter One

Mailer as Man and Legend

It may seem paradoxical to begin a study of Norman Mailer's artistic achievement by devoting a chapter – however brief – to Mailer's biography. There are several good reasons for doing so, however. The beginning student of Mailer's works deserves to know the basic facts underlying what Mailer himself refers to as his "legend."[1] Moreover, both beginning and advanced students should confront the problem of how difficult it is to apply the known facts of Mailer's life to the interpretation of his books. And even a brief review of Mailer's life will necessarily include an overview of his writing career, thus preparing readers for the critical discussions to follow.

The Early Years: 1923-59

Our major source of information on Mailer's life is, of course, Mailer himself. Since 1959 no fewer than 17 of his books have described one or more of his personal experiences, and this does not count any of the "autobiographical" novels. It is rather striking, then, that we still know next to nothing about the first 20 years of Mailer's life. Mailer almost never alludes to his childhood, and even his fictional heroes are notoriously reticent about their "formative" years. Why this should be so is something of a mystery, but Mailer offers a strong hint in *The Armies of the Night.* At one point he writes of his emotions while watching a group of young men turn in their draft cards to protest the war in Vietnam:

> [A]s they did this, a deep gloom began to work on Mailer, because a deep modesty was on its way to him, he could feel himself becoming more and more of a modest man as he stood there in the cold with his hangover, and he hated this because modesty was an old family relative, he had been born to a modest family, had been a modest boy, a modest young man, and he hated

> that, he loved the pride and the arrogance and the confidence and the ego-
> centricity he had acquired over the years, that was his force and his luxury
> and the iron in his greed, the richest sugar of his pleasure, the strength of his
> competitive force. (*AOTN*, 77)

Mailer's "modest" boyhood is clearly something he would rather
forget. The rejection of his Jewish heritage is probably crucial here,
for Mailer grew up in "the most secure Jewish environment in
America" and says that the one self-image he finds intolerable is that
of a nice Jewish boy from Brooklyn.[2] At present, however, such theories must remain speculation.

What we do know about Mailer's early years tends to suggest
that he was a model son, what we would call an "achiever." Born in
1923 to Isaac and Fanny Mailer, Mailer grew up in Brooklyn and
graduated from Boys High School in 1939. An excellent student, he
entered Harvard at 16 and earned a B.S. degree in aeronautical
engineering in 1943. While at Harvard he wrote a great deal of fiction, winning several short story contests and completing two
unpublished novels before entering the army in 1944.[3] That same
year he married Beatrice Silverman, the first of his six wives.

Mailer served in the Pacific at Leyte and Luzon before returning
home in 1946 to begin writing *The Naked and the Dead*. The publication of this novel in 1948 was almost surely the turning point in
Mailer's life. Like Melville, Mailer points to his twenty-fifth year as the
beginning of his "real" existence, for with the enormous success of
The Naked and the Dead his life changed irrevocably:

> My farewell to an average man's experience was too abrupt; never again would
> I know, in the dreary way one usually knows such things, what it was like to
> work at a dull job, or take orders from a man one hated. If I had had a career
> of that in the army, it now was done – there was nothing left in the first
> twenty-four years of my life to write about; one way or another, my life
> seemed to have been mined and melted into the long reaches of the book.
> And so I was prominent and empty, and I had to begin life again. (*AFM*, 92)

There can be little question that in 1948 Mailer did begin to refashion his life and therefore his personality. The young man who wrote
The Naked and the Dead was still modest enough to tell an inter-
viewer, "I think it's much better when people who read your book

don't know anything about you, even what you look like."[4] Eleven years later this man was saying that his major desire was to make "a revolution in the consciousness of our time" (*AFM*, 17). Obviously, something remarkable occurred in Mailer's life between 1948 and 1959.

It is easier to note this change than to specify what brought it about. Mailer discusses this period of his life at great length in *Advertisements for Myself* (1959), and so we might assume that a careful reading of this work would provide ample biographical evidence. In fact, however, the information offered in *Advertisements* is highly selective. Here we discover that Mailer worked as a scriptwriter in Hollywood during 1949-50; that he and his first wife were divorced in 1952; that he married Adele Morales in 1954; that he lived in Mexico at different times in the early 1950s; that he cofounded *The Village Voice* in 1955 and subsequently became a columnist for this Greenwich Village weekly; and that he experimented with sex and drugs, especially while writing his third novel, *The Deer Park* (1955). Beyond these bare facts, however, Mailer tells us surprisingly little abut his personal life.

Advertisements also reminds us that it was during this period that Mailer wrote two rather unpopular novels, *Barbary Shore* (1951) and *The Deer Park*, a number of short stories (collected in *Advertisements*), and one of the more important essays of the post-war period, "The White Negro" (1957). Ultimately, these are the crucial "facts" of the period in question, not only for those of us who admire Mailer's art but for Mailer himself. Mailer introduces biographical materials only when they are relevant to the growth of his ideas and/or individual works, and even then it is not always clear whether he means to argue for a direct relationship between his life and his art. Two examples should suggest the tenuous connection between what we know of Mailer's life and his published works.

One of the more revealing sections of *Advertisements* describes the composition, publication, and critical reception of *The Deer Park* (*AFM*, 228-64). In the course of this lengthy essay Mailer discloses much of what we know about his experiences in Mexico, his experiments with marijuana and peyote, and his quarrels with various New York publishers. The subject matter and tone of this piece almost seem confessional. But what does the essay really tell us about the nature of Mailer's third novel? In an interview with Mailer I once asked him to comment on my theory that *The Deer Park* is his most autobiographical novel. (I had in mind the relationship between Charley Eitel and Elena Esposito, which I took to be a fictional reworking of Mailer's second marriage.) Mailer acknowledged the "personal" sources of the book but declined to elaborate.[5] His essay on *The Deer Park* is even more reticent on this subject. This confirms that Mailer's personal "revelations," here and elsewhere, are seldom introduced to "explain" his works. In his personal essays Mailer contributes odd pieces of lore concerning his life, but these details neither constitute a "thoroughgoing autobiography" (*AFM*, 107) nor assist materially in the interpretation of his art.

The genesis of Mailer's most famous essay, "The White Negro," is an even more telling example. First published in 1957 in *Dissent* and reprinted in *Advertisements*, "The White Negro" analyzes the postwar phenomenon of the hipster, that violent American rebel whom Mailer defends in his most impassioned rhetoric. It might be argued that the whole of *Advertisements* is intended to explain Mailer's conversion to this "cause." Early sections describe his youthful commitment to first political liberalism and then revolutionary socialism; later sections trace his rejection of rationality as an adequate guide to life's complexities. Gradually, over almost 10 years, Mailer discarded his liberal and socialistic sympathies and turned to what he called an "American existentialism," roughly embodied in the hipster and characterized by a deep commitment to instinct as opposed to reason. "The White Negro" climaxed one of the most startling intellectual reversals in American literary history.[6]

Mailer's philosophical shift during this period was therefore drastic, but what led to this change? His war experiences do not seem to be the answer, for Mailer's serious commitment to socialism dates from 1948 to 1951. His stay in Hollywood may have been crucial, but he has never offered a detailed account of that period. The experiments with sex, alcohol, and drugs were obviously relevant, but Mailer's many references to these experiences hardly constitute more than random hints. Finally, Mailer's second marriage may well have been decisive, but he has revealed virtually nothing about this marriage. The plain truth is that we do not know what prompted Mailer's intellectual volte-face. We do not even know if his personal experiences were more important than his reading during this period, for the latter has never really been examined.

We do know that *Advertisements for Myself* was as decisive for Mailer's career as *The Naked and the Dead* had been for his personal life. Written in the wake of Mailer's popular and critical failures with *Barbary Shore* and *The Deer Park*, *Advertisements* reveals the emergence of that proud, arrogant, and egocentric personality Mailer celebrates in *The Armies of the Night*. The emergence of Mailer's "legend" dates from this year too, though Mailer has been filling in its contours for the past 30 years. After the publication of *Advertisements*, it would be a long time before anyone would accuse Mailer of being a nice Jewish boy from Brooklyn.

The Middle Years: 1959-78

Mailer's tone throughout *Advertisements* is calculated to offend most of his readers, but the source of his first real notoriety was "The White Negro," specifically the passage in which he defends as "courageous" the murder of a candy store keeper by "two strong eighteen-year-old hoodlums" (*AFM*, 347). While this defense is heavily qualified and extends the essay's total argument, it is hardly surprising that the American public was less than charmed by the "logic" embodied in the following: "The psychopath murders – if he has the courage – out of the necessity to purge his violence, for if he cannot empty his hatred then he cannot love, his being is frozen with implacable self-hatred for his cowardice" (*AFM*, 347). But, of course, few men achieve legendary status because of what they *write*. What ensured Mailer's dubious reputation was the single most unfortunate event of his life: the stabbing of his second wife less than a year after the publication of *Advertisements*.

Mailer stabbed his wife with a penknife on 20 November 1960, in the aftermath of a rather bizarre party celebrating his decision to run for mayor of New York City. Though the wounds inflicted were superficial and his wife declined to press charges, Mailer was confined to the mental ward of Bellevue Hospital for 17 days. Many people assumed – no doubt with good cause – that the whole affair was a monstrous example of absurd theory leading to absurd practice. These same people were not amused when Mailer published the following poem in 1962:

So long
as
you
use
a knife,
there's
some
love
left.[7]

Nor were they delighted by the appearance of *An American Dream*
(1965), a novel in which Mailer's hero strangles his wife but manages
to avoid prosecution. By the middle of the 1960s Mailer had pretty
well established himself as the most notorious literary figure in
America.

This reputation was strengthened throughout the 1960s as
Mailer's name appeared again and again in semilurid headlines. In
1962 Mailer and Adele Morales were divorced and Mailer married
Lady Jeanne Campbell, the daughter of the duke of Argyll and the
granddaughter of Lord Beaverbrook. One year later Mailer and Lady
Campbell were divorced and Mailer married the actress Beverly
Bentley. During this obviously hectic period Mailer also published a
book in which he lectured John Kennedy on his presidential respon-
sibilities, engaged in barroom brawls that inevitably made the
tabloids, and got himself tried – but not convicted – for resisting
arrest in Provincetown, Massachusetts. These events were followed,
several years later, by his rather more famous arrest at the Pentagon
during the antiwar demonstrations of October 1967. It was after his
release at this time that Mailer went on national television and
exchanged obscenities with Dick Cavett's audience. Indeed, the late
1960s found Mailer a regular guest on late-night talk shows, where
he was usually cast as an American Brendan Behan.[8]

Given Mailer's domestic and personal problems during the
1960s, it is remarkable that this period remains the most productive
of his career. Amid what appears to have been personal chaos Mailer
managed to publish one volume of poems, *Deaths for the Ladies
(and other disasters)* (1962); two miscellanies, *The Presidential
Papers* (1963) and *Cannibals and Christians* (1966); and two novels, *An American Dream* (1965) and *Why Are We in Vietnam?*
(1967). At the same time he completed one play, *The Deer Park*

(1967), and three movies, *Wild 90* (1967), *Beyond the Law* (1967), and *Maidstone* (1968). Most important, Mailer published two works of nonfiction (*The Armies of the Night* and *Miami and the Siege of Chicago* [both 1968]) that restored the literary reputation he first commanded 20 years earlier. When *The Armies of the Night* won both a Pulitzer Prize and a National Book Award, Mailer achieved what must have seemed literary vindication – however temporarily.

From 1968 to 1978 Mailer occupied a more respectable position in both American society and American letters than at any time since the publication of his first novel. His activities remained controversial but much less so than during his "The White Negro" period. Mailer's changing attitudes were no doubt crucial to this transformation. Since 1965 he has grown increasingly suspicious of violence as a means of personal or collective salvation; indeed, he has grown increasingly conservative about life in general. By 1969 Mailer had become sufficiently respectable to run for mayor of New York City in a more or less serious manner, finishing fourth in a field of five candidates in the Democratic primary.[9] His love affairs of this period generated none of the massive publicity attending his previous marriages. It is easy to exaggerate this newly won "respectability," of course, for Mailer was involved in many local controversies during these 10 years, including his public quarrel with women's liberation, his endorsement of a so-called Fifth Estate, or civilian FBI, to watch over governmental agencies, and his $1 million contract with Little, Brown.[10] There was just enough bad publicity to justify Mailer's remark that he was the second most unpopular man in America (Richard Nixon ranking first).[11] Increasingly, however, Mailer was perceived as a serious writer first and an eccentric second, thus reversing his public image of the early 1960s.

Mailer has characterized these 10 years as "a period when, with every thought of beginning a certain big novel which had been promised for a long time, the moot desire to have one's immediate say on contemporary matters kept diverting the novelistic impulse into journalism" (*EE*, ix). These "contemporary matters" ranged from America's space program to graffiti, from the women's movement to Muhammad Ali. Mailer's books on these subjects kept his name before the public as an inveterate critic of the national scene. Nonetheless, the personal revelations occasionally offered in such works should not seduce us into reading them as autobiographical.

As I argue in later chapters, Mailer's nonfiction describes his own experience of various American phenomena in order to get at the real meaning of recent American history, not to offer a stylized form of public confession. In such works as *Of a Fire on the Moon* (1970), *The Prisoner of Sex* (1971), *Marilyn* (1973), and *Genius and Lust* (1976) Mailer cultivated the most attractive side to his public "legend," that of prophetic national commentator. And in the book that concluded the 1970s, *The Executioner's Song* (1979), Mailer demonstrated that he could be such a commentator without the personal references that characterize his earlier nonfiction.

The Later Years: 1979-89

The 1980s were a time of domestic tranquility for Mailer, as he spent the entire decade with one woman, Barbara Norris Church (his sixth and apparently his last wife), and eight of his children. This period was preceded by two of the more spectacular episodes in his personal life, however. In the late 1970s Mailer decided to marry Barbara Norris (whose professional name was Norris Church). Divorce from Beverly Bentley, with whom Mailer had not lived for years, took more than three years and became the messiest of all Mailer's well-documented domestic debacles. When he finally achieved his divorce in 1980, Mailer first married Carol Stevens, an ex-mistress, because he wanted to give his name to an earlier child by Stevens. Mailer and Stevens were married and divorced the same day, and Mailer was then free to marry Norris Church. From 1977 to 1979 Mailer was also at work researching and writing *The Executioner's Song*. At this time he corresponded with a Utah prisoner named Jack Henry Abbott. Mailer helped arrange Abbott's prison release in 1980 and wrote an introduction to Abbott's *In the Belly of the Beast: Letters from Prison* (1981). In 1981 Abbott stabbed and killed a young waiter in New York City, and Mailer's testimony at the subsequent trial became a media event to match his domestic contretemps of the same period.

From 1982 to the present Mailer's life has been far less sensational. In 1981 Mailer played Stanford White in Milos Forman's film version of *Ragtime* (1982). In 1982 his own film adaptation of *The Executioner's Song* appeared, directed by Lawrence Schiller and starring Tommy Lee Jones, Rosanna Arquette, and Eli Wallach. In

1985 Jean Luc Godard asked Mailer to write a modern version of *King Lear,* and Mailer proceeded to draft a script called *Don Learo* in which Lear is the head of a modern Mafia family. (Godard decided not to film this script.)[12] In 1986 Mailer organized the International PEN Conference in New York City, an event that involved him in a lavishly described conflict with old sparring partners, New York's literary feminists.[13] That year Mailer also wrote his third work on Marilyn Monroe, a play called *Strawhead* that he produced at the Actors' Studio with his daughter Kate in the starring role.[14] In 1986 Mailer directed his own film version of *Tough Guys Don't Dance,* a first effort at commercial film that won him the 1987 Golden Raspberry Award for worst director of 1987 (an honor shared with Elaine May for *Ishtar*). More recently Mailer's public efforts have been confined to such familiar acts as recommending a presidential candidate (Jesse Jackson), describing a championship fight (Mike Tyson versus Michael Spinks), and trying to enlist Pope John Paul II into PEN.[15]

I would suggest that the relation between Mailer's life and works during this period is more distant than at any other time in his career. The Abbott affair occurred two years after Mailer published *The Executioner's Song,* and the works of the 1980s have virtually no biographical connections with the events just summarized. In 1980 Mailer published *Of Women and Their Elegance,* an "imaginary memoir"[16] of Marilyn Monroe. In 1983 he finally completed his work in progress since the early 1970s, the monumental Egyptian novel *Ancient Evenings.* The next year he published *Tough Guys Don't Dance,* a murder mystery in the so-called tough-guy tradition. More recently he has published a 1,300-page novel about the CIA, *Harlot's Ghost* (1991).[17] In each case one can see biographical connections, but often they go well back into Mailer's past. Monroe has been a continuing obsession, of course, and the hero of *Tough Guys Don't Dance* somewhat resembles a younger Mailer. *Of Women and Their Elegance* is perhaps Mailer's least distinguished work of prose, however, and the links between Mailer and his protagonist Tim Madden are finally rather weak (much weaker than the ties between Mailer and Stephen Rojack, the protagonist of *An American Dream*). Mailer's *relatively* sober public persona in the 1980s again confirms that there is no easy approach to Mailer's art through his life, even if Mailer the literary critic would no doubt be in earnest search of one.[18]

It may be that I am overly skeptical, in part because of what the two published biographies have *not* done to elucidate Mailer's art. Hilary Mills's 1982 biography supplied new information about Mailer, but her subject's lack of cooperation inevitably limited what Mills could provide in a full-scale biography. As noted by many reviewers, the more serious problem with this book is its total lack of a literary hypothesis. Mills does not so much fail to relate Mailer's life to his art as she disdains such an effort. And, of course, the same point can be made about Peter Manso's *Mailer: His Life and Times* (1985), a massive "narrative" that splices together literally hundreds of interviews by and about Mailer over many years. Manso provides even more information than Mills, but one might seriously question whether Manso's book is best described as a biography.[19] Mailer still needs his Richard Ellmann, and he may have found him in his authorized biographer, Robert Lucid. For some years Lucid has been at work on a comprehensive biography. The single excerpt published to date, as well as Lucid's previous studies of Mailer, suggests that skeptics such as myself may finally have to give the literary biographer his due.[20]

Whatever Lucid's achievement to come, I think it is still best to focus on Mailer's aesthetic achievement. After all, Mailer's career now spans four decades and more than 30 volumes. Though full of personal lore for those interested in Mailer's life, these books are surely more valuable as evidence of Mailer's continuing effort to win approval as *the* American writer of the postwar period. It is time we turned to this evidence, especially to those works I consider Mailer's most impressive individual accomplishments: *The Naked and the Dead, The Deer Park, The Armies of the Night, The Executioner's Song,* and *Tough Guys Don't Dance.* In analyzing these books and the rest of Mailer's ouevre, I cannot hope to do full justice to Mailer as man and legend. But I do hope to show why the man and his legend are of more than passing interest in the first place.

Chapter Two

The Naked and the Dead
The Beast and the Seer in Man

It is often a shock to reread the early work of a writer we have come to admire. The second time around this work usually seems rather thin; we find we have remembered effects that do not exist, values that were never there. Mailer's first novel, *The Naked and the Dead* (1948), is a special example of this phenomenon. To reread Mailer's book is indeed to revise our first impression, but in this case the "revision" is all to Mailer's benefit. What we encounter is a work of enduring power, a power simply incommensurate with the novel's reputation. We find that we have tended to value Mailer's first novel for the wrong reasons: as a guide to combat during World War II, as a work of social criticism, as the best of our recent war novels. *The Naked and the Dead* is all these things, but it is also something quite different and more important. At age 25 Mailer was able to use his military experience as the backbone of a long and complex narrative that transcends the generic boundaries of a "war novel." Forty years later the nature of this achievement is still not generally understood.

Certainly *The Naked and the Dead* is more than the "report" of a sensitive young man who survived active service and returned to tell the tale. Mailer began to plan the novel long before his combat experience at Leyte and Luzon. He has traced its origins to the first days of our participation in World War II: "I may as well confess that by December 8th or 9th of 1941, in the forty-eight hours after Pearl Harbor, while worthy young men were wondering where they could be of aid to the war effort, and practical young men were deciding which branch of service was the surest for landing a safe commission, I was worrying darkly whether it would be more likely that a great war novel would be written about Europe or the Pacific" (*AFM*, 28). Much as his General Cummings plans the campaign of Anopopei, the 19-year-old Mailer was already formulating his strategy for a major novel. He had gone a long way toward fulfilling this ambition before serving a day in the army. While still a student at Harvard Mailer wrote a short novel that can only be considered a trial run for *The Naked and the Dead*.[1] From books published during the war, especially John Hersey's *Into the Valley* and Harry Brown's *A Walk in the Sun*, he got the idea of writing his novel about a long patrol. Indeed, it was this decision that led Mailer to volunteer for service in a reconnaissance outfit.[2] These facts suggest that Mailer went to war in search of combat experience that would enable him to complete a novel he had already conceived. It would be foolish to deny the impact of World War II on the book Mailer finally published, but *The Naked and the Dead* is hardly a transcription of the experiences that came Mailer's way during the war. He seems to have decided rather early that the war could furnish an invaluable *background* for a major novel. His preparation for this work covered a full six years.

Discharged in 1946, Mailer began his book in earnest and saw it published in 1948. From the first it was an enormous popular and critical success.[3] Much as his book was liked, however, Mailer was not given sufficient credit for his *novelistic* abilities. Reviewers tended to assess the book as either a disguised documentary or a work of social criticism. To read the novel in these terms is to minimize Mailer's achievement. It is to overlook what differentiates *The Naked and the Dead* from other major novels of World War II, novels so different as *The Gallery*, *The Thin Red Line*, and *Catch-22*. Unlike these works, *The Naked and the Dead* is unified by a full-scale dramatic action. Features of Mailer's book suggest the documentary or the work of social criticism, but they are integrated with the novel's dramatic structure and are not its raison d'être. To establish this point should help clarify the real achievement of Mailer's "war novel."

The Novel as Documentary

It may seem naive to read *The Naked and the Dead* as a documentary, but there is a persistent tradition of doing just that. Indeed, many early critics assumed that Mailer's intention was to transcribe the crucial events of his army career – thus, Marvin Mudrick's description of the novel as "a manual of soldiering in the tropics"[4] and Ira Wolfert's opinion that in *The Naked and the Dead* "the most powerful talents developed . . . are those of the journalist. The story is reported. It is not so much a reading of life as a description in depth of an event in life."[5]

Such views may appear reductive, but who would deny that Mailer's concern for verisimilitude often seems obsessive? The intricacies of davit machinery; the mechanics of tent building; the aspect of a rotting corpse; the effects of a long, sustained march through jungle – virtually everything in the novel is rendered in elaborate, professional detail, as Mailer follows an army platoon through the several stages of a Pacific campaign. Nor is this practice merely a matter of itemizing the paraphernalia of army life. Repeatedly, Mailer employs his "phenomenal talent for recording the precise look and feel of things" to illumine the conditions his characters must suffer.[6] Nor is he less convincing when dealing with his fictional campaign as a whole. When looking over the shoulder of General Cummings and analyzing the progress of the campaign, Mailer achieves the authority of a retired army officer dictating his memoirs.

But of course Mailer is not dictating memoirs, his own or his characters'. Though many of the novel's episodes derive from his personal experiences, Mailer insists that we should not read the book in this fashion: "In the author's eyes, *The Naked and the Dead* is not a realistic documentary; it is, rather, a symbolic book, of which the theme is the conflict between the beast and the seer in man. The number of events experienced by the one platoon couldn't possibly have happened to any one army platoon in the war, but represent a composite view of the Pacific war" (*Current Biography*, 410). Mailer does not deny that "the book will stand or fall as a realistic novel."[7] What he rejects is a simplistic connection between the novel's techniques and its formal ends. Mailer adopts the realistic conventions of most twentieth-century American fiction, but realistic techniques do not point unerringly to the formal aims of a "realistic documentary." Besides referring to *The Naked and the Dead* as a "symbolic" book, Mailer insists that he is neither a realist nor a naturalist: "That terrible word 'naturalism.' It was my literary heritage – the things I learned from Dos Passos and Farrell. I took naturally to it, that's the way one wrote a book. But I really was off on a mystic kick. Actually – a funny thing – the biggest influence on *Naked* was *Moby*

Dick" (Breit, 20). A book whose aspirations suggest those of *Moby-Dick* should not be discussed as a documentary, "realistic" or otherwise.

The novel's symbolism is one feature that transcends the limits of a documentary, but more important still is the story told. Some of the enormous detail in this book may be attributed to Mailer's indulgence of his special knowledge of war; certain episodes and characters contribute little except as they add to Mailer's "description in depth of an event in life." But Mailer usually manages to relate whatever he describes to the novel's elaborate dramatic action. The conditions on Anopopei, Mailer's mythical Pacific island; the routine of army life; the many actions forced on the men – these things are always seen in relation to the characters and their developing conflicts. Contrast the resulting effect with that of James Jones's *The Thin Red Line* (1962), a work that might truly be called a realistic documentary.

The Thin Red Line resembles Mailer's novel in many obvious ways. It too describes the campaign for a single Pacific island (in this case, Guadalcanal). Like Mailer, Jones observes every facet of the campaign, from the initial landing to the mopping up. Like Mailer, Jones employs the literary device of the microcosm as he follows a representative group of men (C-for-Charley-Company) throughout the campaign. Yet the two books are not really similar, as Mailer himself suggests when he aptly describes *The Thin Red Line* as "so broad and true a portrait of combat that it could be used as a textbook at the Infantry School if the Army is any less chicken than it used to be." He goes to the heart of Jones's intentions: "Jones' aim, after all, is not to create character but the feel of combat, the psychology of men." For Mailer, "*The Naked and the Dead* is concerned more with characters than military action" – and so he cannot see that his book is truly comparable to *The Thin Red Line.*[8]

Mailer's comments are very much to the point. His novel differs from Jones's in that its central concern is to develop its many characters. Jones's characters might as well go unnamed, so little difference does it make who they are or what they do except at the moment Jones happens to use them to illustrate an aspect of combat. Nothing in *The Thin Red Line* is comparable to Mailer's gradual development of the conflicts among his major characters. No effort is made to prepare for shifts in the action. In fact, there is no dramatic action in

The Thin Red Line. As Mailer suggests, Jones is not interested in such an action; his intentions correspond to those Mudrick and Wolfert attribute to Mailer. By contrast, *The Naked and the Dead* is rooted in the traditional development of character through a structured series of episodes. We must judge its documentary features as they do or do not serve in this development.

The Novel as Social Critique

Much the same argument applies to elements of social criticism in *The Naked and the Dead*. The existence of such elements is obvious: the criticism of the army as an institution that informs every incident in the novel; the attack on totalitarianism that emerges from the discussions between General Cummings and his aide, Lieutenant Hearn; the grim portrait of American society developed through the I and R platoon, especially in the "Time Machine" biographies of eight enlisted men and two officers (Cummings and Hearn). Yet we must still ask how these features function in the novel as a whole.

Before we assess their function, however, we should first understand the nature of Mailer's social criticism. Far too often *The Naked and the Dead* is treated as the work of a "young liberal" whose critique of American society is substantially the same as that of Dos Passos, Farrell, and Steinbeck.[9] Prior to World War II Mailer was, in his own words, a "progressive-liberal." And in 1948, *after* finishing *The Naked and the Dead* and traveling through Europe, Mailer did join the campaign for Henry Wallace. Nonetheless, *The Naked and the Dead* is not the work of a political liberal. In *Advertisements for Myself* Mailer suggests that his early short novel, "A Calculus at Heaven," makes "an interesting contrast to *The Naked and the Dead*, for it is an attempt of the imagination (aided and warped by books, movies, war correspondents, and the liberal mentality) to guess what war might really be like" (*AFM*, 28). That the novella was determined in part by "the liberal mentality" certainly makes it an interesting contrast to *The Naked and the Dead*, for we have his own word for it that when he wrote his first published novel Mailer was an anarchist, not a liberal (*AFM*, 271).

This difference helps to explain some common misreadings of the later work. Standard critical procedure goes something like this: first, the critic assumes that *The Naked and the Dead* is a thesis novel and that its thesis resembles those expounded by writers such as Dos Passos, for Mailer's "sympathies" are also progressive; then the critic finds that the novel's action does not consistently support the presumed liberal thesis and so either points out Mailer's failures of execution or begins to talk about trusting the tale and not the teller.[10] This procedure involves at least two fallacies: (a) that *The Naked and the Dead* is a thesis novel and (b) that Mailer uses the book to advance liberal values and a liberal social critique. I will return to these problems after considering the novel's action, where I hope to show that what seems inconsistent or weak to the reader who takes Mailer's liberalism for granted is nothing of the sort if we approach the novel without this presupposition. Here I would simply stress that Mailer did not write his novel to do the work of a sociologist.

Mailer's social vision does emerge during the novel, especially in those sections which trace the men's backgrounds, but his characters are not "examples" in a sociological tract. Consider the "Time Machine" sections. If *The Naked and the Dead* were really a thesis novel, these biographies would function as evidence in Mailer's "argument" concerning the American social scene; however, I think Barry Leeds suggests the real relation between the biographies and the rest of the novel:

> Thus, while *The Time Machine* is used to portray the home of a Midwestern businessman, the slums of Boston, or Harvard Yard, it is the presence on Anopopei of men who have experienced these places, which justifies Mailer's detailed treatment of them, and obviates the possibility of their introduction seeming stilted. Every element of American society dealt with becomes integral to the novel as a whole, not merely because it seems to fit into a re-creation of that society, but because it is drawn from the life of a character in whom the reader has come to believe.[11]

The "Time Machine" may be a laborious device to enrich our experience with the men on Anopopei, but that is its function. Although Leeds cites Martinez, he might have mentioned any number of other characters. When Gallagher learns of his wife's death, for example, he becomes an important figure in the novel for the first time. At this point Mailer introduces a "Time Machine" section on Gallagher's Boston-Irish background, his training in frustrated prejudice.[12] Just as we first see Gallagher as fully human, stunned by the loss of his wife, Mailer highlights his ignorance and bigotry. Paradoxically, we are all the more impressed by Gallagher's intense feeling for his wife. He becomes a more complex and interesting character than would have been possible had his biography or his mourning been presented alone. Thus, Mailer uses the "Time Machine" to illuminate character, introducing the device at just that moment in the narrative when it best supplements the novel's action.

The "Time Machine" differs, then, from similar devices in the works of John Dos Passos.[13] The "Camera Eye," "Newsreel," and biography sections in *U.S.A.*, for example, are clearly intended to complement the narrative in the manner of a thesis novel. These sections are not directly related to the narrative; they do not even concern its characters. Instead, they are determined by and substantiate Dos Passos's attack on the American social system. Mailer's use of a similar device is for a quite different end. The "Time Machine" sections are intended to comment on each character's role in the action. When this does not happen – as in the belated "Time Machine" passage devoted to Polack, a figure of no real significance (*NATD*, 608-20) – the reader is likely to find the material digressive, even intrusive. Mailer's novel differs from Dos Passos's trilogy in its use of social elements to clarify a dramatic action, not a social argument.

The Novel as Dramatic Action

I am suggesting that *The Naked and the Dead* is a rather traditional novel. This is not meant as criticism of the book. If it lacks the stylistic and formal innovations of Mailer's more recent novels, especially *An American Dream* (1965), *Why Are We in Vietnam?* (1967), and *Ancient Evenings* (1983), *The Naked and the Dead* is nonetheless a more successful work. It is successful in its adaptation of a novelistic form we can trace from Richardson and Fielding down to Mailer's immediate precursors, Hemingway and Faulkner. This form emphasizes character and action – staples of fiction as central to *The Naked and the Dead* as they are to the novels of Austen and Dickens. Interpretation should begin with precisely these features.

It may seem rather harmless to argue that *The Naked and the Dead* is essentially "a novel of character," as John Aldridge first suggested and Mailer once confirmed.[14] In fact, however, there are fairly important consequences if we accept this idea. Indeed, we will probably have to reject the more popular interpretations of Mailer's novel. Consider Randall Waldron's "case" against Mailer's conclusion:

> The central conflict in *The Naked and the Dead* is between the mechanistic forces of "the system" and the will to individual integrity. Commanding General Cummings, brilliant and ruthless evangel of fascist power and control, and ironhanded, hardnosed Sergeant Croft personify the machine. Opposing them in the attempt to maintain personal dignity and identity are Cummings' confused young aide, Lieutenant Hearn, and Private Valsen, rebellious member of Croft's platoon. Mailer fails to bring this conflict to any satisfying resolution: at the novel's end Hearn is dead and Valsen's stubborn pride defeated, but likewise Croft is beaten and humiliated and Cummings' personal ambitions thwarted. . . . [T]he conclusion of *The Naked and the Dead* and its total meaning are unclear.[15]

Like Norman Podhoretz and John Aldridge, Waldron dislikes Mailer's ending because it fails to generate the radical "protest" presumably intended.[16] Waldron obviously expects the book to end as this kind of thesis novel is supposed to end – with a clear demarcation between victim and victimizer. Again like Podhoretz and Aldridge, he assumes that Mailer conceived the book as a warning against totalitarian tendencies in America and cannot see that Mailer achieves this purpose by treating his villains in the same manner as his heroes.

But why assume that Mailer intended to write a protest novel? If we make this assumption, the novel's ending – indeed, the coherence of the whole work – is called into question. We would at least expect Mailer to distinguish among his characters sufficiently to clarify his own moral position and to articulate his "warning." As Waldron remarks, Mailer "fails" to do this. My own view is that he never intended to do so. If we stop treating Cummings, Croft, Hearn, and Valsen as representative figures in a political allegory, we should come to see that Mailer prepares all along for the ending Waldron and others find so disappointing. In examining *The Naked and the Dead* as a dramatic action we should not only make sense of what others find "unclear" but also get at the true sources of the novel's power.

Mailer's published remarks on the composition of his novel tend to confirm that he did not organize it around a political or social "thesis." Mailer says that from the first he wanted to structure his book around a long patrol involving a single army platoon (Plimpton 1967, 260). It seems likely that he first intended to write a collective novel in the manner of Dos Passos, using the patrol to examine under stress a group of men broadly representative of American society. While he does something like this in the published novel, Mailer reveals that his book changed as he completed the second draft. It changed because he chose to develop two characters outside the platoon, General Cummings and Lieutenant Hearn: "The part about the platoon went well from the beginning, but the Lieutenant and the General in the first draft were stock characters. If it had been published at that point the book would have been considered an interesting war novel with some good scenes, no more. The second draft was the bonus. Cummings and Hearn were done in the second draft" (Plimpton 1967, 257). As Mailer suggests, the fleshing out of Cummings and Hearn "made" his novel as a work of art. Mailer patterned their relationship after the conflict between Croft and Valsen, the leading members of the platoon and presumably the main characters in the initial draft. *The Naked and the Dead* came more and more to deal with these four major figures; it began to take on the full dimensions of a novel of character.

Mailer's two plot lines are sufficiently similar they might almost be considered a double plot. In each case a character of liberal sympathies fights for his integrity against a fascistic superior; in each the "good" character is defeated while the "bad" character fails in his most ambitious undertaking. Whereas Croft's tactics against Valsen are openly sadistic, Cummings exercises an intellectual tyranny over Hearn. Finally, however, this is a minor distinction, for the results are indistinguishable. These conflicts are reminiscent of much "protest" literature with which *The Naked and the Dead* is often compared. Cummings and Croft seem prototype fascists, the villains of scores of proletarian novels; Hearn and Valsen seem the archetypal victims of such novels. If we take a closer look, however, we should discover subtleties appropriate to Mailer's overall design.

Initially, the feud between Croft and Valsen seems a simple matter of irreconcilable personalities. Certainly this is our impression in part 1, where Croft and Valsen nearly come to blows in a scene that is repeated with variations throughout the novel, until their quarrel is resolved on Mount Anaka. Their "roles" are fixed this early: Croft as the aggressive platoon leader; Red as the recalcitrant private who resists authority and authoritarians (*NATD*, 31-32). Red is presented from the outset as a proud but rather ineffectual man who is capable of feeling "a sad compassion in which one seems to understand everything, all that men want and fail to get" (*NATD*, 14), but who has no hope of translating his feelings into action: "Everything is crapped up, everything is phony, everything curdles when you touch it" (*NATD*, 350). Both his compassion for others and his personal cynicism define Red as Croft's opposite. Croft is an obvious, even a spectacular sadist. As a National Guardsman he kills a striker for no other reason than the pleasure it gives him (*NATD*, 161). On Anopopei he tantalizes a Japanese prisoner with kindness before shooting him in the head (*NATD*, 195), crushes a small bird in his bare hand (*NATD*, 530), and coldly arranges the death of Hearn (*NATD*, 598). Croft loves combat, for only in combat does he find release from his hatred of the world (his "Time Machine" section concludes, "I HATE EVERYTHING WHICH IS NOT IN MYSELF"; *NATD*, 164). Croft must master everything that is not in himself. He is confident that he can do so, for "he had a deep unspoken belief that whatever made things happen was on his side" (*NATD*, 9).

Yet Croft and Valsen are not mere foils, as Mailer reveals in the first half of part 2. This section of the novel moves toward two separate "moments of truth," one experienced by Croft and the other by Valsen. The first such moment climaxes Mailer's account of the Japanese counterattack, a performance as fine as anything in the book. Here we see Croft in his natural element, the violence of war. He controls his men so fiercely that he revives Valsen's hatred (*NATD*, 125, 129). Indeed, he treats the weaknesses of others as if they were personal enemies (*NATD*, 137). Yet the climax of this episode is Croft's moment of *fear* – more precisely, his awareness that he too can be made afraid. This recognition sends "a terrible rage working through his weary body" (*NATD*, 155), and its effects are felt through the rest of the novel, until Croft's rage is expended against Mount Anaka.

The second climactic moment occurs when the men go to search Japanese bodies for souvenirs. This hunt is a nightmare, revealing, in Chester Eisinger's words, "the deepest urge toward violence and debasement in human beings" (Eisinger, 35). Red finds it oppressive because he must pass through piles of rotting bodies. The stench is overpowering, the corpses horribly distorted and maggot-ridden. Suddenly Red is "sober and very weary." Unlike the others, Red understands that he is surrounded by the bodies of *men*. Standing over one such body, he experiences a kind of epiphany: "Very deep inside himself he was thinking that this was a man who had once wanted things, and the thought of his own death was always a little unbelievable to him. The man had had a childhood, a youth and a young manhood, and there had been dreams and memories. Red was realizing with surprise and shock, as if he were looking at a corpse for the first time, that a man was really a very fragile thing" (*NATD*, 216). Different as Croft and Valsen are, their climactic insights in part 2 are quite similar. Each discovers that "a man was really a very fragile thing." They differ, of course, in how they respond to this discovery: Croft tries to exorcise it through violence, while Red accepts it with a "wise" melancholy. This section of the book is structured to reveal the common anxieties underlying their radically different approaches to life.

In the second half of part 2 Mailer develops an even more complex antagonism. Prior to the represented action Cummings more or less adopts Hearn as his protégé. He sees in Hearn an intellectual equal and a sympathetic ear for his theories about the nature of power. When Hearn responds to the general's attentions with something less than gratitude, his fate is to illustrate Cummings's first principle: "There's one thing about power. It can flow only from the top down. When there are little surges of resistance at the middle levels, it merely calls for more power to be directed downward, to burn it out" (*NATD*, 323). Throughout the book we see Cummings trying to "burn out" Hearn's resistance. The conflict here seems quite straightforward. Indeed, critics often refer to Hearn as Mailer's liberal spokesman. Hearn's resistance to Cummings is supposed to represent Mailer's own political feelings and to justify Hearn's role as the novel's "hero."

The problem is that Hearn represents not so much liberalism as the *desire* to be liberal. Surely he is an odd humanitarian: he likes few people (*NATD*, 69, 328), he is a self-confessed snob (*NATD*, 78), and he feels distaste for Jews (*NATD*, 83) and a "trace of contempt" for the enlisted man (*NATD*, 168). Temperamentally, Hearn is an aristocrat. It is not surprising that he defends his liberal notions with faint conviction, for his real commitment is to himself: "The only thing that had been important was to let no one in any ultimate issue ever violate your integrity" (*NATD*, 326). Hearn would protect his "inviolate freedom" and so avoid "all the wants and sores that caught up everybody about him" (*NATD*, 79). His motto is appropriately sterile: "The only thing to do is to get by on style" (*NATD*, 326). Defined by his detachment, his distance from real human concerns, Hearn is best known by his failures to act.

Because he feels no real commitment to his humanitarian interests, Hearn is vulnerable to the same urges that move Cummings and Croft. Hearn is fascinated by Cummings, who has the ability "to extend his thoughts into immediate and effective action" (*NATD*, 77), because Hearn is drawn to power himself: "Always there was the power that leaped at you, invited you" (*NATD*, 353). Resentment of his position vis-à-vis Cummings mingles with his desire to be like Cummings: "he had acquiesced in the dog-role, had even had the dog's dream, carefully submerged, of someday equaling the master" (*NATD*, 313). Hearn comes to believe that "divorced of all the environmental trappings, all the confused and misleading attitudes he had absorbed, he was basically like Cummings" (*NATD*, 392). He even comes to fear that "when he searched himself he was just another Croft" (*NATD*, 580).

What Hearn fears is that he is no less a fascist than Cummings or Croft. But even Cummings is more complex than this might suggest. A self-styled "reactionary," Cummings prefers fascism to communism because "it's grounded firmly in men's actual natures" (*NATD*, 321). To say the least, Cummings has no high opinion of man's nature. He thinks Hitler "the interpreter of twentieth-century man" and believes "there's never a man who can swear to his own innocence. We're all guilty, that's the truth" (*NATD*, 313). But, of course, Cummings does not see himself as he sees others. Indeed, he has a mystical sense of his own destiny: "The fact that you're holding the gun and the other man is not is no accident. It's a product of everything you've achieved, it assumes that you're . . . you're aware enough, you have the gun when you need it" (*NATD*, 83-84). Cummings views himself as the man with the gun. He is speaking of himself, not "man," when he says that "man is in transit between brute and God" (*NATD*, 323).

Cummings's vanity is immense, his ambitions worthy of Ahab. We learn early that his intention on Anopopei is to "mold" his troops, the terrain, and even "the circuits of chance" to the contours of his will (*NATD*, 85). Confident that he can dispose of any obstacle, natural or human, Cummings believes that life is like a game of chess (*NATD*, 180). But his rationality is a disguise, as Mailer makes clear by exposing the real forces at work on Cummings: self-pity amounting to paranoia, and homosexuality.[17] As the novel unfolds we learn that Cummings is no closer to harmonizing "Plant and Phantom,"[18] body and spirit, than are the men of Croft's platoon, or Hearn.

During part 2, then, we come to see the novel's central conflicts as rather more ambiguous than they appeared at first; in each case the antagonists have more in common than we might have supposed. This is made especially clear in part 3, in which the four major figures all suffer a remarkably similar fate. As noted earlier, each "good" character is defeated by his totalitarian opponent. Hearn is the victim of both Cummings and Croft, for Cummings transfers Hearn into a platoon already selected for a dangerous mission and Croft deliberately plots Hearn's death. Red's defeat is not fatal, but it is no less decisive. A man committed to nothing except his own personal integrity, Red is so beaten down he feels relief after he confronts Croft and is defeated: "At the base of his shame was an added guilt. He was glad it was over, glad the long contest with Croft was finished, and he could obey orders with submission, without feeling that he must resist" (*NATD*, 696).

Yet if they triumph over Hearn and Valsen, Cummings and Croft are hardly the novel's "victors." Throughout part 3 Croft's efforts are directed toward conquering Mount Anaka, the great mountain that towers over Anopopei, "taunting" Croft with its "purity" and "austerity" (*NATD*, 497, 522, 527). The mountain becomes for Croft what his troops are for Cummings: the "other" that resists his control and must be molded to serve his will. Like Cummings, however, Croft is unable to control the circuits of chance. When he stumbles over a hornets' nest, the men flee down the mountain and the march abruptly ends (*NATD*, 699-700). Croft is left puzzled and spent: "Croft kept looking at the mountain. He had lost it, had missed some tantalizing revelation of himself. Of himself and much more. Of life. Everything" (*NATD*, 709).[19] This passage recalls the single section devoted to Cummings in part 3. Faced with "mass inertia or the inertia of the masses," the men's resistance to his more grandiose ambitions, Cummings is unable to find a meaningful pattern among the forces at work in the campaign: "There was order but he could not reduce it to the form of a single curve. Things eluded him" (*NATD*, 571). Like Croft, Cummings must finally give the circuits of chance their due. He attempts with his final attack what Croft attempts on Mount Anaka, but the campaign ends in a manner he could never anticipate (the inept Major Dalleson, not Cummings, engineers the final assault). Cummings must admit that "he had had very little or perhaps nothing at all to do with this victory, or indeed any victory" (*NATD*, 716). For Cummings too there comes the knowledge of personal limitation.

As noted previously, Mailer is often criticized for refusing to create ideologically satisfying characters. The assumption here is that Mailer wrote his book to "defend liberalism" (Eisinger, 37), to warn against the antiliberal forces within the American system. But Mailer has made it clear that he "intended" something quite different – something that might even *require* the treatment of character we find in *The Naked and the Dead*. Mailer says that he conceived the book as "a parable about the movement of man through history" ("Rugged Times," 25); he defines its basic theme as "the conflict between the beast and the seer in man" (*Current Biography*, 410). It would seem that for Mailer the movement of man through history is an ongoing struggle between the bestial and the visionary forces in man himself. This idea is not terribly original, of course, but the power of *The Naked and the Dead* depends not on the originality of its ideas but on how well they are embodied in the novel's characters and events.

Moreover, Mailer's ideas are not as schematic as I may have suggested. Unlike the typical proletarian or social novel, *The Naked and the Dead* does not present its beasts and seers in obvious counterpoint. If Croft is set against Valsen in the book, who is the beast and who is the seer? The epigraph to part 3 is relevant here: "Even the wisest among you is only a disharmony and hybrid of plant and phantom. But do I bid you become phantoms and plants?" (*NATD*, 431).[20] This rhetorical question implies that man should be neither "plant" nor "phantom" exclusively; neither all body nor all soul; neither beast nor seer. Man should seek harmony between the physical and the spiritual, though, as Nietzsche observes, even the wisest among us is a "disharmony and hybrid." This is certainly true of the major figures in *The Naked and the Dead*, each of whom carries within himself Nietzsche's bestial and visionary forces. The ultimate effect of Mailer's parallel plots is to emphasize this "disharmony" in each character. When Cummings and Croft suffer defeats comparable to those of Hearn and Valsen, we should realize that Mailer rejects a crude contrast between good and evil. In dramatizing the conflict between the beast and the seer in man, Mailer shows that *all* his characters are subject to the same conflict.[21]

Surely Mailer establishes this kinship between Cummings and Croft. Both are power moralists who rely on fear and hatred in their command of others; both are inordinately ambitious; both function as Hearn's enemy and plan to have him killed. Each is "coldly efficient" (*NATD*, 179), latently homosexual,[22] and obsessed with his wife's infidelity (*NATD*, 182, 200). They share an extreme individualism that is coupled with a strong sense of personal destiny. For Cummings, "the fact that you're holding the gun and the other man is not is no accident"; for Croft, "if a man gets wounded, it's his own goddam fault" (*NATD*, 522) – if Cummings sees himself as the man with the gun, Croft sees himself as the man who will never be wounded. Cummings and Croft are most alike in their common rejection of accident or chance as a determining force in life. Cummings's ambition is nothing less than to mold the circuits of chance, while Croft has "a deep unspoken belief that whatever made things happen was on his side." Each possesses a naive faith that he can work his will on the world.

In their rejection of determinism Cummings and Croft almost justify Podhoretz's suggestion that they are the novel's "natural heroes" (Podhoretz, 387). While Hearn and Valsen suggest vacillation and futility, Cummings and Croft are all energy and commitment. "Natural heroes" is a bit much, however. We should not see Cummings and Croft as mere villains, but neither should we equate Mailer's admiration for certain qualities in Croft with, say, admiration for the character as a whole.[23] In response to the question "Whom do you hate?" Mailer once answered, "People who have power and no compassion, that is, no simple human understanding" (*AFM*, 271). Can we fail to apply this statement to Cummings and Croft?

What prevents these characters from being purely hateful is what Mailer calls their "vision." Croft is moved by a "crude unformed vision" (*NATD*, 156), and Cummings is driven by "one great vision" (*NATD*, 323), momentarily embodied when he observes his first battlefield and experiences "the largest vision that has ever entered his soul": "There were all those men, and there had been someone above them, ordering them, changing perhaps forever the fiber of their lives. . . . *There were things one could do.*" As he surveys the battlefield Cummings is "choked with the intensity of his emotion, the rage, the undefined and mighty hunger" (*NATD,* 415). This hunger is Croft's crude unformed vision; this rage is Croft's "rage" at the frustrations of the final patrol (*NATD,* 527). Moreover, the vision these men share is no mean one. As we have seen, Cummings's greatest urge is to be omnipotent; Croft too is tantalized by "vistas of such omnipotence he must wonder at his own audacity" (*NATD,* 40). The common spirit that links Cummings and Croft is unmistakable. In one sense they are the novel's "seers": confident of the world's tractability, they are determined to achieve destinies commensurate with their mighty hungers.

Unfortunately, Cummings and Croft are also the novel's principal "beasts." There is nothing so despicable in *The Naked and the Dead* as Croft's calculated destruction of the lame bird discovered by one of the men, and Cummings is subject to the same impulses, as we learn when he comes upon a cigarette Hearn has put out on his floor: "If he had been holding an animal in his hands at that instant he would have strangled it" (*NATD,* 318). Hearn discovers early in the book that Cummings is capable of atrocities as great as any Croft will later commit. Behind the general's "facade" is that naked animal closeted with its bone. The naked animal in Cummings finds expression in his power morality, his persecution and finally his execution of Hearn.[24] The conflict between the beast and the seer in man is precisely the conflict within both Cummings and Hearn. The urges that move them are *both* bestial and visionary.

In his portraits of Hearn and Valsen, Mailer further undermines the "structure of protest" readers have expected of him (Aldridge, 138). To achieve such protest, Mailer needed to depict Hearn and Valsen as more or less admirable figures victimized by the representatives of an unjust society. But of course he presents them in a very different light. Whereas Cummings believes that "in the Army the idea of individual personality is just a hindrance" (*NATD,* 180-81), Hearn and Valsen have no commitment except to their individual personalities. Both place the highest value on what Hearn calls "inviolate freedom." They ask nothing more specific from life, because they also share contempt for what life offers: Red's "particular blend of pessimism and fatalism" (*NATD*, 444) is everywhere evident, while Hearn believes that "if you searched something long enough, it always turned to dirt" (*NATD*, 183). Because they have found so little to value in life, Hearn and Valsen have lived as drifters. Unlike Red, Hearn has not literally been a hobo, but his lifestyle might easily be mistaken for Valsen's: "Get potted, get screwed, and get up in the morning, somehow" (*NATD*, 347). Hearn and Valsen are confirmed in their pessimism by what happens to them on Anopopei. Each is made to struggle for his inviolate freedom; each concludes that "there were no answers" in this struggle (*NATD*, 585, 704). The repetition of this exact phrase emphasizes that neither Hearn nor Valsen discovers a sustaining belief. In both men the qualities of the seer are blunted.

We tend to think of Hearn and Valsen in relation to their enemies, but this contrast can be misleading. Hearn discovers in himself many of the qualities that unite Cummings and Croft. Both Hearn and Cummings are "born in the aristocracy of the wealthy midwestern family" (*NATD*, 169); both have domineering fathers who force them into "masculine" activities (boys' camps and athletics for Hearn; military school for Cummings); both become "cold rather than shy" (*NATD*, 407) and suffer a displaced sex life (like Cummings, Hearn "fights out battles with himself" on the bodies of his women [*NATD*, 416]). During a football game Hearn experiences "an instant of complete startling gratification when he knew the ball carrier was helpless, waiting to be hit" (*NATD*, 344) – a clear enough parallel to Croft's sadism. The connection between Hearn and Croft is most obvious during the patrol, where each man tries to redeem his failure early in the campaign and Hearn comes to think of himself as "another Croft."

Although Red does not so clearly resemble Cummings, interesting similarities exist. When the campaign begins to go badly, Cummings undergoes "the amazement and terror of a driver who finds his machine directing itself, starting and halting when *it* desires" (*NATD*, 300). This event echoes Red's discovery of "a pattern where there shouldn't be one" after the death of a young soldier (*NATD*, 39). Red's kinship with Croft has already been suggested. Once he is defeated by Croft, Red finds that he is happy to obey orders without feeling he must resist. When the march up Mount Anaka ends, Croft experiences much the same emotion: "Deep inside himself, Croft was relieved that he had not been able to climb the mountain. . . . Croft was rested by the unadmitted knowledge that he had found a limit to his hunger" (*NATD*, 701). Once their ambitions are thwarted, Cummings and Croft do not seem altogether different from even Red Valsen.

Does the resemblance among these characters "humanize" Cummings and Croft or "expose" Hearn and Valsen? The answer must of course be *both*. Cummings and Croft are not entirely reprehensible; Hearn and Valsen are not quite admirable. The whole action is directed toward these ironic judgments. "Only connect," Forster advised, but none of the major characters is able to balance the beast and the seer within himself. What Red lacks in energy and purpose Croft lacks in compassion and the ability to expand his unformed vision beyond the need for power. It is much the same with Hearn and Cummings. Hearn would seem to be the one most likely to connect the warring forces in himself, but Hearn is perhaps the most incomplete of the major figures. Neither Hearn's sympathies nor his desire for power are ultimately authentic. It is one of the novel's many ironies that Hearn is nonetheless the one character who achieves even a limited dignity.[25] In *The Naked and the Dead* there is no correlation at all between goodness and the fruits thereof.

Even as he dramatizes their conflicts Mailer hints that his characters are basically alike. This does not evidence moral or aesthetic confusion; instead, it makes possible Mailer's rather terrible commentary on his creations. At the end he collapses their several fates into a single fate – disillusionment – and confirms what has been implicit throughout: man is a "disharmony," "corrupted, confused to the point of helplessness" ("Rugged Times," 25), and the world he inherits has no sympathy for his weakness. Croft and Valsen may seem polar opposites, but whether they seek power or personal freedom they are doomed to a common failure. Their apparently different desires represent what Mailer once insisted we see in all his characters: "yearnings for a better world" ("Rugged Times," 25). Mailer does not mock these desires; indeed, nothing else redeems Cummings and Croft even slightly. What he does is show how nearly impossible it is to realize such "yearnings."

Mailer does this in a work that engages our feelings in the manner of all great novels. His primary purpose is not to document the experience of combat or the failure of our political system but to create a dramatic action that embodies more universal concerns. The result is a dark but moving image of the human condition. This image is one Mailer will never again present so starkly in his fiction; indeed, all his subsequent works can be seen as attempts to qualify or even to disavow the bleak implications of his first novel. The "truth" of this image is not really in question, however. What matters is Mailer's success in fleshing out the elaborate dramatic action that unifies his book. A novel of character in the best sense of that phrase, *The Naked and the Dead* remains one of Mailer's most impressive achievements.[26]

Chapter Three

The Deer Park

The Rare Tenderness of Tragedy

Mailer has expressed his pleasure at the authoritative voice he still hears in *The Naked and the Dead:* "[I]t seems to be at dead center – 'Yes,' it is always saying, 'this is about the way it is.' " He has also confessed that this authority was lost, both in his work and in his personal life, with the extraordinary success of his first novel: "Naturally, I was blasted a considerable distance away from dead center by the size of its success, and I spent the next few years trying to gobble up the experience of a victorious man when I was still no man at all" (*AFM,* 92). Eventually Mailer would regain his artistic equilibrium with *The Deer Park* (1955), one of his most important works. Between 1949 and 1955, however, Mailer wandered through such literary excursions as the allegorical *Barbary Shore* (1951) and a massive, de Sade-like novel he contemplated writing before settling for the more modest proportions of *The Deer Park.* Before looking at *The Deer Park* in some detail, we should glance briefly at the fictions written in the aftermath of *The Naked and the Dead. Barbary Shore* may be Mailer's weakest novel, as most of his critics agree, but it nonetheless marks a significant transition in his career. And the several works either written or contemplated between 1952 and 1955 lead directly into Mailer's third – and perhaps best – novel.

Barbary Shore

Mailer is often his own best critic, and his account of the difficulties he faced with his second novel is perhaps the most useful of his self-critiques. Indeed, I quote this account at such length because I think Mailer touches here on all the major issues concerning *Barbary Shore:*

If my past had become empty as a theme, was I to write about Brooklyn streets, or my mother and father, or another war novel (*The Naked and the Dead Go to Japan*), was I to do the book of the returning veteran when I had lived like a mole writing and rewriting seven hundred pages in those fifteen months? No, those were not real choices. I was drawn instead to write about an imaginary future which was formed osmotically by the powerful intellectual influence of my friend Jean Malaquais, and by the books I had read, and the aesthetics I considered desirable, but *Barbary Shore* was really a book to emerge from the bombarded cellars of my unconscious, an agonized eye of a novel which tried to find some amalgam of my new experience and the larger horror of that world which might be preparing to destroy itself. I was obviously trying for something which was at the very end of my reach, and then beyond it, and toward the end the novel collapsed into a chapter of political speech and never quite recovered. Yet, it could be that if my work is alive one hundred years from now, *Barbary Shore* will be considered the richest of my first three novels for it has in its high fevers a kind of insane insight into the psychic mysteries of Stalinists, secret policemen, narcissists, children, Les-bians, hysterics, revolutionaries — it has an air which for me is the air of our time, authority and nihilism stalking one another in the orgiastic hollow of this century. . . . [M]uch of my later writing cannot be understood without a glimpse of the odd shadow and theme-maddened light *Barbary Shore* casts before it. (*AFM*, 93-94)

Mailer identifies his book's obsession with the postwar political situation, the profound influence of Jean Malaquais and other radical writers, and the difficulties he experienced in trying to maintain aesthetic poise while working in new literary territory. Moreover, Mailer offers his own thematic reading by touting the novel's "insane insight" into what he calls psychic mysteries. For Mailer, *Barbary Shore* is a book in which authority and nihilism stalk each other on a very large stage indeed, "the orgiastic hollow of this century."

As John Henry Raleigh says, Mailer appears to be "an appreciative audience of one" for his second novel.[1] When the book first appeared, Mailer's commitment to "a far-flung mutation of Trotsky-ism" may have been a factor in its popular and critical failure (Plimpton 1967, 262); over the years, however, Mailer's aesthetic strategy has been the real problem for his friends and detractors alike. *Barbary Shore* seems to encourage a fatal lack of attention. Consider the odd fact that two authors of books on Mailer misspell the name of his heroine. Guinevere[2]; consider as well that (a) one of these critics alleges that Mikey Lovett has "a short affair" with Guine-vere (Lovett's fondest wish!) and (b) the other repeats a common misconception among reviewers when she speaks of the protagonist's "suicide" (McLeod is in fact murdered at the end of the novel) (Bufithis, 32; Radford, 85). Presumably, the novel's partisans would argue that such details are insignificant, because *Barbary Shore* is an allegory rather than a traditional novel. Yet even in reading allegories we usually remember the heroine's name and understand what happens to the protagonist.

Barbary Shore has been treated as at least two different kinds of allegory. John Stark proposes that the main characters stand quite directly for political movements or ideas: McLeod, an ex-Soviet official, represents bolshevism; his wife, Guinevere, stands for the masses; Hollingsworth, an FBI agent, embodies the capitalist state; and fellow travelers Lannie Madison and Mikey Lovett represent Trotskyism.[3] Stark's formula is balder than those offered by other critics and is no doubt open to Robert Begiebing's complaint that *Barbary Shore* is too often read as a "rigid allegory" (Begiebing 1980, 14, n. 4). But if we compare Stark's admittedly crude categories with Mailer's own thematic terms in the long passage just quoted, we may well wonder whether the author of *Barbary Shore* is not practicing a form of "conscious fabulism," and practicing it rather crudely. "Conscious fabulism" is Begiebing's phrase for the sort of explicit allegorizing we associate with medieval drama, political satire, and modern dystopian works like Aldous Huxley's *Brave New World* and George Orwell's *1984*. Begiebing argues that Mailer's form is "visionary allegory," which seems to differ from conscious fabulism in that its themes emerge "naturally" and do not dictate the nature or actions of the characters. A visionary allegory is one in which the author does not *plan* his allegorical implications. As it happens, this notion fits very well with Mailer's revelation (or is it confession?) that when he wrote *Barbary Shore* he had no idea from one day to the next what he was going to have his characters do.[5] I remain skeptical, however, as to whether Begiebing's distinction points to artistic mastery or even artistic control.

Mailer identifies one of his novel's major problems when he refers to its "collapse" into a late chapter of political speech. McLeod's conversations with Hollingsworth in the final third of the book read all too much like the rather unpalatable political essays Mailer published in the early 1950s.[6] These speeches bring the action to a complete stop while adding little to the novel's ideologi-

cal debate. The book's problems do not start with these late chapters, however. All the characters are shadowy figures from the outset.
Lovett is the vaguest of Mailer's sensitive but naive narrators; Lannie
is an impossibly contradictory character; McLeod is a very pale pre-
liminary draft of Charles Francis Eitel, the protagonist of *The Deer
Park;* and Guinevere seems to have wandered into a novel that has
no use for her fantastic personality. Indeed, the very interesting
Guinevere exposes Mailer's inadequate grasp of the fabulator's art,
for Mailer uses Guinevere to pursue his novel's psychic mysteries
while failing to advance its political implications.[7] In the first edition
of this book I somewhat carelessly accused *Barbary Shore* of being a
"rigid allegory," but the novel's real problem is that it is *alternately*
such an allegory and an impressionistic pursuit of Mailer's psychic
mysteries: Stalinism, the secret police, narcissism, children, lesbians,
hysterics, revolutionaries. Notice that some of these items are political and some are not. The list accurately reflects Mailer's interests
from chapter to chapter but also suggests the unassimilated narrative
concerns randomly poured together. At the end there are too many
things we do not know, even if we do know that Hollingsworth kills
McLeod. Mailer's odd mixture of allegory and a traditional literary
action anticipates his technical problems with *An American Dream*
(1965) and *Why Are We in Vietnam?* (1967), but the effect here is
much more devastating.[8]

Rather than pursue the novel's various improbabilities, I will
close this brief discussion by suggesting that the most serious problem with *Barbary Shore* is the style in which it is written. Among the
reviewers, Irving Howe notes that the novel is badly written, and
many years later Robert Solotaroff adds his own illustrations.[9] My
examples merely confirm theirs. The novel's narrator, Mikey Lovett,
speaks throughout in a cramped, excessively literary manner Mailer
will struggle to refashion in later narrative voices. Early in the book
Lovett remarks of his apartment, "Even at four dollars a week the
bargain was not conspicuous, but I was enamored of it."[10] Later he
describes his Brooklyn surroundings: "For a June morning the sidewalks were still cool, and the brownstone houses were not without
dignity" (*BS*, 12-13). Later yet he writes, "The hot summer afternoon
dragged by, carrying me with it in torpor. I tried to read, I thought of
working, but neither was practicable" (*BS*, 57). "Enamored," "not
without dignity," "practicable" – never again will Mailer write so

stiffly. Indeed, he will devote the next several years to remaking the style of Lovett's successor, Sergius O'Shaugnessy, the narrator of *The Deer Park* and "The Time of Her Time" (1959). Mailer has written at length about his arduous effort to transform Sergius's prose style (*AFM*, 234-45), an effort he might have brought to *Barbary Shore* as well. *Barbary Shore* is Mailer's first step away from a literary form in which it is sufficient to report "the way it is," and perhaps it was a necessary first step. Nonetheless, it remains one of Mailer's least successful works.

An Eight-Volume Novel and "The Man Who Studied Yoga"

In the wake of his problems with *Barbary Shore* Mailer turned to writing war stories that required little time or commitment. In 1952 he published "The Paper House" and "The Dead Gook"; in 1953, "The Language of Men" (as well as a fourth story, "The Notebook"). (These stories are reprinted in *Advertisements for Myself*, 109-53.) Good as these stories are, Mailer himself notes their uncharacteristic modesty (*AFM*, 108). By contrast, Mailer's next project was to include a prologue about a character named Sam Slovoda and no fewer than eight volumes: "The eight novels were to be eight stages of [Slovoda's] dream later that night, and the books would revolve around the adventures of a mythical hero, Sergius O'Shaugnessy, who would travel through many worlds, through pleasure, business, communism, church, working class, crime, homosexuality and mysticism" (*AFM*, 154). As Mailer remarks, this is hardly a modest scheme: "one would need the seat of Zola and the mind of Joyce to do it properly" (*AFM*, 154).

Although Mailer has some claim to both Zola's seat and Joyce's mind, his eight-part epic was not to be. After working on the first volume dedicated to "pleasure," Mailer found that he could not go on unless he settled for a "simpler" novel based on his original characters. This realization came after he had completed the prologue and the first draft of *The Deer Park*, and so he was reconciled to abandoning the larger project with "The Man Who Studied Yoga" and *The Deer Park* to show for his efforts (*AFM*, 155-56).

"The Man Who Studied Yoga" (written in 1953 or 1954 but first published in 1956) is one of Mailer's better works. Mailer acknowledges that his short fiction is "neither splendid, unforgettable, nor distinguished," but he also claims that "The Man Who Studied Yoga" is "superior to most good short fiction."[11] Mailer is right on both counts. Even the best of his short fiction betrays insufficient care with the fundamentals of craft. Indeed, "The Man Who Studied Yoga" is "not entirely functional," as Mailer himself points out (*AFM*, 156). Having written this piece as the prologue to his since-abandoned masterwork, Mailer declined to revise the story for "reasons which are probably sentimental" (*AFM*, 156). This is regrettable, for "The Man Who Studied Yoga" is a powerful story, interesting in its own right as well as in its relationship to *The Deer Park*.

"The Man Who Studied Yoga" describes a day in the life of Sam and Eleanor Slovoda. Sam is "a small frustrated man, a minor artist manqué" (*AFM*, 154): desiring to be a serious novelist, he is instead "an overworked writer of continuity for comic magazines" (*AFM*, 158). Sam is therefore a somewhat comic version of Charles Francis Eitel, the hero of *The Deer Park*. Sam is even credited with one of Eitel's most revealing remarks: "it is the actions of men and not their sentiments which make history" (*AFM*, 163). For both Sam and Eitel this insight is ironic; each is strong on sentiment but weak on action. Sam's relationship with his wife also reminds us of *The Deer Park* and its central love affair between Eitel and Elena Esposito. Like Eitel and Elena, Sam and Eleanor come to know a cruel sadness because they are not brave enough to make their marriage work and so fail to grow: "As Sam is disappointed in life, so is Eleanor. She feels Sam has cheated her from a proper development of her potentialities and talent, even as Sam feels cheated" (*AFM*, 160).

Mailer's story dramatizes the melancholy essence of this marriage. When they gather with friends to watch a pornographic movie, Sam and Eleanor move toward the kind of experience they have always denied themselves; they are confronted by the possibility of an orgy. Mailer does not offer this potential orgy as an absolute good; instead, he uses it to embody that "orgiastic vision" (*AFM*, 176) Sam and Eleanor have repressed by accepting the values and rituals of a comfortable middle-class routine. Sam and Eleanor are not up to facing their "orgiastic vision" and its possibilities for growth (or, as Mailer *always* says, its possibilities for evil). They watch the movie and make polite conversation about it with their friends; finally they are unchanged by it. They are not like Cassius O'Shaugnessy, "the man who studied yoga"; if Cassius has "done about everything" (*AFM*, 171), Sam and Eleanor have done precisely nothing. Near the end of the story Sam is described as "a man who seeks to live in such a way as to avoid pain, and succeeds merely in avoiding pleasure" (*AFM*, 185). In this respect Eleanor is his perfect mate. Eitel and Elena will demonstrate greater resources, but *The Deer Park* deals with the same plague that afflicts the Slovodas.

"The Man Who Studied Yoga" feeds directly into *The Deer Park*, then, but it is also related to "The Time of Her Time" and "Advertisements for Myself on the Way Out," sections of a 1,000-page novel Mailer began to write after he finished *The Deer Park*. As published in *Advertisements for Myself* (479-503, 513-32), these later narratives again employ Sergius O'Shaugnessy and other characters from *The Deer Park*. As everyone notices, however, the Sergius of "The Time of Her Time" is a transformed character, one of the most interesting in all Mailer's fiction. We do not really know why Mailer gave up on this 1,000-page version of his earlier, eight-part monster, though James Rother offers some interesting speculations.[12] In any case, the excellences of "The Man Who Studied Yoga" and "The Time of Her Time" (if not the rather flatulent "Advertisements for Myself on the Way Out") confirm that Mailer's successful transition in the 1950s is away from *both* the naturalism of his first novel and the allegory of his second.

The major work of this period is *The Deer Park*, however, and so we should look more closely at this vastly underrated novel. Mailer thinks that 100 years from now *Barbary Shore* may be considered the richest of his first three novels (*AFM*, 94). But let us hope not. Let us hope instead that in something less than 100 years Mailer's third novel will be recognized as the book in which he regained his sense of "the way it is" and gave us one of the best American novels published since World War II.

The Deer Park

For a novel this exceptional, *The Deer Park* was a long time in even finding a publisher. Mailer has provided a full account of his troubles with the book, its conception, composition, revision, publication, and reception (*AFM*, 228-67). What stands out in this account is that seven publishing houses refused *The Deer Park* before G. P. Putnam's Sons finally accepted it (*AFM*, 231). The source of this hostility was revealed in the novel's reviews – Mailer's reward for his long, tortured struggle with *The Deer Park* was to discover that a good many readers thought it a dirty book. Sidney Alexander went so far as to suggest *The Deer Park* was "not even good pornography," though he assured us it *was* pornography: "Norman Mailer's new novel makes one think of a vice-squad man who goes in to investigate and stays to participate."[13] It is hard to understand how a novel so mild by contemporary standards could arouse such alarm. It is amusing to read that Mailer revised *The Deer Park* with the fear of censorship in the back of his mind (*AFM*, 241-42). It is not so amusing to discover that a majority of the novel's first critics saw in it little more than a crass preoccupation with sex. Strange that a writer who hates pornography as much as Mailer does should be plagued by the accusation that his own works are obscene.[14]

If *The Deer Park* is not a sensational work, a "shocker" in the great tradition of Irving Wallace and Harold Robbins, what, then, is it? Mailer's critics tend to classify *The Deer Park* as a "Hollywood novel," much as *The Naked and the Dead* is often labeled a "war novel." Michael Millgate suggests as much in defining "the essential theme" in serious novels about Hollywood: "Reality is distorted, human values are inverted or destroyed, and commercialism is always and everywhere the enemy. This is the essential theme of all serious Hollywood novels. It is at the heart of the struggle between Stahr and Brady in *The Last Tycoon*, between Fineman and Sammy Glick in *What Makes Sammy Run?*, between Halliday and Milgrim in *The Disenchanted*, between Eitel and Teppis in *The Deer Park*."[15] Indeed, Mailer has said that he first thought the conflict between Eitel and Teppis would be central: "The original title of *The Deer Park* was *The Idol and the Octopus*. The book was going to be about Charles Francis Eitel, the Director, and Herman Teppis, the Producer, and the underlying theme was the war between those who wished to make an idol out of art, the artists, and the patron who sued art for power, the octopus" (Plimpton 1967, 269).

This is the book Millgate addresses – the book Mailer *was* going to write but did not. Mailer's success in detailing the world of Hollywood has obscured the fact that his central concern is the love affair between Charley Eitel and Elena Esposito. Mailer has revealed that he ended up changing the novel's style to reflect the character of his narrator, Sergius O'Shaugnessy. The result, in Mailer's view, was to transfigure the story told by Sergius. This story is said to involve "two people who are strong as well as weak, corrupt as much as pure" (*AFM*, 238) – Eitel and Elena. As Mailer says elsewhere, *The Deer Park* is about "a movie director and a girl with whom he had a bad affair" (*AFM*, 242). Its reviewers and critics to the contrary, *The Deer Park* is a love story.

I emphasize this point because critical discussions of the novel tend to focus on Mailer's satiric presentation of Hollywood; to regret the fact that Eitel is the central character[16]; or, as with Millgate, to misrepresent Mailer's interest in Eitel. Each of these tendencies leads us away from Mailer's real achievement. If Eitel was first conceived as a representative artist in dubious battle with the Philistines (Herman Teppis, Collie Munshin, the congressional investigating committee), he came to interest Mailer rather more in the nuances of his affair with Elena. Gradually Mailer came to place this affair at the center of his book, using the other characters and episodes to define its significance. Eitel's affair with Elena is not, as Richard Chase suggests, "a small masterly novel within a novel."[17] It *is* the novel, at least its central movement.

Few critics have been moved to speak of a central movement in their readings of *The Deer Park*. It has been assumed that Mailer used the book to indulge a variety of his personal interests – Hollywood, the precarious position of the artist in America, the sexual revolution, the advent of the hipster, and so on – and that he divided his narrative interest more or less equally among three characters, Sergius, Eitel, and Marion Faye. It has been assumed, in other words, that *The Deer Park* has no center, no structural or thematic unity. The novel has been respected – *when* it has been respected – for its local successes, its successful parts: its humor, its satire on the movie world, at times its delineation of the Eitel-Elena love affair. What Chase says about this affair is really quite typical, for he assumes that in a novel so loosely organized this episode must be considered apart from its context in Mailer's narrative.

My own view is that *The Deer Park* is a work of much greater unity than anyone has yet acknowledged. The novel is only incidentally a satire on Hollywood or an outlet for Mailer's philosophical predilections; at heart it is the story of a rather tragic love affair. In dealing with the novel's minor and major characters, I hope to show that Mailer uses both his fictional world and his several subplots to enrich the central action of Eitel's "bad affair." I would also suggest that in the gaudy and seemingly unique mores of Hollywood Mailer discovered the materials for his most impressive critique of postwar America.

Desert D'Or: "That Gorge of Innocence and Virtue"

It is easy to see why *The Deer Park* is often taken as a formal satire. Its fictional world of Desert D'Or (Palm Springs) is a satirist's delight. It is a world marked by the varieties of sexual experience – a world of "sandwiches" and "balls," multiple infidelities, even sexual intercourse in telephone booths[18]; a world whose hero is *glorified* by rumors that he is an alcoholic, a drug addict, and a satyr (*TDP*, 28); a world whose most admirable figures are "a girl who's been around" (*TDP*, 186) and a professional pimp. Small wonder that Mailer is credited with detailing the lower regions of hell.[19]

That is not really Mailer's intention, however. His point is that the excesses of Hollywood only mirror our common tendencies. Moreover, what we share with Hollywood is something quite different from its apparent "liberation." In the passage that follows Mailer is discussing contemporary America (circa 1959), but notice how well he describes the world of *The Deer Park:*

> We have grown up in a world more in decay than the worst of the Roman Empire, a cowardly world chasing after a good time (of which last one can approve) but chasing it without the courage to pay the hard price of full consciousness, and so losing pleasure in pips and squeaks of anxiety. We want the heats of the orgy and not its murder, the warmth of pleasure without the grip of pain, and therefore the future threatens a nightmare. . . . We've cut a corner, tried to cheat the heart of life, tried not to face our uneasy sense that pleasure comes best to those who are brave. (*AFM*, 23)

Just so, the world of *The Deer Park* is one in which everyone pursues a good time while looking about furtively for the cops. What Mailer remarks about Desert D'Or is not so much its immorality as its profound sentimentality. The people of Desert D'Or *think* in terms of traditional American values, whatever they may actually *do*.[20]

Desert D'Or betrays this discrepancy everywhere. This "all new" (*TDP*, 1) society is committed to "love" yet unable to avoid the most vulgar commingling of love and lucre, sex and commercialism. Its "art" is well represented by the sentimental movies Collie Munshin wants to make from Eitel's screenplay and Sergius's life (*TDP*, 178-80, 192-93). And while apparently free of traditional moral restraints, Desert D'Or is not free of a sentimental conformity. This is best seen in the community's respect for the congressional committee investigating "subversives" and in Teppis's opinion that we should all *love* society (*TDP*, 270). Desert D'Or's respect for the committee is consistent with its pathetic efforts to keep up appearances – witness its love for publicity shots, proof positive of Teppis's claim that his studio, Supreme Pictures, is "a big family" (*TDP*, 90); its obsession with achieving "decent healthy mature relationship[s]" (*TDP*, 58); its willingness to abandon men like Eitel who stand for a time against "the public and professional voices of our sentimental land" (*TDP*, 374). Mailer's distaste for this world is implicit in the novel's epigraph, a courtier's description of the pleasure court at Versailles: "the Deer Park, that gorge of innocence and virtue in which were engulfed so many victims who when they returned to society brought with them depravity, debauchery and all the vices they naturally acquired from the infamous officials of such a place."

Mailer's attitude toward his fictional world informs his portraits of Collie Munshin and Herman Teppis, two of Desert D'Or's more infamous officials. Munshin should be credited with the phrase Norman Podhoretz cites as most typical of Desert D'Or's hypocrisy (Podhoretz, 385): in conversation with Elena and Sergius, Munshin suggests that what Elena really wants is "a decent healthy mature relationship" (*TDP*, 58). Munshin is also given to protesting that he is "a good liberal" (*TDP*, 57, 181), though his liberalism, like his respect for "mature" relationships, is not much in evidence. In his operations as a Hollywood producer Munshin in fact bears some resemblance to the notorious Sammy Glick.[21] His father-in-law, Herman Teppis, embodies even more impressively the division in Desert D'Or between public image and private fact. Publicly, Teppis has a most cheerful respect for traditional values. "I don't know people who feel respect for society any more," he laments. "In my day a man got married, and he could be fortunate in his selection or he could have bad luck, but he was married" (*TDP*, 64). Teppis has "a

large warm heart" for everyone (*TDP*, 265) but especially for society:
"I love society. I respect it" (*TDP*, 270). But even Teppis knows this
simple piety is a fraud. Immediately after forcing one of his stock girls
to engage in fellatio, Teppis murmurs, "There's a monster in the
human heart" (*TDP*, 285). Certainly there is a monster in Teppis's
heart in his dealings as a Hollywood mogul. The trappings of his
office testify to that large, warm heart he claims for himself: "a
famous painting of a mother and child was set in a heavy gold frame,
and two hand-worked silver cadres showed photos of Teppis' wife
and of his mother, the last hand-colored so that her silver hair was
bright as a corona" (*TDP*, 263-64). Yet it is beneath these pictures
that Teppis carries on his campaign to marry Lulu Meyers to a homosexual actor for the publicity values involved (*TDP*, 263-85). Like
Mushin, Teppis embodies Desert D'Or's schizophrenic blend of the
sentimental and the amoral.

Mailer's critique of his fictional world is crucial because it is
America that he confronts in *The Deer Park*, not just an exotic,
atypical community of Hollywood stars, starlets, and executives. In
the machinations of Munshin and Teppis, Mailer catches Hollywood
in the act of producing what he elsewhere describes as "the sentimental cheats of the movie screen" (*AFM*, 23). But the typical Hollywood movie resembles Mailer's America. It pursues pleasure
"without the courage to pay the hard price of full consciousness"; it
tries "to cheat the heart of life"; it evades what Sergius calls the "real
world . . . a world of wars and boxing clubs and children's homes on
back streets . . . a world where orphans burned orphans" (*TDP*, 47).
In short, it evades the reality of evil and suggests that we can get
what we want at no real cost to ourselves. This sentimental faith is
what America shares with Hollywood. In Munshin, Teppis, and the
rest of Desert D'Or's "prospectors for pleasure" (*TDP*, 4) Mailer
gives us the apostles of this tender creed.

It is also important that we see how this portrait of Desert D'Or
functions in the novel as a whole. Mailer does not render the moral
vagaries of Desert D'Or for satiric purposes alone. Like Fitzgerald in
The Great Gatsby and Hemingway in *The Sun Also Rises*, Mailer uses
his fictional world to define both the state of modern life and the
moral status of his main characters. Just as we respect Gatsby's vision
and Jake Barnes's courage partly because of the visionless and self-
pitying people who surround them, so we appreciate Mailer's central

figures – Eitel and Elena, Sergius and Marion – because of the contrast they make with their environment. Mailer's detailed creation of this world also establishes the moral context in which Eitel and Elena must act. Mailer's hero and heroine command respect because they try to get beyond their social world and its sentimental cheats; they would reject the accommodations of others for the risks and commitment necessary to growth. But if the commercialism, sentimentality, and hypocrisy of Desert D'Or make a vivid picture of what Eitel and Elena try to rise above, they are also the temptations to which Eitel especially falls prey. The value we place on this affair and the ultimate grounds for its failure cannot be understood apart from the context of Mailer's fictional world.

Sergius and Marion

The subplots involving Sergius and Marion are usually seen as much less functional than the novel's setting. Sergius is often discussed as the rather undistinguished hero of *The Deer Park,* and Marion has been called "a dark and unassimilated presence" (Weinberg, 150). But their stories should not be judged as independent lines of action. They are of value insofar as they comment on the fate of Charley Eitel, the novel's true protagonist.

It is particularly important that we understand the limited role assigned to Sergius, for if we isolate his story we are likely to be rather dissatisfied with it. Like Mikey Lovett, Sergius is the rootless narrator of his own story. Brought up in an orphanage, Sergius has "no place to go, no family to visit" after he is discharged from the air force at the beginning of the novel. Although he goes to Desert D'Or in search of "a good time" (*TDP*, 1), his quest has more to do with identity than with pleasure. What Sergius lacks is a solid sense of self. In his first months at Desert D'Or he admits to feeling like an unemployed actor (*TDP*, 5), an impersonator (*TDP*, 19), and a spy and a fake (*TDP*, 21, 46). His experience of the world is that of an alien: "I was never sure of myself, I never felt as if I came from any particular place, or that I was like other people" (*TDP*, 21). As a fighter pilot in Korea Sergius found a temporary refuge, but "that home fell apart" (*TDP*, 45) when he discovered the consequences of his bombing missions. His experiences in Desert D'Or are no happier. Like Bellows's Augie March, he comes to feel that he must look elsewhere for

a fate good enough; he must, it seems, renew his quest in the bullrings of Mexico and the lofts of Greenwich Village (*TDP*, 349-54).

But what is Sergius looking for? Even as the novel ends, he cannot really tell us: "[D]o we not gamble our way to the heart of the
mystery against all the power of good manners, good morals, the fear
of germs, and the sense of sin? Not to mention the prisons of pain,
the wading pools of pleasure, and the public and professional voices
of our sentimental land. If there is a God, and sometimes I believe
there is one, I'm sure He says, 'Go on, my boy. I don't know that I
can help you, but we wouldn't want all *those* people to tell you what
to do' " (*TDP*, 374). By the end of the book Sergius has evaded the
sense of sin and the wading pools of pleasure; he has stopped lis-
tening to the public and professional voices of our sentimental land.
But if he has arrived at the heart of the mystery, he does not reveal
its secret. Mailer tells us that Sergius was "the frozen germ of some
new theme" (*AFM*, 236). This theme is Mailer's "American existentialism," his belief that we must create our own identities in a world
we *always* make. Alas, it is a theme still frozen in the figure of
Sergius. Mailer dramatizes enough of his narrator's encounter with
Desert D'Or and its infamous officials to justify Sergius's retreat from
the resort and subsequent search for a different life-style, but Mailer
hardly prepares us to accept Sergius's bullfighting or his bullfighting
school as forays into the heart of the mystery. Mailer argues that "a
life which is directed by one's faith in the necessity of action is a life
committed to the notion that the substratum of existence is the
search, the end meaningful but mysterious" (*AFM*, 341). Presumably,
we are to see Sergius as carrying on this search from the bullrings of
Mexico to his loft in Greenwich Village, yet this whole final episode
lacks conviction.

This should not be the final word on Sergius, however. Mailer
never intended that we should take Sergius as the novel's hero. In
his essay on *The Deer Park* Mailer refers to the offer Sergius receives
of a movie career and the consequences of his refusal – his separation from Lulu Meyers and his withdrawal from Desert D'Or; Mailer
remarks that this entire episode "had never been an important part
of the book" (*AFM*, 243). As I have suggested, the *important* part of
the book concerns Eitel and Elena. We should judge Sergius's story
as it relates to Eitel's.

Sergius comes to Desert D'Or in search of a viable self; in Charley Eitel he finds a model. At first Sergius is very much the innocent and Eitel the wise instructor. When Eitel says that his Romanian mistress was "passionate in a depressing way," Sergius demands, "How can passion be depressing?" (*TDP*, 35); later Sergius sees nothing ridiculous in his hope that Lulu will "give up the movies" (*TDP*, 229). Sergius understands neither himself nor the world; in Mailer's terminology, he does not know how things work.[22] Through his friendship with the older Eitel, Sergius quickly learns some of the necessary discriminations. Early in the novel he is an uncritical member of Dorothea O'Faye's notorious "court"; after meeting Eitel, however, Sergius finds that "Dorothea's charm had turned, and the better I came to know her the less I was impressed by her" (*TDP*, 139-40). Sergius also achieves a more critical attitude toward such hangers-on as Jay-Jay and real insight into the complexities of Marion Faye (*TDP*, 140-41, 147). He becomes progressively more reliable as a guide to the moral climate of Desert D'Or.

Ironically, this change is most significant as it affects Sergius's views on Eitel. Precisely because Sergius becomes more reliable, his doubts about Eitel become the reader's doubts. Sergius first sees Eitel as a victim of that "real world" Sergius discovered in Korea: "I had the notion that there were few kind and honest men in the world, and the world always took care to put them down. For most of the time I knew Eitel, I suppose I saw him in this way" (*TDP*, 23). Sergius both identifies with and idealizes Eitel: "I felt that he was a man like me, only many times smoother and he knew more" (*TDP*, 29). Later, commenting on what he has learned in Desert D'Or, Sergius says, "Eitel is very different from me" (*TDP*, 100). Between these last two statements we have Sergius's development in *The Deer Park*. Sergius comes to see that Eitel is as much at fault as the "world" – precisely the point Mailer later made concerning the tragedy of Eitel and Elena (*AFM*, 238). When Sergius finally turns on Eitel, his judgment may lack something in compassion but it lacks nothing in authority (*TDP*, 302-8).

Mailer builds his judgment into the very structure of his book, for he counterpoints Sergius's growth and Eitel's moral decline. At the beginning of the novel each man is recovering from the most devastating experience of his life – for Sergius, the breakdown that follows his recognition of the "real world"; for Eitel, the loss of his career because of his stand against the investigating committee. Each is afflicted with impotence (both literal and figurative). During the novel the two men undergo similar experiences. Each enters into a love affair that resolves the immediate problem of impotence but leads to a more serious moral dilemma; each is tempted by the commercialism of Hollywood (commonly represented by Munshin and Teppis); and each is forced to decide whether he was meant to be an artist. The two stories make an ironic contrast. As Sergius detaches himself from Lulu Meyers, rejects the temptation of Hollywood, and dedicates himself to becoming a writer, Eitel fails in his affair with Elena, gives in to Munshin and Teppis, and admits that he is not an artist. As Sergius grows, Eitel declines. Sergius is therefore of great value to Mailer in defining the more central action of Eitel's moral failure. Mailer's rather vague treatment of Sergius at the end is unfortunate, but it would be a major flaw only if the book focused on Sergius's "education." As the novel stands, it is enough that we last see Sergius still in search of a better life, no longer "one of those boys for whom losing came naturally" (*TDP*, 20), for this tends to highlight Eitel's too-graceful acceptance of defeat before the public and professional voices in America and in himself.

Mailer's existentialist leanings are also relevant to his treatment of Marion Faye. Marion anticipates Mailer's interest in the hipster, the American existentialist. In "The White Negro" (1957) Mailer argues that the hipster is a product of this century's countless atrocities, especially the invention and use of the atom bomb. Because we have been forced to live with death as a constant possibility, the honest response to our condition is "to accept the terms of death, to live with death as immediate danger, to divorce oneself from society, to exist without roots, to set out on that uncharted journey into the rebellious imperatives of the self" (*AFM*, 339). Mailer sees the hipster as engaged in just such a journey. The hipster's faith is good existentialist doctrine: one must divorce oneself from society and shape reality to the form of one's needs; the rebellious imperatives of the self must be obeyed or one will go under, for "life is a contest between people in which the victor generally recuperates quickly and the loser takes long to mend" (*AFM*, 349). Life is a war, and help must come from within or not at all. As Mailer says, "The unstated essence of Hip, its psychopathic brilliance, quivers with the knowledge that new kinds of victories increase one's power for new kinds of perception; and defeats, the wrong kind of defeats, attack the body and imprison one's energy until one is jailed in the prison air of other people's habits, other people's defeats, boredom, quiet desperation, and muted icy self-destroying rage" (*AFM*, 339). Which is not a bad account of what happens to Sergius (the "victor"), to Eitel (the "defeated"), and to Marion himself.

For many readers, Marion is the hipster incarnate. Mailer remarks of hipsters that, while they are few in number, "their importance is that they are an elite with the potential ruthlessness of an elite." Marion is nothing if not an elitist with a potential – nay, a kinetic – ruthlessness. Mailer distinguishes the hipster from the pure psychopath by the hipster's "absorption in the recessive nuances of one's own motive which is so alien to the unreasoning drive of the psychopath" (*AFM*, 343). Again, Marion's self-scrutiny is almost obsessive. In addition, Mailer describes both the *ideal* hipster and the *actual* hipster as of 1957. In the passage that follows he speaks of the psychopath but means to define the hipster (a "philosophical psychopath"; *AFM*, 343) as he exists at present:

> At bottom, the drama of the psychopath is that he seeks love. Not love as the search for a mate, but love as the search for an orgasm more apocalyptic than the one which preceded it. Orgasm is his therapy – he knows at the seed of his being that good orgasm opens his possibilities and bad orgasm imprisons him. But in this search, the psychopath becomes an embodiment of the extreme contradictions of the society which formed his character, and the apocalyptic orgasm often remains as remote as the Holy Grail, for there are clusters and nests and ambushes in his own necessities and in the imperatives and retaliations of the men and women among whom he lives his life, so that even as he drains his hatred in one act or another, so the conditions of his life create it anew in him until the drama of his movements bears a sardonic resemblance to the frog who climbed a few feet in the well only to drop back again. (*AFM*, 347)

Marion is much like the frog. Repeatedly, he tries to purge his "compassion" and cleanse himself of what he calls the world's "bullshit," thus forging his own character despite "the conditions of his life." Marion is this kind of hipster – a *failed* hipster.

But even this perspective is misleading. Mailer suggests that both the ideal and the actual hipsters are searching for an "apocalyptic orgasm" – not Marion's style at all. Mailer speaks of "the hipster, rebel cell in our social body, [who] lives out, acts out, follows the close call of his instinct as far as he dares" (*AFM*, 363); he approves

of the hipster's emphasis on "the need of his body" (*AFM*, 341); and
he defines hip as "the affirmation of the barbarian" (*AFM*, 355).
Instinct, body, barbarian – these terms are not easily associated
with Marion Faye. Marion is profoundly distrustful of his instincts:
"He could be impregnable if sex was of disinterest to him and that
was how to be superior to everybody else" (*TDP*, 156). In fact, Marion is the hipster's opposite number, always acting from reason and
never from instinct. When his rational decisions fail because his emotions intrude, Marion feels "defeated" instead of liberated (*TDP*,
341). Marion is a much more complex figure than the programmatic
hipster of Mailer's essay; all he really shares with that romantic figure
is a sense of *mission*. The end of Marion's search, like that of
Mailer's hipster, is "meaningful but mysterious." Mailer might have
been thinking of Marion when he came to write of the hipster's
"goals": "What is to be created is not nearly so important as the hipster's belief that when he really makes it, he will be able to turn his
hand to anything, even to self-discipline" (*AFM*, 351). Marion's
"black heroic safari" (*TDP*, 328) is such a quest for greater self-con-
trol. Neither he nor his creator can be more specific.

It follows that Marion's values are exclusively negative – we are
repeatedly told what he does *not* like. The essence of his thought is
that "the whole world is bullshit" (*TDP*, 17). The expression *bullshit*
is shorthand for the fabulous illusions we live by, the values we read
into our acts. One such illusion is man's faith in love, and Marion has
his remedies for this pretension: "No one ever loved anyone except
for the rare bird, and the rare bird loved an idea or an idiot child.
What people could have instead was honesty, and he would give
them honesty, he would stuff it down their throats" (*TDP*, 155). As
Sergius notices, Marion is an inverted saint whose message is the
vileness of human nature and whose single consolation is the honest
acceptance of one's corruption. This perverse integrity is what makes
Marion so useful to Mailer, for Marion's role is to comment on and to
influence the novel's action. The book's "evil genius" (Plimpton
1967, 270), Marion stands apart from the other characters and casts
a very cold eye on their inconsistencies and vices.

Marion is most often employed as Eitel's conscience. As such, he
is crucially involved in several of Eitel's more important decisions. It
is Marion who reinforces Eitel's desire to resist the subversive committee, arguing that to capitulate would merely allow Eitel to go on

making commercial motion pictures: "You'll just keep cooking slop till you die" (*TDP*, 41). Later it is Marion who tempts Eitel with the possibility of being unfaithful to Elena (*TDP*, 186-87). These two episodes mark, respectively, the high point in Eitel's moral history and the end of his struggle to make it with Elena. In each case Marion encourages an action that will epitomize Eitel's moral condition of the moment. Marion is also crucial to the aftermath of the second episode, Eitel's liaison with the call girl Bobby. When he demands that Bobby pay him $167 of the $500 Eitel has given her, Marion helps define our complex response to Eitel's gesture. Marion's demand points up Eitel's sentimental weakness in giving Bobby so much money, while it also creates sympathy for Eitel's more compassionate treatment of the girl. The grounds for Eitel's tragedy are implicit here, for Eitel is both weak *and* compassionate.

Marion also helps shape our views on Elena. He first sees her as potentially one of his "girls": "Charley, you know like I know, she's just a girl who's been around" (*TDP*, 186). Marion tries to think of Elena as he thinks of Bobby: as someone who must have honesty stuffed down her throat. He has considered instructing Bobby in her own nature by humiliating her sexually, but for Elena he has greater plans. He senses the profound loneliness in Elena; he thinks that her nature is suicidal and that she must be taught this truth about herself: she must be made to commit suicide. But Marion cannot rid himself of "a pure lump of painful compassion" for Elena (*TDP*, 334) – she is more than a girl who's been around, and finally he cannot deny this greater depth in her. Of particular relevance is Marion's opinion of Elena when he thinks she is dead: " 'She was better than the others,' he said to himself. 'She was the strongest of the whole lot' " (*TDP*, 340). It is a sign of the times that Mailer should use Marion Faye as a reliable commentator, but such is the case. Marion's last words on Elena measure her ultimate stature in the novel.

Marion's own story is concluded in these final pages. This is the story of his unhappy love affair with an idea. Marion's "idea" follows from his belief that the world is "bullshit." Everything is phony; the world's advice is worthless; to listen to the world is to invite what Marion hates most in life – slavery (*TDP*, 15). "Slavery" is anything that restricts freedom of the will: ethical prescriptions, the demands of a business, even compassion ("Compassion was the queen to guilt"; *TDP*, 160). Marion's "idea" is that life must be dominated through a merciless exercise of reason and will. Our emotions are taught us by the world and the world is a whore.

Marion's nihilism makes him an excellent witness against the hypocrisies of others, but it is not an easy philosophy to live by. This is especially true for Marion, who is by nature sensitive, even tender. Marion must *teach* himself to resist his emotions. Because he feels fear at night, he must leave his house unlocked (*TDP*, 150-51). Because he is afraid he will attach a sentimental value to sex, he must become a pimp. Because he "burns" for Paco, a poor Mexican boy in need of a fix, he must refuse the boy money – he must beat off compassion or play the victim to his emotions (*TDP*, 160). Such a program for stifling one's feelings must end in failure. Though he rejects the mystique of sex by becoming a pimp, Marion ends up "in trade," a common businessman – an exchange of one "prison" for another (*TDP*, 328). His efforts to make Elena kill herself are a conscious attempt to break out of this prison and give his life a diabolic "purpose," but he cannot follow through: "he had his drop of mercy after all" (*TDP*, 341).

From our point of view, Marion's "defeat" is his victory. His story is a thematic inversion of Eitel's, for while Eitel struggles to live up to his feelings for Elena, Marion struggles to rid himself of his emotions altogether. Both men "fail," but their failures mark very different endings. We must take Eitel as we find him at the end of the novel, for he has lost the desire to *search*. It is different with Marion. We last see Marion on his way to a real prison, but his final words are not those of a defeated man: "I have the feeling I'm just getting on to it" (*TDP*, 347). Perhaps Marion has begun a search less self-defeating than his quest for an omnipotent will. We cannot be sure, no more than we can be sure that Sergius will discover the "meaningful but mysterious" end to *his* search. But this very uncertainty is what deepens our sense of Eitel's contrasting, irreversible commitment to the coward in himself who has chosen the easy route of prestigious mediocrity. In his last appearance, as throughout the novel, Marion thus contributes to our understanding of Eitel.

Eitel and Elena

If Mailer skillfully integrates his fictional world and his several subplots into the novel's action, his most impressive achievement is still his treatment of Eitel and Elena. I agree with Richard Foster that "as we move toward the core of this book – the affair between Elena and Eitel – surely we move from the impressive into the field of force of something like 'greatness' " (Foster, 39). Whatever its other virtues (and vices), *The Deer Park* is strongest at its center.

Because the novel is about the moral defeat of its hero, Charles Francis Eitel, it should be helpful to summarize Eitel's career prior to the represented action. Mailer provides such a summary early in the book when he reveals that Eitel represents the generation of Americans born into the Great Depression. The son of immigrant parents and the "first of his family to go to college" (*TDP*, 30), Eitel marries young and pursues his own interest (the theater) as well as his wife's (radical politics). His work in the New York theater brings him a reputation as a promising director and finally a call from Hollywood. There he manages to make three low-budget films that are still valued as realistic masterpieces. In the years that follow, Eitel involves himself in the Spanish Civil War (a final gesture of "commitment" to the Left); returns to Hollywood and sheds his wife (he will go through two more divorces); and achieves, in 15 years and 28 pictures, a huge commercial success largely based on technical virtuosity rather than art. Like many men of "humble beginnings," Eitel works hard to achieve a dubious celebrity. Once dedicated to the art of the theater, he comes to realize that "he would always be making the studio's pictures . . . his true marriage was with the capital" (*TDP*, 36).

As we first meet him, of course, Eitel is making no pictures at all. After years of compromising his integrity, Eitel loses everything as a result of one principled action: his refusal to cooperate with the congressional investigating committee. For this admirable gesture he is blacklisted in Hollywood. We first see Eitel during his exile in Desert D'Or, where he is working on a new film script that he views as "another chance" (*TDP*, 44), an artwork that will redeem his years in Hollywood. This work has gone badly, for Eitel discovers that he cannot function without the nourishment of Hollywood's fortune and esteem. A fabled lover, Eitel is reduced to impotence by his forced withdrawal from the protective atmosphere of Hollywood. He is plagued by self-doubt and the fear that he has lost his capacities for art and pleasure alike; he has no answer for the voice in himself that says he cannot succeed without Hollywood.

At this point Eitel meets Elena Esposito, Munshin's former mistress. Inspired by his ability to make love to Elena, Eitel recaptures his lost vitality and returns to his film script. In the long course of his novel Mailer charts the consequences of this affair for Eitel's talent and character. Ultimately, however, we are concerned more with the affair itself than with the question of whether Eitel can be restored to achievement and self-esteem by a love affair. It is Elena, not his script, that represents "another chance" for Eitel.

This is to suggest that Mailer's basic subject is Eitel's love affair. Eitel's relationship to Hollywood, cited by Millgate and others as the novel's focal point, is resolved before the book is half over. Eitel capitulates to Munshin by page 178, where he admits to himself that his projected masterpiece is "impossible." The rest is detail: eventually he will arrange to work for Munshin and Teppis as he has always done. Surely we are not intended to see this decision as in any sense climactic. Rather, it is an important stage in the disintegration of Eitel's affair with Elena. The rest of Mailer's novel traces the unhappy history of this affair.

If this is not obvious, one reason is that Mailer also develops the affair between Sergius and Lulu Meyers. This second affair should be seen as a comic foil, however. Each affair begins with a marvelous first night that rids the man of his temporary impotence; each leads to an immediate increase in the man's self-esteem ("How I loved myself then," Sergius thinks after making love to Lulu [*TDP*, 96]; "Loving himself, loving her body as it curled against him . . . [Eitel] fell asleep a happy man" [*TDP*, 103-4]); each goes from a first-night extravaganza to a morning-after depression (*TDP*, 104, 130); and each costs the man great anguish when he is first separated from his beloved (*TDP*, 113-15, 129-30). More generally, each affair is as unpredictable as Lulu's moods, and much of our interest is in following the irrepressible ups and downs the two couples are always suffering. Mailer's use of counterpoint in this matter is quite deft. With their obvious parody of the all-American couple (both are blond, blue-eyed, and beautiful), their games of seduction ("I was the photographer and she was the model; she was the movie star and I was the bellhop; she did the queen, I the slave" [*AFM*, 138]), and Lulu's superb capriciousness, Sergius and Lulu tend to set off the very human anxieties and greater seriousness of Eitel and Elena. Indeed, Eitel and Elena play for higher stakes than do their younger counterparts. When Eitel and Elena fail, it is not an experience to assimilate and value. In Hemingway's phrase, it is truly the end of something.

Mailer develops this crucial affair with an almost-Proustian sense for nuance. In this respect his treatment of Eitel and Elena is unique, for nowhere else in Mailer's fiction is a love relationship developed so fully. The passages devoted to Eitel and Elena are alternately amusing and pathetic, inspiriting and painful. Above all, they are human. They do complete justice to Mailer's distinction between fictional "characters" and "beings" – Mailer suggests that "a character is someone you can grasp as a whole, you can have a clear idea of him, but a being is someone whose nature keeps shifting" (Plimpton 1967, 270). Mailer offers Lulu as an example of the latter, but the real "beings" in *The Deer Park* are Eitel and Elena. This is especially true of Elena, Mailer's one totally successful female character.[23] Like other American writers of the first rank, Mailer has had his troubles with the subject of sexual love, but *The Deer Park* shows he is capable of treating the ambiguities of love with a fine sensitivity.

We may come to sympathize with Elena rather more than with Eitel; nonetheless, the story Mailer tells is still basically Eitel's. Mailer dramatizes Eitel's inability to redeem his past and traces this failure to Eitel's romantic belief that the past can be redeemed without radical change of the self. Eitel sees in sex a sufficient antidote for all the bad habits he has accumulated in Hollywood, but Mailer endorses Sergius's remark that Eitel is "profoundly sentimental about sex" (*TDP*, 110). The evidence for this view is the rest of *The Deer Park*, for what are we shown if not the failure – the inevitable failure – of Eitel's most cherished and sentimental hopes?

Eitel's dream is that "together each of them would make something of the other" (*TDP*, 110). Together they will try to confirm Eitel's most secret conviction: "[T]he core of [his] theory was that people had a buried nature – 'the noble savage' he called it – which was changed and whipped and trained by everything in life until it was almost dead. Yet if people were lucky and if they were brave, sometimes they would find a mate with the same buried nature and that could make them happy and strong" (*TDP*, 121). The last of the romantics, Eitel hopes to uncover and nourish the buried nature in Elena and himself. Indeed, he hopes that their natures are common. But they are not common, as Eitel must finally acknowledge (*TDP*,

257). Although a "noble savage" exists within Elena, its equivalent in
Eitel has been irreparably changed, whipped, and trained by everything in the life he has chosen to live for too many years. Eitel's
belief that Elena has revivified his buried nature is indeed profoundly sentimental – as if growth could come to him as a gift and
not through his own acts.

This is not to say that Mailer lacks sympathy for Eitel and his
romantic aspirations. If Eitel's dream is romantic, so is his creator.
Mailer has said that "the sickness of our times for me has been just
this damn thing that everything has been getting smaller and smaller
and less and less important, that the romantic spirit has dried up,
that there is almost no shame today like the terror before the romantic" (AFM, 382). In this spirit Mailer has proposed any number of
"romantic" alternatives to our pragmatic and deadening social life
(for example, we should combat juvenile delinquency by holding
"medieval jousting tournaments in Central Park" [TPP, 22]; we
should elect John F. Kennedy in order to restore "the dynamic myth
of the Renaissance – that every man was potentially extraordinary"
[TPP, 39]). Mailer has also shown an exceptional – and romantic – concern for such religious concepts as salvation and damna-
tion, not, it would seem, because he is religious in a conventional
sense but because such beliefs infuse life with meaning. Eitel shares
this desire for the romantic but lacks Mailer's conviction that we
must *earn* our romanticism. In Mailer's view, we pay for everything
we get in life and to deny this hard truth is to entertain a profound
sentimentality. As he says in a passage quoted earlier, "We want the
heats of the orgy and not its murder, the warmth of pleasure without
the grip of pain." It is so for Eitel, who must act in new ways and
embrace new values if he is to have Elena but cannot force himself to
do so.

Mailer portrays Eitel's failure in three stages. In the first stage,
the beginning of the affair, Eitel comes to imagine a future transfigured by the power of sex. In chapters 14 through 16, however,
Mailer describes Eitel's reversion to old, old habits. At the start of
chapter 14 we see Eitel, depressed and disillusioned, six weeks into
his affair. Before returning to follow his movements during these
weeks, we learn that Eitel has already been unfaithful to Elena.
Mailer removes suspense while inviting us to follow the history of

Eitel's failure. We are to concern ourselves not with the question of *whether* Eitel will fail but *how* he has failed.

At the beginning of his affair Eitel believes he is insulated from the seductive pull of Hollywood. The visit of a former assistant, Nelson Nevins, teaches him otherwise. It turns out that Nevins has inherited Eitel's women as well as the movies Eitel used to make (*TDP*, 165). Nevins inspires in Eitel "the pang of jealousy, call it more properly the envy he felt that he was being forgotten" (*TDP*, 167). Nevins's visit prepares for the reappearance of Collie Munshin, who has often worked with Eitel and hopes to do so again despite Eitel's status as a pariah. Eitel must make a crucial decision at this point, for if he is to work for Munshin he must give up his conception of the script he is writing and accept Munshin's "improvements," all of them dishonest and sentimental but commercially viable (*TDP*, 178-80). This decision is crucial, because to accept Munshin's proposition is to abandon the desire to be an artist.

Eitel capitulates soon after he begins to meet with Munshin. He has had a terrible time writing his script about "a modern saint" who first rises to fame by exploiting the miseries of others on a television show, then leaves the show to live amid the poverty and suffering he has exploited, and finally ends a suicide (*TDP*, 126-27). This script is at once a reworking of *Miss Lonelyhearts*[24] and a warning from Eitel to himself that he must not go back to his former life. Like the hero of his script, Eitel has been willing to "market sentiment and climb the heights of his own career" (*TDP*, 126), all the while contemptuous of the audience he feeds with false and crippling emotion. Like his hero, Eitel must reject his "success" and begin anew. Unfortunately, he cannot imagine a life that embodies his newfound integrity. The suicide of his hero foreshadows Eitel's "selling" himself to Munshin (*TDP*, 199).

Eitel thinks that his affair begins to fail because "the world had come" (*TDP*, 164) in the form of Nevins and Munshin, enticing him with its comforts and prestige. But Nevins and Munshin are only catalysts who revive Eitel's longing for his old status. They bear the message that Elena must go, for Eitel believes that if he is to take up his former role in Hollywood he must do so without Elena. She has none of the talents she would need as the wife of a famous director. She is "timid with people" and "crude in her manners" (*TDP*, 103);

even "medium clever" conversation ruins an evening for her (*TDP*, 172). By Hollywood's standards, Elena is a "fifth-rate woman," Eitel a "second-rate man" (*TDP*, 204). How would they ever manage together in Hollywood? This logic points to the more serious problem of Eitel's snobbery, for Eitel also regards Elena as a fifth-rate woman. His dream is that together they will make something of each other, but it is *Elena* who must change. She is a "fishwife" (*TDP*, 166) and "such poor material" (*TDP*, 167) for his remodeling program; "she was only what he could make of her" (*TDP*, 115). Eitel can never forget that the two of them are, at the very least, very different people. His arrogance is most evident in the conceit he invents while preparing Elena for the announcement that they must part: she becomes his "one hundred and fourteen pound sailfish" who must be maneuvered with "professional disinterest" (*TDP*, 203). The columnist who remarks that Eitel is doing a "buodoir Pygmalion" with Elena is vulgar but not necessarily wrong (*TDP*, 121).

Yet mixed with Eitel's arrogance is his profound guilt. Because Elena represents everything that Hollywood is not, Eitel is submerged in bad faith after submitting to Munshin and comes to desire "an affair with a woman for whom he cared nothing" (*TDP*, 205). Eitel's disastrous liaison with Bobby climaxes the second stage of his affair. The events of the third and final stage are virtually inevitable. Indeed, just as Mailer depicts Eitel *after* he has been unfaithful and then traces the steps that brought Eitel to this act, so now Mailer informs us that Eitel and Elena have separated *before* he returns to narrate the final stages of their estrangement (*TDP*, 290). As before, the effect is tragic. Simply by adjusting the chronology of his narrative, Mailer lends a sense of inevitability first to Eitel's indiscretion and then to his separation from Elena. Of necessity, we are concerned with the process of their failure and how they respond to it, not the question of whether they will succeed or fail.

The last movement of Eitel's affair begins the evening he attends one of Dorothea O'Faye's nightly parties. This party, as described in chapters 18 and 19, inevitably recalls the party given by Teppis some months earlier. At that time Eitel and Elena took strength from their infatuation; Eitel retained sufficient courage to flaunt Elena before Teppis and his daughter, Lottie Munshin (*TDP*, 91-93). Now Eitel and Elena are nearing their end together. Eitel spends most of the evening in conference with a congressman who has come to negotiate a second committee appearance for the suddenly "cooperative" Eitel (*TDP*, 242-45). This submissive posture is repeated a few days later when Eitel and Elena participate in a "ball" at Don Beda's. Here Eitel's nerve collapses entirely and he cannot forgive Elena for enjoying herself. He is utterly blind to Elena's stake in the experiment, the loneliness she momentarily escapes in the adoring eyes of Don Beda and his wife (*TDP*, 293-94). Eitel leaves Elena well before she leaves him to live with Marion.

Eitel is left with the comforts of rationalization: "What seemed most odious to him was that they had been tender to each other, they had forgiven one another, and yet he did not love her, she did not love him, no one ever loved anyone" (*TDP*, 297). Eitel knows better. He knows that, in cold fact, "it was his own fault, finally it was always one's own fault" (*TDP*, 164). Eitel thinks this much earlier, after his night with Bobby, but he is no less honest with himself now. He admits to Sergius that he has given in to Munshin because he wants his career with its attendant rewards: " 'You see,' Eitel was saying into my ear, 'it took me until now to realize I wanted such things very much, and that was why I stayed in the capital' " (*TDP*, 226). He can tell himself that "if he had learned nothing else, he had learned that he was not an artist, and what was a commercial man without his trade?" (*TDP*, 298). Eitel is even harder on himself in describing the messy details involved in retracting his testimony before the congressional committee: "So for the first time in my life I had the sensation of being a complete and total whore in the world." Eitel's one consolation is that he *knows* he is "disgusting" (*TDP*, 306).

Later Eitel will look back on these months in Desert D'Or as "the end of his overextended youth" (*TDP*, 373) – as if he had salvaged maturity from his experiences of this period. The price has been high, however. He has not given himself to his affair with Elena; he has feared the changes he must make, the risks he must embrace. His reward is guilt and a timid repentance, for as Eitel realizes, "there was that law of life so cruel and so just which demanded that one must grow or else pay more for remaining the same" (*TDP*, 346). Because he does not grow, Eitel must pay. Ironically, he must pay in part by marrying Elena. After her auto accident with Marion, Elena is helpless. She asks Eitel to marry her and he can only comply; though he does not love Elena, he is responsible for her. Finally, Eitel is married to his past as well as to Hollywood. We last see Eitel in his sad maturity, engaged in the professional routine of his career and an affair with Lulu Meyers. Always he must live with the knowledge that he and Elena have not made something of each other. They have instead arrived at a compromise in which Eitel goes his own way and Elena is stranded in "that domain where her problems were everyone's problems and there were no answers and no doctors, but only that high plateau where philosophy lives with despair" (*TDP*, 372).

The conclusion of *The Deer Park* recalls Mailer's indebtedness to Hemingway. Mailer has said of Hemingway, "It is certain he created my generation – he told us to be brave in a bad world and to be ready to die alone" (*TPP*, 73). Mailer tells us something like this too. As Robert Solotaroff remarks, *The Deer Park* shows Mailer "clearly working his way toward the position that courage is the primary virtue" (Solotaroff, 56). This is Hemingway's lesson, of course: in a bad world (Desert D'Or, say) the one imperative is to have courage; to lack courage is to end as Eitel and Elena end. Yet Mailer's moral vision differs significantly from Hemingway's. Recall Frederic Henry's reflections at the end of *A Farewell to Arms:* "If people bring so much courage to this world the world has to kill them to break them, so of course it kills them. . . . It kills the very good and the very gentle and the very brave impartially." Frederic's thoughts represent Hemingway's mature conviction that life itself is a tragedy.[25] Mailer agrees that to live in this world demands enormous moral stamina, but he does not blame our failures on the world alone. Throughout *The Deer Park,* in long passages of severe introspection, Mailer portrays Eitel's endless struggle with his conscience. Mailer thus makes it clear that Eitel is not simply acted on by the world of Desert D'Or or Hollywood. It is as Mailer says: because Eitel and Elena "do more damage to one another than to the unjust world outside them," there is a hint of "the rare tenderness of tragedy" to their moral failure (*AFM*, 238). There is certainly a cruel sadness to it, emphasized by the fates of Sergius and Marion, who continue to struggle with the "unjust world" and so mark by contrast the complacency to which Eitel and Elena are reduced in the end.

This "rare tenderness of tragedy" applies more to Elena than to Eitel. Elena comes from the most depressing background; as Eitel says, "My God, her parents brought her up with a meat cleaver" (*TDP*, 186). Once she leaves school her life is a series of affairs with men who appreciate only her talents in bed. She has no real chance to grow into the social role Eitel demands of his wife; she is, all too painfully, a "social book-end" (*TDP*, 86). Indeed, Elena seems no more than what Marion first calls her, a girl who's been around. But she is much more than this, as first Eitel and then Marion discover. Eitel learns at once that outside the unfamiliar territory of "society" Elena is another person: "Never had he seen such a change. Where she was timid with people, she was bold with him; where crude in her manners, subtle with intuition" (*TDP*, 103). At first this insight only convinces Eitel that Elena is an extraordinary lover. Later he is to see the justice in Munshin's remark that Elena is "a person who hates everything that is small in herself" (*TDP*, 57). He is to confirm what Sergius sees immediately: that Elena is "very proud" (*TDP*, 81).

Elena's dignity is fully evident for Eitel (and for the reader) only with the letter she sends Eitel following their separation (*TDP*, 309-18). This letter is an ungrammatical but highly perceptive analysis of their affair. Repeatedly, it captures the faults each of them brings to the affair, and in its tone it suggests an instinctive wisdom Elena has had little opportunity to cultivate. It also reveals the terrible loneliness so evident in Elena's childish delight at being "the center of attention" (*TDP*, 296) with the Bedas and perceived by Marion to be the core of her character (*TDP*, 327). Her loneliness makes Elena as fearful as Eitel; it robs her of the chance to act on her very decent insights. She sees, for example, that both she and Eitel want the other to solve all of life's problems: "that's what you were asking me and what I was asking you and *I resented it as much as you did*" (*TDP*, 315). Fearful of losing Eitel and being alone once again, Elena remains silent and lets this sickness grow until it is too late, Eitel's cowardice asserts itself, and they have lost all chance of truly changing each other.

Elena's fear is much more understandable than Eitel's, yet it too illustrates the theme that runs throughout *The Deer Park* and much of Mailer's later work. This is the theme Mailer first formulated in the passage from *Advertisements for Myself* cited earlier as a description of both contemporary America and the world of *The Deer Park* (*AFM*, 23). The theme is not sex. Rather, Mailer's subject is our moral evasiveness. He offers his fictional world as an embodiment of this evasiveness, as the temptation Eitel and Elena must confront; he offers the stories of Sergius and Marion as alternative responses to this world and therefore as indirect comments on the more central and representative actions of Eitel and Elena. Basically, however, Mailer dramatizes his theme in Eitel and Elena themselves. It is a prime virtue of this novel that as we read we are aware only of their pathetic – perhaps tragic – plight. That their failure may also be America's failure only deepens the pathos and increases the tragedy.

Chapter Four

Mailer as Fabulist

The Novels of the 1960s

Most of Mailer's fictions from 1948 (*The Naked and the Dead*) to 1955 (*The Deer Park*) can conveniently be labeled traditional or realistic. Only *Barbary Shore* (1951) represents a break with this fictional tradition, and *Barbary Shore* is Mailer's one conspicuous early failure. After 1955, however, Mailer seems to have reconsidered the premises on which his novels had been based, for a nine-year hiatus ensued in which no new novel appeared, and this silence was broken with such innovative fictions as *An American Dream* (1965) and *Why Are We in Vietnam?* (1967). It is generally agreed that these books represent a dramatic shift in Mailer's career as a novelist. In these novels, we are told, Mailer abandons the realistic tradition that nurtured his earlier works. But if Mailer's more recent novels mark a radical departure, what is the nature of this new direction? If Mailer gave up the realistic ghost when he serialized *An American Dream* in 1964, what novelistic form did he embrace in doing so? These questions have seldom been asked, let alone answered, but I think they are essential to our understanding of Mailer as novelist. *An American Dream* and *Why Are We in Vietnam?* have been applauded and deplored in the most extravagant terms, but it is hard to see how praise or condemnation can be meaningful unless we first grasp the formal nature of Mailer's experiments.

Of course, Mailer's critics usually feel no such reservation, for they are confident they do understand what Mailer is about in these books. Those who condemn the two novels are certain they are grotesque, unintentional parodies of the traditional novel; those who praise them are just as certain they replace that form with versions of the postmodern novel. My purpose in this chapter is to argue that in a real sense both positions are correct – and wrong. Mailer did attempt something radical in his later novels, but the results suggest that he did not understand the full implications of his experiment. *An American Dream* and *Why Are We in Vietnam?* are what I would call *formal* failures, for they incorporate several fictional strategies without achieving the unity of any single strategy. Their problems confirm Sheldon Sacks's argument that a coherent fiction must be governed by a single synthesizing principle, whatever the variety of its parts.[1] They also point to an unfortunate marriage of theory and practice, for in both works Mailer fleshes out his own theories about the novel – theories that are simply incommensurate with the possibilities of prose fiction. These rather large claims must be clarified, of course, but first we must examine the two novels in some detail.

An American Dream

In the January 1964 issue of *Esquire* Mailer's first novel in almost 10 years began to appear in serialized form. Eight installments later it was finished, and in 1965 Mailer issued the book in a slightly revised, hardcover edition.[2] It was called *An American Dream,* and none of Mailer's previous books had received quite the reception that awaited this one. Granville Hicks wondered whether the book was "a bad joke"; Philip Rahv argued that it lacked "verisimilitude, even in the most literal sense"; Elizabeth Hardwick dismissed it as "a fantasy of vengeful murder, callous copulations and an assortment of dull cruelties."[3] Others were even more hostile, if that is possible.[4]

Any summary of the book's contents will quickly reveal what offended its reviewers. *An American Dream* describes 32 hours in the life of its hero, Stephen Richards Rojack, an ex-war hero and ex-congressman who is now employed as a university professor whose works expound "the not inconsiderable thesis that magic, dread, and the perception of death were the roots of motivation."[5] At the beginning of the novel Rojack is suffering the pains of estrangement from his wife, Deborah, but more generally he is gripped by a sense of spiritual failure amid the trappings of material success. Before the first chapter is over he begins to remedy his condition by murdering his wife. Much of the subsequent action involves Rojack's efforts to pass off her death as a suicide, but the police interrogations are only a small portion of our hero's activities. He also makes love to two different women a total of four times; he falls in love with a blond named Cherry, now involved with a gangster but formerly the mistress of Rojack's powerful father-in-law, Barney Oswald Kelly; he defends his right to Cherry by beating up her present lover, Shago Martin, a black whom Rojack considers "the most talented singer in America" (*AAD*, 181); he engages in a fierce, climactic confrontation with Kelly, who is associated not only with the criminal element in America but also with Satan himself; he suffers the loss of Cherry, who is killed by a friend of Shago's; and he resolves to go west, to Las Vegas. All this, as the reviewers were quick to point out, in slightly more than a single day. Once he arrives in Las Vegas, Rojack has fantastic luck at the gambling tables, wins enough money to pay off his debts in New York, and decides to desert America. We last see him preparing to light out for the primitive wilds of Guatemala and Yucatán.

It is a commonplace that any plot summary will distort a writer's achievement, but the one just offered has the additional limitation of not suggesting all the offending features in *An American Dream*. My summary should suggest why Rahv could not discover his cherished verisimilitude, or why Hardwick would speak of callous copulations. What it does not convey is the pervasive role of magic in the novel, those innumerable occasions where events are apparently determined by irrational "forces" rather than by human choices or chance, as if Rojack's "not inconsiderable thesis" about magic, dread, and the perception of death were Mailer's thesis as well. The novel does not so much describe Rojack's confrontations with the people in his life or such social representatives as the police as it details his traffickings with white and black magic, the phases of the moon, and a host of instinctual "powers" that tell him what to do at all crucial moments and are associated quite seriously with God or the devil. For many readers, including the reviewers cited earlier, the ultimate vulgarity of Mailer's novel is its powerful suggestion that violence (including violent sex) is not an intolerable aberration but, rather, an extreme example of life's essential irrationality.

When his book first appeared, then, Mailer stood accused of violating both the canons of novelistic decorum and simple good sense. Since 1965, however, *An American Dream* has been defended by most of Mailer's serious critics. Indeed, it is often cited as the best of Mailer's novels, an opinion first advanced by the author himself.[6] Critics explain the novel's oddities with one of three theories: (a) Mailer was writing a kind of Chaucerian or Dantean "dream-vision,"

not a realistic novel[7]; (b) Mailer was writing in the American tradition
of romance rather than the "great tradition" of nineteenth-century
English fiction[8]; or (c) the book's extravagant events are the literary
creations of its narrator-protagonist and are not to be confused with
the literal occurrences we expect in a novel.[9] All three theories share
a basic assumption: to read *An American Dream* as a realistic novel
is to misread it altogether. This sort of thinking has been so influen-
tial that I can think of no one who has questioned its plausibility
since Leo Bersani offered the first counterattack on Mailer's reviewers, remarking that "Mailer's latest novel has had the further distinction of provoking a quaint resurgence of neoclassical canons of
taste" (Bersani, 603). Anyone who questions the persuasiveness of
Mailer's novel should apparently be aligned with the Rymers, John-
sons, and Popes of contemporary criticism. Although there are far
worse things than espousing the critical standards of Samuel Johnson, I think the issue here is not whether Mailer has a right to the
kind of imaginative freedom a neoclassicist might find suspect but
whether Mailer has in fact abandoned the conventions of realism, as
his defenders so confidently assume.

It happens that Mailer has provided a number of comments on
the formal nature of *An American Dream:* "When I wrote the novel,
I had decided to take a pretty conventional movie story, or movie
melodrama, and make it into a realistic novel"[10]; "I wanted to write a
novel of action, of suspense, of character, of manners against a violent background. . . . *An American Dream* in a funny way becomes a
novel of manners."[11] Now we are all familiar with the intentional
fallacy and its pitfalls. Indeed, these quotations may illustrate the latter, for I am sure that Mailer's conception of a realistic novel is not
Philip Rahv's or Elizabeth Hardwick's. Nonetheless, Mailer's remarks
suggest that it is too easy to dismiss the illogical elements in *An
American Dream* as conventions of romance. We must face the possibility that in developing the details of his novel Mailer was, in
Robert Solotaroff's phrase, "serious-serious" (Solotaroff, 137).

Mailer has offered another, more indirect commentary on *An
American Dream*. Having learned that Hardwick's scathing review
was to appear in *Partisan Review*, Mailer paid for "A Short Public
Notice" in the same issue. In this two-page reply to Hardwick, Mailer
reprinted a condensed version of the John Aldridge review that first
appeared in *Life*. Mailer remarks of Aldridge's review, "I cannot pre-

tend I was displeased to see it there [in *Life*], but I'm nearly as satisfied to see it here."[12] Presumably, then, Mailer endorses Aldridge's reading of the book:

> The novel explores, in what will surely be called morbid and salacious detail, the possibilities, not for damnation, but for salvation to be found in some of the most reprehensible acts known to our society – murder, suicide, incest, fornication and physical violence. It dramatizes the various ways a man may sin in order to be saved, consort with Satan in order to attain to God, become holy as well as whole by restoring the primitive psychic circuits that enable him to live in harmony with himself and find his courage, regardless of whether his courage seeks its test in the challenges of love or the temptation to murder, whether he ends by becoming saint or psychopath. It is, in short, a radically moral book about radically immoral subjects, a religious book that transcends the conventional limits of blasphemy to expose the struggle toward psychic redemption which is the daily warfare of our hidden outlaw selves.[13]

Perhaps the most interesting point about this passage is that Aldridge speaks of how Mailer's book transcends the conventional limits of blasphemy, not the conventional limits of the novel. This point is important, for it explains how Mailer can approve Aldridge's paraphrase and yet speak of his book as "realistic." The truth is that *An American Dream* was intended as "a religious book that transcends the conventional limits of blasphemy" *and* as "a novel of action, of suspense, of character, of manners against a violent background." Further, I think it can be shown that the book Mailer intended to write is also, for better or worse, the book he did write. *An American Dream* fails *because* of what Mailer tried to do, not because he failed to do it.

If we accept Aldridge's paraphrase, it seems clear that one thing Mailer tries to do is to chart his hero's exemplary struggle toward spiritual health. As Aldridge says, Rojack sins in order to be saved, consorts with the devil in order to attain to God. His involvement with murder, sodomy, fornication, and other forms of physical violence is the necessary prelude to his "psychic redemption," for Mailer believes that only in successfully engaging our hidden outlaw selves can we revitalize a peculiarly American myth, "that each of us was born to be free, to wander, to have adventure and to grow on the waves of the violent, the perfumed, and the unexpected" (*TPP,* 39). Solotaroff demonstrates that Rojack's story illustrates one of

Mailer's first principles: we can grow only if we have the courage to
confront our most violent possibilities, for true growth derives from
what Mailer likes to call "existential" situations, that is, situations in
which the outcome is both serious and uncertain.[14] Seen in this
light, *An American Dream* is precisely what Solotaroff calls it: "a fictional rendering of Mailer's ontology" (Solotaroff, 133). And thus
seen it becomes something like a Dantean dream vision, as so many
critics argue.

On the other hand, the situation Mailer describes in *An American Dream* is not simply archetypal. This is, after all, an *American*
dream, as several commentators acknowledge by citing as the locus
classicus for critical discussion the following passage from
"Superman Comes to the Supermarket" (1960): "Since the First
World War Americans have been leading a double life, and our history has moved on two rivers, one visible, the other underground;
there has been the history of politics which is concrete, factual, practical and unbelievably dull if not for the consequences of the actions
of some of these men; and there is a subterranean river of untapped,
ferocious, lonely and romantic desires, that concentration of ecstasy
and violence which is the dream life of the nation" (*TPP*, 38). This
passage suggests that we should see Rojack not as Anyman working
his way back to those primitive psychic circuits Mailer associates
with God but, rather, as a modern American, living in *the* modern
city, New York, and suffering from the distinctly American
schizophrenia just summarized. For Mailer, the "forces" that work
on Rojack are both ontologically and socially real. In reading Mailer's
one-volume encapsulation of the *Inferno, Purgatorio,* and *Paradiso*
we have no need for a fourfold critical analysis, or even a twofold
analysis, for the literal and the analogical are one.

This is the theory of it, at any rate. The practice is a good deal
less persuasive, for uniting such diverse intentions leads to formal
confusion, the frustration of any definite narrative expectations. In
effect Mailer tries to combine the narrative forms of action and apologue. Sacks defines an action as "a work organized so that it introduces characters, about whose fates we are made to care, in
unstable relationships which are then further complicated until the
complication is finally resolved by the removal of the represented
instability." Examples are *Tom Jones, Pride and Prejudice,* and
Great Expectations. Sacks defines an apologue as "a work organized

as a fictional example of the truth of a formulable statement or a series of such statements" (Sacks, 26). Examples are *Rasselas, Candide, Pilgrim's Progress,* and indeed *The Divine Comedy.* If I am right, *An American Dream* reads like a cross between *Great Expectations* and *Rasselas!* Though this suggestion may seem fanciful, isn't it the case that Mailer's reviewers read his book as a contemporary *Great Expectations* – albeit a perverse version of Dickens's classic? And isn't it fair to say that Mailer's defenders credit his novel with the form and moral seriousness, if not the moral stance, of Johnson's eighteenth-century fable?

As noted earlier, these positions are both right and wrong, for each isolates certain features of the text while ignoring others. Like such traditional novels as *Great Expectations, An American Dream* employs realistic devices to create sympathy for its central character, to define the "instability" he must overcome, and to trace the course of events leading to removal of the instability. When Rahv said that *An American Dream* was "written in the realistic convention" (Rahv, 4), he was not imposing an alien tradition on the work of a "new" novelist. Rather, he was responding to Mailer's manifest desire to create believable, complex characters whose actions might seem extreme but not incredible. He was responding to scene after scene in which Rojack's psychological state and social situation are recorded with all the concern for "reality" we would expect of Jane Austen. In short, he was responding to those features which explain Mailer's reference to the book as "a novel of manners." On the other hand, it is hard to credit Mailer's remark that "any intellectual aspects of *An American Dream* will have to be dredged up by the critics,"[15] for one critic has shown that nearly every episode illustrates Mailer's basic intellectual commitments. Solotaroff's brilliant discussion of the novel – essentially an elaboration of Aldridge's paraphrase – should persuade any reader that Mailer wanted to embody his philosophical/religious notions in the manner of Johnson, Voltaire, or Dante himself. Whether he did so successfully is, of course, another question.

Indeed, it is a real question whether Mailer's novel succeeds as an action *or* as an apologue. As an action, *An American Dream* represents a slight modification of the form Sacks describes, for Mailer does not so much introduce characters in unstable relationships as he introduces *a* character in unstable relationship with himself. The "represented instability" is internal, not external, for Rojack is a man whose plight corresponds to Mailer's account of modern anomie: "Postulate a modern soul marooned in constipation, emptiness, boredom and a flat dull terror of death. . . . It is a deadening existence, afraid precisely of violence, cannibalism, loneliness, insanity, libidinousness, hell, perversion, and mess, because these are the states which must in some way be passed through, digested, transcended, if one is to make one's way back to life" (*TPP,* 283). Rojack is a man who must pass through these very "states," for in no other way can he achieve what Mailer values most, "a single identity at [his] center" (*CC,* 76). As an action, *An American Dream* describes this dark rite de passage, which perhaps explains why our sense of Rojack's inner life is immensely more vivid than our sense of the world around him, including the novel's other characters.

The first problem with the novel as an action is that Mailer does little more than "postulate" Rojack's desperate situation. It seems that Rojack's condition has something to do with his wife, the manner in which he capitalized on his war record, and his tendency to lecture about the motivating powers of magic and dread rather than to engage these powers directly. We know all this because Rojack tells us about it in a five-page summary of his life just before he murders his wife. This summary is neither persuasive nor affecting, with the result that, in Sacks's terms, we do not *care* enough about Rojack. We identify with him to the degree that we identify with any first-person narrator, but we never feel the kind of sympathy a successful action requires. Certainly we do not feel the kind of sympathy *this* protagonist requires when he plunges into acts of murder, sodomy, and psychic warfare. To create sufficient concern for such a hero, Mailer had to persuade us that Rojack's inner state is truly desperate, that he is on the verge of spiritual death at the hands of devilish social agents. But to do so would have required something like the hundreds of pages Dickens devotes to the social forces that have made Pip what he is.

The problem is that Mailer could not enter into such "novelistic" detail without detracting from the metaphysical implications of Rojack's rite of passage. Dante could introduce his hero's situation in a single stanza, remarking only that "Dante" had lost his way and ended up in a dark wood, because the mode of Dante's great poem does not require that we care about its protagonist in a personal way. The protagonist's fate concerns us only as it is exemplary, and so Dante is well advised to ignore the specifics of his hero's departure from the straight road. In trying to have it both ways, Mailer merely creates a sketchy and enigmatic murderer who is scarcely acceptable as an exemplary figure, even if his creator thinks of him as one.

This failure to generate sufficient concern for Rojack is the novel's major problem as an action, but there are other difficulties as well, chief among them the nature of Rojack's quest for authenticity. Rojack submits to violence, insanity, libidinousness, perversion, and so on because he has come to believe "in grace and the lack of it, in the long finger of God and the swish of the Devil" (*AAD*, 35). Such beliefs lead him to believe as well in following his instincts, his "inner voice." In this he merely practices what Mailer has often preached: "To learn from an inner voice the first time it speaks to us is a small bold existential act, for it depends upon following one's instinct which must derive, in no matter how distorted a fashion, from God" (*TPP*, 194). Rojack's inner voice tells him to kill Deborah, to approach Cherry, to remove Cherry's diaphragm during sexual intercourse, to fight Shago Martin, to confront Barney Kelly, and to walk a parapet 30 floors above the sidewalks of New York City. Rojack listens and obeys in each case, and so these events would seem to be the concrete stages in his quest for psychic redemption.

Yet this inner voice and the actions it demands are also associated with the world of black magic and taboo, the world of the irrational. Rojack makes just this association at one point: " 'God,' I wanted to pray, 'let me love that girl [Cherry], and become a father, and try to be a good man, and do some decent work. Yes, God,' I was close to begging, 'do not make me go back and back again to the charnel house of the moon' " (*AAD*, 162). This desire to pull back from a perverse quest is not a momentary weakness on Rojack's part; it is repeated later when he argues with the inner voice that tells him to risk a dangerous journey to Harlem: "Let me love her some way not altogether deranged and doomed. It makes no sense to go to Harlem. Let me love her and be sensible as well" (*AAD*, 208). And it is repeated yet again at the end of the novel when Rojack thinks, "I wanted to be free of magic, the tongue of the Devil, the dread of the Lord, I wanted to be some sort of rational man again" (*AAD*, 255).

What are we to think of Rojack's reservations about his quest? Indeed, what are we to think of the quest itself?

These questions lead to a more fundamental query: what kind of action does the novel represent? Many readers see Rojack as a victim of neurotic, perhaps even psychotic tendencies. They sympathize with him at precisely those moments when he expresses the desire to be free of magic and its capricious demands. Can we be sure – from the text alone – that these readers are wrong? Can we share Aldridge's confidence that Rojack finally achieves salvation, in which case his reservations are only momentary signs of weakness? The book offers only Rojack's point of view, as Mailer himself reminds us,[16] and Rojack seems quite ambivalent on the issue. I think it is hard to avoid Stanley Gutman's suggestive conclusion: "The reader can never finally determine whether Rojack has, through magic, cut through rational conventions to a hidden significance, or whether he has entrenched himself more firmly in the illusory world of the psychotic" (Gutman, 100). Gutman does not seem to think this is an artistic problem, but I would suggest it is a fatal, not an enriching, ambiguity. The story of a sick man who achieves health by cutting through rational conventions is a different story from that of a sick man entrenching himself more firmly in the illusory world of the psychotic. If we can never be sure which kind of story is unfolding, our response at all points must be quizzical, detached, essentially intellectual. The novel as an action is crippled by such aesthetic distancing, for Rojack and his quest can never elicit the sort of emotional response Mailer presumably intended.

It would seem that Mailer expected us to read *An American Dream* with a close knowledge of his other works as an interpretive guide. Having written so often of the moral "plague" that invaded American life after World War II, Mailer presents his brief notations concerning Rojack's personal history as sufficient explanation for his hero's spiritual malaise. After all, doesn't Rojack suffer from all the telltale signs of that very plague? Having expressed his personal views in so many quarters, Mailer expects us to understand that Rojack is achieving authenticity when, for example, he interrupts the sexual act with Cherry to remove her diaphragm (*AAD*, 127). Don't we all know how much our author detests contraception? But, of course, not all of us do know this; nor should we be expected to. If *An American Dream* cannot be understood without a working knowledge of *The Presidential Papers* and *Cannibals and Christians* – volumes that collect Mailer's nonfiction of the early 1960s – no better explanation can be offered for the novel's failure as an action, for we can hardly be moved by characters and events that require an external gloss to be understood.

Much the same problem arises with the novel as an apologue. Solotaroff argues that *An American Dream* makes "fine sense as an exposition of ideas" (Solotaroff, 171), but this is true only for those who are well versed in Mailer's private mythology. To make intellectual sense of the novel, we must again resort to Mailer's other works. The result is that Mailer's "formulable statement" is unacceptably private or obscure. This is the case at almost any stage in the novel's "argument," but I think the point can be made by looking at two examples of Mailer's method.

Early in the novel Rojack tells of a war experience in which he saved his army company by killing four German soldiers. He explains that this action was made possible by "the clean presence of *it*, the grace" (*AAD*, 5), an inspiration later defined as the sort of instinctual prompting Rojack must learn to trust at all times, not just intermittently. Just before he killed the fourth German, however, Rojack made the mistake of looking into his victim's eyes, and in their presence he lost his "grace" and barely managed to kill the fourth soldier. Rojack says that these eyes "had come to see what was waiting on the other side, and they told me then that death was a creation more dangerous than life" (*AAD*, 7). This experience continues to haunt Rojack in his subsequent career as a political, social, and academic lion in New York. Indeed, the message in these eyes precipitates the crisis that culminates in the murder of Rojack's wife. It is fair to ask, then, what this "message" really amounts to.

The novel itself never answers this question, though it offers a belated hint or two. At the end Rojack sees such eyes again when he examines a cancer victim on an autopsy table (*AAD*, 265-67). This event is a strong clue for anyone who knows something of Mailer's theories about cancer. For Mailer, cancer results when the cells "betray" the body, when "they refuse to accept the will, the dignity, the desire, in short the *project* of the person who contains them" (*TPP*, 205). Cancer is a condition that comes to people who are dying spiritually, whose "projects" are inauthentic. What Rojack saw in the fourth German's eyes was a cancerous state. But how does this lead to the message that death is a creation more dangerous than life?

It leads to this idea via Mailer's notions about the human soul, death, and the possibility of life after death. Mailer has affirmed the latter so many times that it is impossible not to take him at his word.[17] He believes that "we feel dread when intimations of our death inspire us with disproportionate terror, a horror not merely because we are going to die, but to the contrary because we are going to die badly and suffer some unendurable stricture of eternity" (*TPP*, 151). We die "badly" if we die in the state Mailer calls "cancerous" – the state of the fourth German soldier and the man on the autopsy table. Death is indeed a dangerous creation, for it may well involve the eternal loss of one's soul. This fear is what Rojack reads in the German's eyes and what comes upon Rojack himself when he refuses the moon's invitation to commit suicide in the novel's first chapter (*AAD*, 11-13).

It is dangerous to dismiss this early episode as fantasy, for the call of the moon is perilously close to those other irrational messages which appear everywhere in the novel. After not responding to this call, Rojack asks, "Will you understand me if I say that at that moment I felt the other illness come to me, that I knew then if it took twenty years or forty for my death, that if I died from a revolt of the cells, a growth against the design of my organs, that this was the moment it all began, this was the hour when the cells took their leap?" (*AAD*, 13). What we are to understand is that this is the moment Rojack becomes cancerous ("a revolt of the cells"), and not, I fear, in any metaphoric sense. Behind Rojack's anxiety at this moment – the cause of his debilitating repression – is very much "a fear of dying," as Brom Weber calls it[18]: a fear "that death is not the end of anything, but is instead a continuation of the worst terrors of life" (*CC*, 363), the absolute worst being that the soul might "cease to exist in the continuum of nature" (*TPP*, 214).

Now all of this is perfectly clear – to anyone who ponders Mailer's essays or the more recent *Ancient Evenings* (1983). I cannot believe that a reader deprived of this guidance could understand the metaphysical implications of these early scenes. To the degree this is true, the novel as an apologue must suffer. But the novel also suffers when Mailer's implications are all too obvious, when his thought is relatively clear but insufficiently demonstrated, perhaps undemonstrable. The novel's climactic scene offers perhaps the best example. Throughout the book Rojack faces a series of moral and physical challenges, each requiring an extraordinary act of courage. This series culminates when he decides to walk the parapet on Barney Kelly's terrace. Rojack succeeds in negotiating the parapet once, but his inner voice warns him that the walk must be made *twice* – once for himself, once for Cherry. Because Kelly intrudes, Rojack does not make the second walk. The result? Rojack rushes back to Cherry's apartment and finds she has been beaten to death.

Cherry's death cannot be seen as mere coincidence. Rojack refuses to commit suicide when "instinct was telling [him] to die" (*AAD*, 12), and so the cells rebel and he becomes cancerous; Rojack and Cherry engage in authentic, loving sex (once that devilish diaphragm is removed), and so Cherry conceives a child (*AAD*, 176); Rojack does not "protect" Cherry by walking the parapet a second time, and so she dies. The world of *An American Dream* is one in which "good" (that is, brave) actions are rewarded and "bad" (that is, cowardly) actions are punished, a world in which poetic justice is writ very large. We can only conclude that one of Mailer's intellectual propositions goes something like this: acts of personal cowardice lead the powers that be to punish us by destroying what we value most. Such a conclusion is as hard to avoid as it is to accept.

The episodes involving the fourth German soldier and Cherry's death illustrate the novel's two major problems as an apologue. The former confirms that Mailer neither develops nor clarifies his rather complicated – and idiosyncratic – beliefs. (Indeed, it is hard to see how he could have done either, given the attention he must also devote to the novel's "realistic" elements.) An apologue is supposed to persuade us that certain propositions are true, but Mailer takes our assent for granted when he presents his ideas in such a condensed, cryptic fashion. The inevitable result is obscurity. Conversely, the episode climaxed by Cherry's death suggests that some of Mailer's ideas cannot be dramatized convincingly. This view may seem arrogant, but I doubt that the greatest artist could have presented the novel's climactic scenes so that their implications were persuasive.

Both problems are compounded by Mailer's insistence that the world of his novel is *real*.[19] This may explain his decision to mix the narrative modes of action and apologue, for in Mailer's view the world of his hero is our world as well. But novelists have enough trouble persuading us that their fictional worlds are either real *or* exemplary. Sacks argues that the forms he defines as action and apologue are mutually exclusive, that a work of fiction cannot be organized coherently as part action, part apologue. Whether this is true of all novels needn't concern us here, but the example of *An American Dream* suggests that it is all too true of Mailer's fiction.

Why Are We in Vietnam?

Curiously, no one has remarked that Mailer's next novel, *Why Are We in Vietnam?*, suffers from the same formal problem as its predecessor. Even Solotaroff, the one critic who questions the "mixed modes" of *An American Dream*, argues that *Why Are We in Vietnam?* is entirely coherent and vastly superior as a novel. I would agree that *Why Are We in Vietnam?* is a much better book, but I hardly think it achieves "one constant, if complex, focus" (Solotaroff, 173).[20] If anything, Mailer mixes the modes of action and apologue even more radically here than in his previous work. The result is a brilliant but finally incoherent work, the one Mailer novel that justifies the common complaint that his works do not succeed as wholes despite their fascinating parts.

The novel as an action again focuses on its narrator-protagonist, in this case the 18-year-old Ranald Jethroe, or D. J. ("Disk Jockey to the world"). D. J.'s remarkably obscene narrative describes a hunting trip in Alaska when he was 16. The participants include D. J.; his best friend, Tex Hyde; his father, Rusty Jethroe; two of Rusty's subordinates at Central Consolidated Combined Chemical and Plastic, a Texas-based corporation; and Luke Fellinka, head guide for the Moe Henry and Obungekat Safari Group. The action centers on D. J.'s relationship with his father, whom D. J. describes as "the cream of corporation corporateness" and "the most competitive prick there is."[21] The action includes three distinct stages, as D. J. first rejects his father and the upper-middle-class culture he represents, then embraces the "new man" his father seems to become during the hunt, and finally rejects his father altogether once the change is revealed as illusory. These vacillations correspond to the early, middle, and late stages of the hunt itself, though this aspect is often obscured by the onrushing scatological commentary of our young hero, a self-proclaimed "genius." For anyone who discovers the sensitive young man beneath the hip locutions and defiant brashness of D. J.'s rhetoric, the action is movingly developed. Its very simplicity, so unlike the exotic complexities of *An American Dream*, seems to revive Mailer's unique gifts for narrative.

These gifts are everywhere evident, especially in those set pieces which describe the killing of a wolf (*WAW*, 68-70), the tracking of a bear (*WAW*, 135-41), the investigation of an arctic wilderness (*WAW*, 173-204), or D. J.'s past and present experiences with his father (*WAW*, 40-42, 127-34, 137-38). Indeed, Mailer achieves some of the most old-fashioned effects associated with the novel as a form, for the *experience* of encountering a wilderness like the Alaskan Brooks Range filters through D. J.'s monologue with a force reminiscent of Conrad or Faulkner. In Conrad's sense Mailer makes us *see* what the natural world is like in ways that compare with the best passages in *The Naked and the Dead.* In his portraits of Rusty, Rusty's flunkies, and the compromised old hunter, Luke Fellinka, Mailer does even more: he justifies D. J.'s extreme alienation from his father's "civilized" world by rendering the careerism, hypocrisy, and vanity of these contemporary Americans, most tellingly in the scenes in which the party uses helicopters to hunt wild game (*WAW*, 98-105). We can therefore sympathize with D. J.'s endless tirade against what he calls "implosion land," "this Electrox Edison world" (*WAW*, 8), for its debilitating effects are seen everywhere in the novel's adult characters. We can also sympathize with D. J.'s efforts, late in the novel, to work himself free of "mixed shit" (*WAW*, 184) by engaging the primitive world of Brooks Range without the "aid" of his father, such "guides" as Luke Fellinka, or even the tools of our technological age. And we can feel the pathos of D. J.'s failure, signaled at the end by his decision to volunteer for active service in Vietnam, because the forces that have shaped him are finally intractable.

The novel's virtues as an action could be described at much greater length. More to the point, however, is that they are compromised by Mailer's insistence on burdening a tale of unhappy initiation with the materials of political and social allegory. The book's very title implies that Mailer's aims are those of an apologue. The title hints that we are concerned here with more than the story of one's boy's struggle with his family and culture. We are concerned with nothing less than an inquiry into the nature of contemporary America, specifically the sickness in the American character that led to the infamous war in Vietnam. Unavoidably, we are encouraged to see the novel's characters and events as types. I believe that the artistic consequences are disastrous, for it is one thing to see a character like Rusty Jethroe as a certain kind of American personality, and quite another to see him as America itself.

The allegorical elements in *Why Are We in Vietnam?* have often been cited, perhaps because they are so obvious. The chapter devoted to itemizing every piece of weaponry Rusty and his companions bring with them to Alaska (*WAW*, 77-90); the scenes depicting the use of helicopters to hunt wild animals; Rusty's story about the foul eagle, nature's most notorious scavenger (*WAW*, 132-33) – these sections all too clearly represent, respectively, America's overwhelming material advantage over the Vietcong, America's cowardly bombing tactics, and the scavengerlike nature of America's general enterprise in Vietnam. These scenes and others like them embody Mailer's intense hatred for our bullyish behavior in Vietnam, our obscene disregard for both nature and human life. The implications of such scenes are reinforced by D. J.'s commentary, which excoriates our amoral "Electrox Edison world" and suggests that the corporate types present on the Alaskan hunt fully represent the American character. The novel as an apologue seems to insist that we are in Vietnam because, as Richard Poirier puts it, "we are as we corporately are" (Poirier 1972, 129). What we are, in Mailer's paraphrase, is "a demented giant" suffering from "a fearful disease": "Greed. Vanity. . . . The Faustian necessity to amass all knowledge, to enslave nature" ("Mr. Mailer Interviews Himself," 40). What we are is sick.

The parabolic episodes cited earlier testify to this American sickness without offering a very precise diagnosis of its nature. They do not really tell us, in other words, why we are in Vietnam. Given Mailer's theory, however, it is perhaps unreasonable to expect a more specific analysis. Elsewhere Mailer explores the same problem discursively, and his explanations are almost invariably as general ("America is sick") as that proposed by his novel. In "A Speech at Berkeley on Vietnam Day," for example, Mailer offers this "explanation": "The great fear that lies upon America is not that Lyndon Johnson is privately close to insanity so much as that he is the expression of the near insanity of most of us, and his need for action is America's need for action; not brave action, but action: any kind of action; any move to get the motors going. A future death of the spirit lies close and heavy upon American life, a cancerous emptiness at the center which calls for a circus" (*CC*, 77-78). The following year, 1966, Mailer confirmed the drift of this analysis: "As is evident by now, the only explanation I can find for the war in Vietnam is that we are sinking into the swamps of a plague and the massacre of strange people seems to relieve this plague" (*CC*, 91). It was not until 1968 that Mailer came to suggest the nature of this "plague," which he defined as "a state of suppressed schizophrenia so deep that the foul brutalities of the war in Vietnam were the only temporary cure possible for the condition." He characterized this American schizophrenia as devotion to the contradictory mythologies of Christianity and science ("The love of the Mystery of Christ . . . and the love of no Mystery whatsoever"; *AOTN*, 188). This idiosyncratic analysis really rests, of course, on Mailer's hatred of technology and its dehumanizing effects on any people who allow it to dominate their lives.

Mailer's entire canon testifies to his conviction that to embrace technology is to embrace as well "the Faustian necessity to amass all knowledge, to ensnare nature." Thus, it is possible to square Mailer's paraphrase of the novel's meaning with his later, more analytical account of America's motives in pursuing the war in Vietnam. What defies credibility is that we should be expected to see a man like Rusty Jethroe (or his underlings) as acting from a Faustian desire to amass all knowledge. Rusty and the others are, if anything, the mindless products of a system we might call Faustian, given Mailer's definition of the term; as such, however, they are effects, not causes. While it might seem presumptuous to ask that Mailer get at the *causes* of our American sickness, his own title generates this expectation. That his book does not satisfy such expectations perhaps explains why we sense something pretentious in Mailer's efforts to "expand" the significance of his work beyond the confines of D. J.'s personal story.

The novel as an apologue suffers from other problems we have already seen in *An American Dream*. Again Mailer fails to fuse those events crucial to his hero's personal story and those events crucial to his fictional argument (if such a merger is even possible); again he depends on our knowledge of his other works to understand the implications of his fable. Both problems can be illustrated by examining one episode toward the end of the book. When he turns away from the "mixed shit" of the hunting party, D. J. heads into the more remote wilds of the Brooks Range, accompanied only by his friend Tex Hyde. What ensues is an awe-inspiring confrontation with perhaps the last of the American frontiers, climaxed by a night spent under the aurora borealis during which D. J. receives two messages: (a) that "God was here, and He was real and no man was He, but a beast, some beast of a giant jaw and cavernous mouth with a full cave's breath and fangs, and secret call: come to me" (*WAW*, 202), a God who admonishes, "Go out and kill – fulfill my will, go and kill" (*WAW*, 203), and (b) that D. J. should overcome his fears and engage Tex in homosexual relations (*WAW*, 202). What are we to make of D. J.'s God, and what are we to think of D. J. when he fails to act on his desire for Tex? Presumably, these are important rather than peripheral questions, for they arise at the very end of both the hunting trip and Mailer's novel.

D. J.'s "discovery" that God is a beast leads to his enlistment in Vietnam, where he and Tex Hyde, his "killer brother" (*WAW*, 204), can begin to satisfy this God's command to fulfill his will, go and kill. Knowing how Mailer feels about the war in Vietnam, several critics assume that D. J.'s God must be his own creation, the product of his enforced training in an overly competitive culture.[22] On the other hand, critics familiar with Mailer's other writings identify this God with that instinctual "voice" both Rojack and D. J. must learn to trust.[23] If the first reading is true, Mailer wants to warn against the unchastened expression of our competitive instincts, instincts we project onto our God to justify such abominations as the war in Vietnam. If the second reading is true, Mailer means to warn against *not* acting from such instincts, and it then becomes a real question as to why we should oppose the war. Surely it makes a crucial difference which view is correct, but how can we choose between them? The novel ends a few pages after D. J. experiences the presence of this God, and Mailer does nothing to clear up the scene's ambiguity. This may well be intended to illustrate Mailer's belief that we can never be absolutely certain whether it is God or the devil who "speaks" to us[24]; nevertheless, what it tells us about the American character or the war in Vietnam is anybody's guess.

The meaning of D. J.'s sexual repression is also completely ambiguous. For Robert Langbaum, "The story suggests that the idyll ends in failure because the sexual experience to which it has been leading, an expression of bisexuality, is inhibited."[25] This view seems to agree with Mailer's exhortation to trust our instincts, formulated throughout his works in pronouncements like the following: "Our emotions are a better guide to what goes on in these matters [sexual conception] than scientists [are]" (*TPP*, 143) and "[I]f there is a strong ineradicable strain in human nature, one must not try to suppress it or anomaly, cancer, and plague will follow" (*TPP*, 22). Yet Poirier remarks of D. J.'s relationship with Tex, "Their love for each other is a minority element already sickened by a homoerotic lust for masculine power. Such, in general, is Mailer's view of the possibilities of homosexual love, as in his writing about Genet in *The Prisoner of Sex*" (Poirier 1972, 149). Like Langbaum, Poirier takes his cue from Mailer's other works, in this case Mailer's many hostile statements about homosexuality. Mailer's handling of this episode has led his critics to seek external guidance concerning his meaning, but such steps have not prevented disagreements like the one between Langbaum and Poirier, for Mailer's comments on homosexuality betray hopeless contradictions. Mailer opposes homosexuality because it is "unnatural" but praises the man who suppresses his homosexual instincts: "It was put best by Sartre who said that a homosexual is a man who practices homosexuality. A man who does not, is not homosexual – he is entitled to the dignity of his choice" (*TPP*, 243). This is to praise an act of will at the expense of instinct, precisely the opposite of what Mailer usually recommends.

Such intellectual confusion is devastating to the novel's pretensions as an apologue. In turn, those pretensions have a crippling effect on the novel as an action. I have no doubt that Mailer intended D. J.'s final efforts to achieve a redeeming authenticity as the climax both to his hero's personal plight and to his own inquiry into America's role in Vietnam. In either case, however, we can only know that we are in the presence of failure, D. J.'s and/or America's. What *kind* of failure is altogether obscure. Insofar as D. J.'s fate fails to illuminate the fate of America, the novel as an apologue remains unresolved. Insofar as our attention is diverted to that larger, national issue, the novel as an action loses much of its emotional power. Like *An American Dream, Why Are We in Vietnam?* teaches

the hard lesson that it is easier to talk about combining different
novelistic traditions than to actually do so.

Mailer's Marriage of Theory and Practice

I refer to *talking* about the fusion of novelistic traditions because
Mailer does just that in much of his literary criticism. Years ago
Mailer could say that one of his early novels was about "a movie
director and a girl with whom he had a bad affair" (*AFM*, 242), but
this relatively humble fictional intention is alien to Mailer's literary
discussions after 1959. The latter are invariably informed by the
apocalyptic conception of the artist Mailer began to formulate in
Advertisements for Myself. Here Mailer tells us that the artist should
be "as disturbing, as adventurous, as penetrating, as his energy and
courage make possible" (*AFM*, 276); that "the final purpose of art is
to intensify, even, if necessary, to exacerbate, the moral consciousness of people" (*AFM*, 384); that to turn "the consciousness of our
time" is "an achievement which is the primary measure of a writer's
size" (*AFM*, 465). No surprise, then, if Mailer uses this work to publi-
cize his new goal as a novelist: to create "a revolution in the consciousness of our time" (*AFM*, 17). This messianic conception of the
writer's role is evident in almost everything Mailer has published
since 1959. In 1966 he even went so far as to condemn Hemingway
and Faulkner – "perhaps . . . the two greatest writers America ever
had" – for refusing their chance to "save" America (*CC*, 99).
    A writer so fiercely interested in ideas and their power to inten-
sify our moral consciousness is well advised to write the kind of fiction Robert Scholes calls *fabulation.* As Scholes defines it, fabulation
is a form essentially concerned with "ideas and ideals" (Scholes, 12):
"For the moment, suffice it to say that modern fabulation, like the
ancient fabling of Aesop, tends away from the representation of reality but returns toward actual human life by way of ethically controlled fantasy. Many fabulators are allegorists. But the modern fabulators allegorize in peculiarly modern ways" (Scholes, 11). If I am
right about Mailer's intentions and achievement, *An American
Dream* and *Why Are We in Vietnam?* are the works of a late-blooming fabulist whose allegorical methods are indeed peculiar because
they presuppose that the representation of reality and ethically
controlled fantasy are the same thing. This assumption is undercut

by the works of Vladimir Nabokov, Thomas Pynchon, and John Barth, representative fabulists who seem intuitively to understand what Sacks insists on in formal argument – that we cannot have our cake and eat it too.

It will seem to many that in judging Mailer's novels of the 1960s I exaggerate the importance of what Poirier calls "merely formal resolutions" (Poirier 1972, 120). Poirier would protect the extraordinary passages in these novels against judgments based on mechanical concepts of form that stress neatness and symmetry. But it is not a lack of neatness that I object to in Mailer's novels of this period. Rather, it is the fact that expectations are constantly aroused only to be unfulfilled, as Mailer tries vainly to reconcile Charles Dickens and Samuel Johnson. This is a crucial failure, for as Kenneth Burke argues, "*Form* in literature is an arousing and fulfillment of desires. A work has form in so far as one part of it leads a reader to anticipate another part, to be gratified by the sequence."[26] I do not condemn formal irresolution, but the lack of significant form throughout. Mailer's early novels are superior to his later ones because they achieve an emotional impact only possible when the work's parts come together to form a unified whole. It may be that Mailer was dimly aware of this himself, for he did not publish his next novel until 1983. The delay suggests that he again felt the need to reconsider the assumptions underlying his fiction. At any rate, his major achievements in the 1960s and 1970s are works of nonfiction, as we shall see in the next four chapters.[27]

Chapter Five

Mailer's Miscellanies
The Art of Self-Revelation

It has become a commonplace that Mailer's *real* achievement is to be found in his nonfiction. There, it is argued, we come upon Mailer "happily mired in reality, hobbled to the facts of time, place, self, as to an indispensable spouse of flesh and blood who continually saves him from his other self that yearns toward wasteful flirtations with *Spiritus Mundi*" (Foster, 41). If it seems a bit harsh to describe Mailer's novels as wasteful flirtations with *Spiritus Mundi,* many of us would still agree with Richard Foster's basic point: Mailer's nonfiction *is* a pleasant subject if one has any sympathy for his pretensions as a major writer. This is why it is curious that Mailer's much-admired nonfiction should generate so little critical commentary. From the attention (or lack thereof) it has received, one might think that Mailer's early nonfiction is no more than artful journalism, as his enemies no doubt believe and his friends have failed to dispute.

Mailer has filled the breach himself, of course, arguing at every opportunity that his realistic nonfiction should not be confused with factual journalism. He once said that "the superb irony of his professional life" was to receive the highest praise as a journalist, "for he knew he was not even a good journalist and possibly could not hold a top job if he had to turn in a story every day."[1] For Mailer, journalism is a matter of producing factual reports intended for the mass media. It is an affair of *facts,* a ceaseless inquiry into who did what to whom, at what place, and at what time. If he is not unreliable as a journalist, Mailer is hardly in competition with the daily reporter. Indeed, the whole thrust of his nonfiction is away from "factual" history. "For once let us try to think about a political convention without losing ourselves in housing projects of fact and issue" – so begins Mailer's first important essay of the 1960s, "Superman Comes to the Supermarket" (*TPP,* 27). Mailer would replace housing projects of fact and issue with a sense for the mysteries of personality and the relations among such mysteries (interests obviously taken over from the house of fiction). He has argued that "there is no history without nuance,"[2] and this statement suggests his goal as a "journalist": to capture the nuances of recent American experience and so define its true, as opposed to its *statistical,* meaning.[3]

The concern for nuance and the rejection of fact underlie Mailer's "engaged" reportage, a literary form closer to the novel than to traditional journalism. This form is best embodied in *The Armies of the Night* (1968), Mailer's first extended foray into the political history of our time. It also shapes more recent works: *Miami and the Siege of Chicago* (1968), *Of a Fire on the Moon* (1970), *The Prisoner of Sex* (1971), *St. George and the Godfather* (1972), *Marilyn* (1973), and *The Fight* (1975). Contrary to widely held opinion, however, these books did not come to us as unanticipated and unique achievements. As early as 1959 Mailer began the nonfictional innovations that made his more recent books possible. I want to consider this early work here, both as the preparation for Mailer's writings after 1967 and as an independent achievement that deserves more attention than it usually receives. By tracing the gradual emergence of Mailer's "subjective" approach to nonfiction, we should come to see what A. Alvarez means when he says that Mailer's early essays now seem "like so many training flights" for *The Armies of the Night.*[4] But we should also come to see that as Mailer turned to the techniques of fiction he was able to succeed in the essay form as never before. This is no mean achievement – among his contemporaries only James Baldwin surpasses Mailer as an essayist.

Although Mailer's nonfiction is usually assumed to have been received more generously than his fiction, this is not obvious to anyone who reads through the reviews of Mailer's early collections. Presumably, the people who now speak of Mailer's "brilliant" journalism were not available to review *Advertisements for Myself, The Presidential Papers,* and *Cannibals and Christians.*[5] Neither the reviewers nor Mailer's later admirers discuss these collections as more than compilations. While the best case for Mailer's nonfiction is not to be made by arguing that the collections are unified wholes, Mailer's efforts to give them unity should be acknowledged. These books reveal Mailer's fascinating attempt to make art by juxtaposing his most brilliant and ephemeral pieces. They bespeak his literary courage if not his common sense.

The First Three Collections

Mailer once referred to his "optimistic love affair with the secret potentialities of this nation" (*CC*, 71), as if to acknowledge that his argument with America has been a lover's quarrel. This quarrel is at the heart of Mailer's first collection, *Advertisements for Myself* (1959), a sermon delivered to America by a troubled American, as Mailer's rhetoric constantly reminds us: "So, yes, it may be time to say that the Republic is in real peril, and we are the cowards who must defend courage, sex, consciousness, the beauty of the body, the search for love, and the capture of what may be, after all, an heroic destiny" (*AFM*, 23-24). A few pages earlier Mailer remarks that "the shits are killing us" (*AFM*, 19) – thus the sense of urgency in the lines just quoted; thus *Advertisements for Myself*, a book that explores the many ways in which the "shits" are killing us (or at the very least, how they are killing one of us). As such *Advertisements* is a work of social criticism in which Mailer is his own first (and last) example. But of course *Advertisements* is many other things as well: an exercise in personal therapy, an act of propaganda, a "muted autobiography" (*AFM*, 335), and what I will later define as a literary autobiography. *Advertisements* is any and all of these things because its materials are so diverse. Mailer reprints whole or in selection almost *everything* he wrote prior to 1959: fiction, essays and articles, journalism, interviews, poetry, plays (fragments thereof), and auto-biography (some would say confession). Whatever the principle of selection at work in the making of *Advertisements*, it was not quality alone. The first question about this book must be whether it has any artistic unity whatsoever.

Mailer's better critics "explain" *Advertisements* on the theory that Mailer used the book as literary or personal therapy. According to Barry Leeds, "The process of establishing an ordered form within which to present the various pieces which make up *Advertisements* was a project intended to provide Mailer with a clearer view of what he had done and what he wished yet to do in his writing" (Leeds, 224). According to Donald Kaufmann, "Mailer is writing as much for himself as for his readers. Mailer in effect is serving as his own therapist" (Kaufmann, *Countdown*, 151). Mailer acknowledges using his writing for therapeutic ends, as when he once wrote a weekly column for the *Village Voice:* "So my readers suffered through more than one week, while the column served as therapy for me: I was eliminating some of the sludge of the past. My style then came into being out of no necessity finer than a purgative to bad habit" (*AFM,* 283). But even if we assume that *Advertisements* was such a purgative, how does this advance our understanding of the artistic principles that unify the work? Such an approach simply skirts the issue and implies that *Advertisements* can be explained only as a "solution" to its author's personal problems. If we look to the work and not the author, we should do rather better than this.

Advertisements may not be an unappreciated masterpiece, but its pieces and parts do fit into several complementary patterns. The first of these is frankly propagandistic. At one point Mailer explains that *Advertisements* is an attempt to keep his name before the public and set the stage for a major novel to which he will devote the next 10 years of his life: "If it is to have any effect, and I can hardly look forward to exhausting the next ten years without hope of a deep explosion of effect, the book will be fired to its fuse by the rumor that once I pointed to the farthest fence and said that within ten years I would try to hit the longest ball ever to go up into the accelerated hurricane air of our American letters" (*AFM,* 477). In one sense, then, *Advertisements* is literally an advertisement. The reader is invited to sample Mailer's previous work and several selections from his next novel (its prologue, a poem by one of its characters, and "The Time of Her Time"). On this basis he or she is to await The Great American Novel that Mailer will soon be offering to an alerted public. Understood in this light, *Advertisements* has no great claim on literary immortality. Mailer has not even produced his advertised masterpiece (unless one takes *Ancient Evenings* to be the thing itself); like many advertisers, Mailer has promised rather more than he has delivered.

Apart from its role in Mailer's public relations, however, *Advertisements* is obviously a kind of autobiography. Mailer introduces each of his pieces with commentary he calls "advertisements," and these sections form, in Mailer's words, the "muted autobiography of the near-beat adventurer who was myself" (*AFM,* 335). Mailer's commentary is what his critics reviewed when *Advertisements* was first published. According to his reviewers, Mailer stood revealed as "a literary terrorist" and "a dotty messiah," and his book as a whole confirmed nothing less than his "artistic crack-up."[6] The reviewers give the impression that Mailer's commentary is the least attractive part of *Advertisements;* however, Mailer says he tried to make the advertisements "more readable than the rest of his pages" (*AFM*, 7), and I think he succeeded. What he did not do is write a true autobiography. All the advertisements reveal something about their author, but only a few sections tell us much about Mailer's personal life. Like Fitzgerald's *The Crack-Up, Advertisements* includes autobiographical materials without becoming a traditional autobiography. As Mailer says early in the book, "It is certainly not my aim to make this a thoroughgoing autobiography" (*AFM*, 107).

Advertisements is more aptly described as a *literary* autobiography.[7] Mailer makes this clear about two-thirds of the way into his book: "In 'The White Negro,' in 'The Time of Her Time,' and in 'Advertisements for Myself on the Way Out' can be found the real end of this muted autobiography. . . . With these three seeds, let us say the book has its end" (*AFM*, 335). *Advertisements* is a biography of the *writer* Norman Mailer. It is an illustrated chronicle of the writer's search for his true role as an artist. Its final sections reveal the climax to this search as Mailer comes upon the subject of hip. Because hip is to furnish the material for his projected masterpiece, Mailer can also use these sections to cap his self-advertisement. Insofar as all the materials in the book are related, however, these final "seeds" are evidence that the writer's artistic voyage has been successful.

This structure gives Mailer's book unity but is ultimately self-defeating. It allows Mailer to include anything he wants to include: stories written in college, stories he could not previously publish, political essays described as "on the tiresome side" (*AFM*, 186), essays that are "no more than expanded notes" (*AFM*, 390). These pieces do illustrate Mailer's several literary directions prior to his present course, but they are also unmistakably dull and often valueless. Mailer was aware of this problem. In "Advertisement for Part Three" he writes, "This next part of the collection is put together almost entirely of writings on the fly. They are superficial, off-balance, too personal at times, not very agreeable. There would be little excuse for including such bits if I had not decided to use my personality as the armature of this book" (*AFM*, 219). Alas, there are too many such "bits" in *Advertisements*, too many articles, poems, fragments, and fragments of fragments that can interest only those of us fascinated by Norman Mailer. The form Mailer gives *Advertisements* is too much a rationalization for reprinting juvenilia, false starts, and since-abandoned projects. These pieces do set off the later, more mature essays and stories – if the reader gets to these later selections. Though it includes such fine things as "The White Negro," "The Man Who Studied Yoga," and "The Time of Her Time," *Advertisements* is finally a book for Mailer's fans.

The Presidential Papers (1963) suffers from much the same defect. In this second miscellany Mailer again resorts to a "defense for the superficial" to justify some of the material he chooses to reprint (*TPP*, 99). This time around, however, there is less need for such a defense. Except for the so-called poems and the concluding philosophical dialogue, "The Metaphysics of the Belly," the individual pieces are excellent. Even the brief columns from *Esquire* and *Commentary* are of greater intrinsic interest than columns from *The Village Voice* reprinted in *Advertisements;* even the open letters to Kennedy and Castro are readable.

At the beginning of *The Presidential Papers* Mailer again tries to persuade us that his various materials are intimately related. In this case Mailer's personality is not the "armature" of his book; instead, its focal point is John F. Kennedy, archetype of the modern hero (or potential hero). Mailer tells us that *The Presidential Papers* was written for Kennedy's benefit. The various selections are included "because their subject matter is fit concern for a President." Mailer adopts the pose of "a court wit, an amateur advisor" (*TPP*, 1) who brings together in his collection writings about and for President Kennedy, a man who has every virtue but one – imagination (*TPP*, 3). Mailer offers himself as Kennedy's imagination. He would introduce the president to the principle of existential politics, an imaginative principle for which Kennedy has great need.

The skeptical will reply that *The Presidential Papers* includes very little that is fit concern for a president. Though he takes up such issues as juvenile delinquency, the Negro emergence, the CIA, and totalitarianism, Mailer also deals with the nature of dread, the dialectic of God and the devil, sex of upper classes and lower classes, cannibalism, and digestion and the unconscious. (These are some of the "topics" listed at the beginning of the book; Mailer's phrasing is preserved [*TPP*, 7].) Moreover, he deals with all these subjects in much the same way. His method is notoriously impressionistic – a most unpolitical method. But for Mailer, this quality is precisely what recommends his book to a man like Kennedy. Mailer argues that the president has for too long dealt with the same old issues in the most "objective" manner possible. Kennedy suffers from "intellectual malnutrition" because he is given "predigested" information (*TPP*, 1-2); he needs a different kind of adviser, for he is now offered "not nuances but facts" (*TPP*, 2). Again, Mailer's aim is to capture nuance wherever he finds it – in the processes of digestion as well as the architectural style of urban renewal – for nuance *is* reality, and politics ought to deal with reality. The president – by extension, all of us – should begin to concern himself with the realities of our situation, even if these realities are not traditionally political. He should come to appreciate the fine lesson of existential politics: "Existential politics is simple. It has a basic argument: if there is a strong ineradicable strain in human nature, one must not try to suppress it or anomaly, cancer, and plague will follow. Instead one must find an art into which it can grow" (*TPP*, 22).

The Presidential Papers charts the anomaly, cancer, and plague that have come to America and proposes a number of solutions, all based on the principle that we must not suppress our desires but, rather, channel them into artful activities. A real thematic consistency runs through the book's separate pieces, as Mailer takes up different features of his old enemy, technology land ("A tasteless, sexless, odorless sanctity in architecture, manners, modes, styles"; *TPP*, 43). Those pieces not concerned with describing our descent into plague offer a solution to this drift. (This is most obviously the case in "Superman Comes to the Supermarket," Mailer's long essay on Kennedy.) When Mailer writes that "totalitarianism has been the continuing preoccupation of this book" (*TPP*, 175), we must grant the implicit claim: this book is sufficiently of a piece to have a continuing preoccupation. Using the figure of Kennedy to represent America – much potential marred by too little imagination, too little insight – Mailer offers a volume almost worthy of the promotion on its paperback cover: "a brilliant, slashing portrait of the Kennedy years by the most controversial writer of our time."

Not everyone would agree, of course. Many reviewers seemed to think that Mailer had betrayed the muse by turning from the novel to publish what one reviewer termed "a collection of magazine pieces . . . essentially the oddments turned out by a novelist who is not writing a novel."[8] Richard Gilman stated outright what many reviewers hinted at in so many ways – that Mailer had abandoned art in pursuit of his "naive and addled philosophical bases."[9] No one came forward to reply that in such essays as "Superman Comes to the Supermarket" and "Ten Thousand Words a Minute" Mailer had in many ways *advanced* his art. No one ventured to suggest that Mailer was perhaps onto something with his "unprofessional" approach to our social and political life. In fact, as we will see in reviewing the growth of Mailer's nonfictional techniques, *The Presidential Papers* includes more of Mailer's successful essays than we find in any of his other collections.

It is more than a little ironic, then, that *Cannibals and Christians* (1966), the least successful of Mailer's first three miscellanies, received a much better press. The book consists in part of articles written in the early 1960s but not collected in *The Presidential Papers*. It includes one selection, "The Metaphysics of the Belly," reprinted from *The Presidential Papers* as an introduction to its sequel, "The Political Economy of Time." *Cannibals* is therefore burdened with not one but two of Mailer's "philosophical" dialogues. (Indeed, if we count the brief "The First Day's Interview," there are *three* such dialogues.) Mailer also sees fit to publish more of his poems.[10] He refers to them here as "short hairs" and explains that they are interspersed throughout *Cannibals* as "seasoning" (*CC*, xii). These "short hairs" take up no fewer than 67 pages altogether, and *Cannibals* would have to offer a very feast to overcome such uninspired seasoning. Moreover, *Cannibals* suffers when compared with the earlier collections because it includes fewer interesting selections. The political writings of part 1 are especially unexciting if set beside comparable essays in *The Presidential Papers,* and Mailer's "philosophical dialogues" must have been read from beginning to end only by myself and a dozen other academics at work on Mailer. *Cannibals* sometimes reminds one of a graveyard for Mailer memorabilia.

Yet Mailer argues that the separate pieces in *Cannibals* "have relations with one another. . . . [T]he writings are parts of a continuing and more or less comprehensive vision of existence into which everything must fit" (*CC*, xi). Sometimes these "relations" are obscure (for instance, the thematic connection between Barry Goldwater's nomination and the emergence of camp). Occasionally they are simply spurious. For example, Mailer begins an essay on the history of American literature by remarking, "There has been a war at the center of American letters for a long time" (*CC*, 95), a conflict presumably related to the struggle between Cannibal and Christian that Mailer sees as the latest stage in our dialectical evolution. In fact, however, Mailer is referring to the antagonism between naturalism and the genteel tradition. Only a relations hunter extraordinaire could see this "war" as one version of the Cannibal/Christian dialectic.

Mailer's theme – the war between Cannibal and Christian in contemporary America – does inform much of the rest of the book. Mailer's penchant for the dialectical had been obvious since *Advertisements*, in which he developed the contrast between the hipster and the white Protestant whose "ultimate sympathy must be with science, factology, and committee rather than sex, birth, heat, flesh, creation, the sweet and the funky," the provinces of hip (*AFM*, 388). In *The Presidential Papers* Mailer came to perceive this conflict as rather more universal, as we see in the passage quoted earlier in which he describes America's "double life" of politics and "untapped, ferocious, lonely and romantic desires, that concentration of ecstasy and violence which is the dream life of the nation" (*TPP*, 38). In *Cannibals and Christians*, as the title implies, Mailer returns to this notion of America's dialectical development as embodied in his Cannibals and Christians. The Cannibals are the right wing of our political life, obsessed with American mediocrity and confident "one can save the world by killing off what is second-rate." The Christians are to be found not in Christian churches but popping up across the political spectrum from moderate Republicans to Communists, united by their belief that "science is the salvation of ill" and "death is the end of discussion." Humanitarian and pacifistic, the Christians have nonetheless succeeded in "starting all the wars of our own time, since every war since the Second World War has been initiated by liberals or Communists." The Cannibals' accomplishments are no less paradoxical, for if they "think of Jesus as Love," they also "get an erection from the thought of whippings, blood, burning crosses, burning bodies, and screams in mass graves" – the Cannibals are not irrelevant to Vietnam (*CC*, 4). Mailer finds both groups unappealing: "Sellah, sellah – is it better to be a foul old Cannibal or a Christian dying of nausea?" (*CC*, 91).

Mailer's Cannibal/Christian dichotomy is the latest attempt in his early miscellanies to explain America's social illness. In *Advertisements* he rails against "national conformity" (*AFM*, 283). In *The Presidential Papers* he decries the many forms of totalitarianism that have come to America. *Cannibals* is the logical result of Mailer's growing pessimism, evident in the shifting terms of his protest. Whereas earlier he attacked first conformity and then totalitarianism, now he refers to his "continuing obsession . . . that the world is entering a time of plague" (*CC*, 2). There is no antidote for this latest sickness. No case is made in *Cannibals* for "the creative nihilism of the Hip" (*AFM*, 325); no brief is set forth for "existential politics" (*TPP*, 22, 43). Now there is only a lament for the devastation we have brought on ourselves.

The lament in *Cannibals* is profoundly conservative and thus marks a real transition to Mailer's later writings. In 1968 Mailer established his identity as a left conservative,[11] but already in *Cannibals* the ex-revolutionary socialist has replaced Marx with Edmund Burke; already he is writing that "1964 was also a year in which a real conservative still had a great deal to say to the nation" (*CC*, 47). This real conservative is Mailer himself, and what he says to the nation is worthy of Burke: "There seems at loose an impulse to uproot every vestige of the past, an urge so powerful one wonders if it is not with purpose, if it is not in the nature of twentieth-century man to uproot himself not only from his past, but from his planet" (*CC*, 235). The misfortune of this collection is that Mailer lifts his lament to the level of art only in the essay on Goldwater and several literary articles not connected to the volume's fundamental theme.

Mailer's miscellanies are simply too heterogeneous to reward his efforts to make them unified wholes (*The Presidential Papers* is perhaps an exception). The fiction in the collections is not up to the standards of Mailer's novels; much of the nonfiction is occasional in the extreme. Hostile critics might say that *most* of the selections, not just a few political essays, read as if they were no more than expanded notes. But this is only to say that Mailer's worst work does not measure up to his best. Lodged in his first three miscellanies are some of Mailer's most accomplished performances. Collectively, these essays form a rather slim volume – slimmer than any of the published collections. But the volume I envision is one of the more significant works in contemporary American literature. It includes the best of Mailer's early essays – except for a few pieces by James Baldwin and Joan Didion, the best essays by an American in the postwar period. Among Mailer's collections, it is this hypothetical gathering of his better pieces that should be considered in detail.

The Early Essays

This hypothetical volume would include a moderate variety of materials, not the great variety of Mailer's published miscellanies. Missing would be the interviews and self-interviews, open letters to Fidel Castro, correspondence with the editor of the *New York Review of Books*, refutation of a gossip columnist, therapeutic columns for *The Village Voice*, and remarks on the sexual implications of the T formation, among other items. If variety is the spice of life, mediocrity is the death of attention. Our ideal volume would be limited to the introductory materials written especially for the first three collections, much of the literary criticism, and those essays published after *Advertisements* which focus on specific American events (for example, political conventions, championship fights, and televised tours of the White House).[12] I agree with the critical consensus that Mailer's reputation as a "journalist" rests largely on the last-mentioned items. His essays on the political conventions of 1960 and 1964, his essay on Jackie Kennedy, and his coverage of the first Floyd Patterson-Sonny Liston heavyweight fight seem to me by far the most impressive items in his early nonfiction. To this list we must add only one earlier piece, "The White Negro," to flesh out our hypothetical volume of Mailer's better essays. Because these essays range from 1957 to the early 1960s, they should allow us to trace the growth of Mailer's unique approach to nonfiction.

Like their author, Mailer's political and social essays have changed remarkably over the years. The pieces that go back to the 1950s hardly anticipate the essayist who will brood over the psychic forces at work in a championship prizefight; whether their subject is David Riesman, homosexuality, Marx, or *Sputnik*, they all betray the

radical intellectual who once dissected Western defense for readers
of *Dissent*. Significantly, Mailer has all but repudiated his earliest
essays: "whenever I sat down to do an article, I seemed to thicken in
the throat as I worded my sentences and my rhetoric felt shaped by
the bad political prose of our years" (*AFM*, 186). Indeed, such essays
as "The Meaning of Western Defense," "David Riesman Reconsidered," and "The Homosexual Villain" are unpleasant reading for
anyone who admires Mailer's prose style. Since collected in *Advertisements*, these articles suggest that Mailer has no real gift for the
closely reasoned, "objective" essay.

"The White Negro" (1957) is Mailer's one significant essay of the
1950s. In one sense an almost-scholarly discussion of the hipster,
this piece succeeds where Mailer's other early essays do not because
it goes beyond the analysis of a cultural or political situation to create what Mailer calls a sociological "fiction" (*AFM*, 196). Mailer's
fiction – the hipster as revolutionary elitist – is not, of course, a
wholly imaginative creation. Mailer tries to describe a real
phenomenon with real historical roots. He traces the birth of the
hipster to the catastrophes of the twentieth century and views this
figure as a rebel against society – that "collective creation" revealed
by World War II to be "murderous" and by the postwar era to suffer
from "a collective failure of nerve" (*AFM*, 388). Mailer is also careful
to identify the source of the hipster's life-style: the black culture
based on jazz, marijuana, and sexuality (hence Mailer's title).[13] But
starting with these observations on the hipster's genesis, Mailer is
quick to take up a partisan defense of the hipster's intuitions. The
true thrust of his "analysis" is not descriptive but prophetic, for he
sees the hipster as the "dangerous front-runner of a new kind of
personality which could become the central expression of human
nature before the twentieth century is over" (*AFM*, 345). The more
inspired passages in "The White Negro" always reject the generally
analytical tone of the essay for a more lyrical evocation of the new
hero who has come among us. This passage is representative:

> It is this knowledge which provides the curious community of feeling in the
> world of the hipster, a muted cool religious revival to be sure, but the element
> which is exciting, disturbing, nightmarish perhaps, is that incompatibles have
> come to bed, the inner life and the violent life, the orgy and the dream of love,
> the desire to murder and the desire to create, a dialectical conception of exis-
> tence with a lust for power, a dark, romantic, and yet undeniably dynamic

> view of existence for it sees every man and woman as moving individually
> through each moment of life forward into growth or backward into death.
> (*AFM*, 342-43)

The "knowledge" Mailer refers to is the hipster's supposed awareness of what is good or bad for his own psyche. Mailer begins by remarking this "knowledge" and ends with nothing less than his claim for the hipster's "dialectical conception of existence." Jean Malaquais calls this claim "a gorgeous flower of Mailer's romantic idealism" (*AFM*, 362), and I doubt that many of us would disagree. Insofar as "The White Negro" is sociology as we tend to think of it, Mailer's achievement is limited by such excessive claims for his subject. But "The White Negro" is really a lyrical defense of Mailer's conversion to hip, an American existentialism that differs from the French variety because it is based on "a mysticism of the flesh" rather than "the rationality of French existentialism" (*AFM*, 314). Mailer succeeds in "The White Negro" to the degree he persuades us that hip has "a dark, romantic, and yet undeniably dynamic view of existence," not that it literally derives from black culture or is a major social force. Despite its sometimes ponderous tone, "The White Negro" therefore anticipates the strategies of Mailer's more recent essays. Like these essays, it is distinguished by the quality of Mailer's brooding and most partisan reflections on what he has observed.

If "The White Negro" was an advance, the real turning point for Mailer's nonfiction was *Advertisements for Myself*. After 1959 Mailer's essays are marked by the strong personal voice he developed in writing the "advertisements" for his first collection. At first the difference is only stylistic, as Mailer cultivates this personal voice and so avoids the "thickening" in the throat that came to him while writing those political essays influenced by "early, passionate, and injudicious reading of the worst sort of Max Lernerish liberal junk" (*AFM*, 186). But gradually Mailer came to introduce his personality as well as his personal voice into his "journalism." His writings from 1960 to 1968 represent a continuing effort to focus his exploration of recent American history by transforming this personal element into a functional persona.[14]

Before he could do this, however, Mailer had to discover the value of fictional techniques for a work of nonfiction. He seems to have made this discovery in "Superman Comes to the Supermarket" (1960). Ostensibly a report on the 1960 Democratic National Convention, this essay is really a glorification of John Fitzgerald Kennedy, the convention's nominee. Mailer has acknowledged the highly partisan, even propagandistic character of the piece: "I was forcing a reality, I was bending reality like a field of space to curve the time I wished to create. I was not writing with the hope that perchance I could find reality by being sufficiently honest to perceive it, but on the contrary was distorting reality in the hope that thereby I could affect it. I was engaging in an act of propaganda" (*TPP*, 60). In other words, Mailer was trying to get Jack Kennedy elected. "Superman Comes to the Supermarket" appeared several weeks before the 1960 election (the piece was printed in *Esquires* November 1960 issue), and Mailer's hidden purpose was to encourage unenthusiastic Democrats to vote for Kennedy. Mailer believes he was successful; he thinks that he, as much as anyone, deserves credit for Kennedy's narrow victory (*TPP*, 60-61, 88-89). Disregarding this claim – the merciful thing to do – we can say that Mailer's covert intentions do not discredit his essay as literature. Mailer's partisanship here is similar to his position vis-á-vis the hipster in "The White Negro," where his enthusiasm for his subject generates some of his finest prose.

Impressed by Kennedy's charisma rather than his politics (which were traditionally liberal, if not a bit conservative), Mailer sets out to dramatize the mysterious allure of Kennedy's personality. Toward this end he employs numerous literary devices, most of them novelistic: character analysis, character sketches, shifts in chronology, and the juxtaposition of contrasting characters and events, among others. But his first tool is sheer rhetoric. He remarks at the beginning of his essay that he will "dress" his argument in "a ribbon or two of metaphor" (*TPP*, 28), and the "argument" is indeed metaphoric. Kennedy is variously described as "a great box-office actor," "a hero central to his time," and "a prince in the unstated aristocracy of the American dream" (*TPP*, 38, 41, 59); he is said to have "a patina of that other life, the second American life, the long electric night with the fires of neon leading down the highway to the murmur of jazz" (*TPP*, 31). Kennedy is contrasted throughout with the sort of candidate desired by the bosses of the convention – the totally political, totally predictable candidate like Richard Nixon. Mailer laments that we have embraced the security of Eisenhower and become technology land itself. We are a country of mythical heroes, but we have lost faith in such heroes. We are therefore in need of a Kennedy, an American prince who will rekindle our faith in the American dream. The nation will reveal itself by its selection of Kennedy or Nixon: "One would have an inkling at last if the desire of America was for drama or stability, for adventure or monotony" (*TPP*, 58). Will the American people be so courageous as to embrace their own lonely and romantic desires?

Needless to say, the "argument" here is some distance removed from "fact and issue." It is a novelist's argument, and throughout "Superman Comes to the Supermarket" Mailer performs the good novelist's task of heightening his protagonist by treating everything else in a manner that can only set off Kennedy's contrasting excellence. The scene at the convention is described so as to make Kennedy appear not only a matinee idol but a savior come unto heathens. Los Angeles is "a kingdom of stucco, the playground for mass men"; the Biltmore Hotel, convention headquarters, is "one of the ugliest hotels in the world" (*TPP*, 33); the people at the convention are either political hacks or party professionals like Lyndon Baines Johnson ("when he smiled the corners of his mouth squeezed gloom; when he was pious, his eyes twinkled irony; when he spoke in a righteous tone, he looked corrupt"; *TPP*, 35). It is to *this* city, *this* hotel, and *these* people that Kennedy comes, the movie star come to the palace to claim the princess (*TPP*, 38). Mailer also places in evidence Nixon's incredibly mawkish remarks upon receiving the Republican nomination: " 'Yes, I want to say,' said Nixon, 'that whatever abilities I have, I got from my mother . . . and my father . . . and my school and my church' " (*TPP*, 45). He dismisses with contempt the Republican National Convention that followed and offers yet another judgment on that convention's nominee: "The apocalyptic hour of Uriah Heep" (*TPP*, 58). He describes in detail Adlai Stevenson's presence at the Democratic convention, for Stevenson plays the passive antihero to Kennedy's hero (*TPP*, 50-51). The "events" Mailer describes in this essay were selected by a professional novelist, not a political journalist. The very texture of his essay validates Mailer's attractive "creation" of John Kennedy – a creation soon to be adopted by the country at large.

"Superman Comes to the Supermarket" reveals the novelist's hand but does not include the device most characteristic of Mailer's

more recent nonfiction – the use of himself as participant as well as
spectator. For this we must look to the later essays, beginning with
Mailer's second convention piece, "In the Red Light: A History of the
Republican Convention in 1964" (1964). As its subtitle suggests, this
essay is about the Republican National Convention rather than its
leading man. (Goldwater is the most important character, but he is
hardly the hero of the piece.) The essay is formally divided into three
parts: (a) a history of events prior to the convention, including
Goldwater's rise to power in the Republican party; (b) a description
of the convention up to Goldwater's nomination; and (c) a spectator's views on Goldwater's acceptance speech. Only at the end does
Mailer abandon the pose of reporter to reflect on Goldwater's
ascendancy and the state of the union in this year of Johnson versus
Goldwater. Yet Mailer's interpretive presence is felt throughout. This
"presence" is what distinguishes "In the Red Light" from journalistic
accounts of the convention.

Mailer's role begins to emerge in the political portraits of part 2.
Here Everett Dirksen is seen as "an old organist who could play all
the squeaks in all the stops, rustle over all the dead bones of all the
dead mice in all the pipes," and we can *hear* Dirksen as Mailer
describes him, "making a sound like the whir of the air conditioning
in a two-mile tunnel" (*CC*, 34). And once we read Mailer's description of George Romney as "a handsome version of Boris Karloff, all
honesty, big-jawed, soft-eyed, eighty days at sea on a cockeyed passion" (*CC*, 31), we can never see Romney again without visions of
Frankenstein's monster. These examples suggest that Mailer is not
exactly a disinterested historian. This is most obvious in his
"analysis" of the Goldwater crusade. Goldwater delegates are presented as "a Wasp Mafia where the grapes of wrath were stored"
(*CC*, 16); they are seen as "a frustrated posse, a convention of hang-
men who subscribe to the principle that the executioner has his
rights as well" (*CC*, 27); their representatives in the California delegation are said to resemble Robert Mitchum playing the mad reverend
in *Night of the Hunter* (*CC*, 36). Mailer even senses this fanaticism in
the bagpipers who play throughout the convention, for theirs is "the
true music of the Wasps" in which we detect "the Faustian rage of a
white civilization . . . the cry of a race which was born to dominate
and might never learn to share" (*CC*, 25). Mailer's metaphoric rendering of the convention can be charged with bias, but many of us

will sympathize with the underlying assumption: what really happened at the convention can be captured only by a human voice concerned with human acts. Even where Mailer is on shakiest ground as a reporter – his characterizations – most of us will find that *his* Scranton, Goldwater, or Eisenhower at least suggests the man we all observe, rather than the faceless political "figure" we encounter in the newspapers. But the point is perhaps obvious. Dealing with the convention as he would in a novel, Mailer achieves the same imaginative authority in what is formally an essay.

Mailer's impressionism is justified because "In the Red Light" is about his response to the ascending right wing rather than the phenomenon itself. Mailer attaches such weight to his impressions because he assumes they are representative. They are also terribly ambivalent, which accounts for the dramatic tension so characteristic of the essay. The Goldwaterites impress Mailer as a WASP Mafia, but their demonstration for Goldwater suggests that their "inner condition" is both more ominous and more appealing: "There was an unmistakable air of beauty, as if a rainbow had come to a field of war, or Goths around a fire saw visions in a cave. The heart of the beast had loosed a primitive call. Civilization was worn thin in the center and to the Left the black man raised his primitive cry; now to the Right were the maniacal blue eyes of the other primitive. The jungles and the forests were readying for war. For a moment, beauty was there – it is always there as tribes and clans gather for war" (*CC*, 34). The appeal in this passage is suggested earlier when Mailer remarks, "I had been leading a life which was a trifle too pointless and a trifle too full of guilt and my gullet was close to nausea with the endless compromises of an empty liberal center. So I followed the four days of the convention with something more than simple apprehension" (*CC*, 26). This passage goes far to explain Mailer's fascination with Goldwater, for Goldwater is an answer to the empty liberal center. Finally, of course, he is an unacceptable answer ("He was humbug. . . . Goldwater was a demagogue"; *CC*, 40), but he does provide Mailer with a rather ominous clue to our condition as a people, for if someone like Mailer feels the attraction of a Goldwater, then Mailer's conclusion is probably true: "America has come to a point from which she will never return. The wars are coming and the deep revolutions of the soul" (*CC*, 45). Mailer renders the convention so persuasively that such prophecies seem virtually inevitable.

We can be grateful for Mailer's fascination with Goldwater – his account of the Republican convention is much richer than it might otherwise have been. Elsewhere, however, Mailer uses his own personality not only to focus coverage of an event or movement but as his basic subject. He treats himself as a character in one of his novels might be treated and so brings the essay form to the borders of fiction. Witness "An Evening with Jackie Kennedy, or, The Wild West of the East" (1962). The final section of this essay reads much like "In the Red Light," for Mailer first describes Jackie Kennedy's televised tour of the White House and then uses the occasion to speculate on the depressing condition of America and what Mrs. Kennedy might be able to do about it were she somewhat less "phony" (*TPP*, 97). But the final section is no more than one-third of the essay. By first reporting his personal encounters with Mrs. Kennedy, Mailer places in evidence his initial impressions of the First Lady; he also, however, provides a portrait of Norman Mailer, necessary, he implies, if his criticisms of Jackie Kennedy are to be fairly assessed by his readers (*TPP*, 88). It is this self-portrait that is original in "An Evening with Jackie Kennedy." Mailer dramatizes not only his initial conversation with Mrs. Kennedy but also the domestic details surrounding it, from an argument with his wife the day he interviews the Kennedys to his wife's conversation with Jackie Kennedy the next day (*TPP*, 84, 87). Here Mailer writes about himself with real comic detachment, observing that he was in a "Napoleonic mood" at the time he received a letter from Jackie Kennedy, noting that he replied "in the cadence of a Goethe" (*TPP*, 87).

Not that self-deprecation is the essence of Mailer's self-portrait. Mailer is typically earnest when it comes to representing his own ideas; he even admits that the essay's middle section is "needlessly long and close to comic in its intensity, for it sails under a full head of sermon" (*IAO*, 12). Moreover, much of the personal material is used to introduce his meetings and correspondence with Jackie Kennedy, still the essay's subject. Nonetheless, we have here the beginnings of Mailer's more recent, more objective self-portraiture – Mailer with irony, so to speak. The emphasis on Mailer's interaction with his subject anticipates the strategies of his later nonfiction.

These strategies are most successfully employed in "Ten Thousand Words a Minute" (1962), Mailer's account of the first Patterson-

Liston fight. Here Mailer emphasizes his own role in a public event almost to the exclusion of the event itself. He may have hit upon this strategy through necessity rather than choice, for the fight itself was a one-round "fiasco" (*TPP*, 307). In any case, Mailer's title is a sly hint that he is concerned here with something more than the coverage of a championship fight. Mailer does write nearly 20,000 words about a two-minute fight – *and* about what he takes to be its symbolic meaning, his relation to it that week in Chicago, and his reaction to its outcome. These latter concerns are what justify the length of "Ten Thousand Words a Minute," the longest and the best of Mailer's essays.

I do not mean to suggest that Mailer neglects his duties as a reporter. In part 1 he gives a fascinating account of the men surrounding the two fighters; in part 2 he offers a very professional report on the Patterson and Liston training camps; in part 3 he presents what must be the most vivid published account of the fight itself; and in part 4 he manages to cover all the postfight activities, including Liston's press conference the next day. Impressive as Mailer's reportage can be, however, "Ten Thousand Words a Minute" is still about Norman Mailer's coverage of a prizefight rather than the fight itself. We sense this as early as part 2, where Mailer dramatizes not only his observations of Patterson and Liston but also his conversations with such men as Cus D'Amato, Patterson's manager, and Jim Jacobs, Patterson's public relations assistant. The humor here is at Mailer's expense; like the self-deprecating passages in "An Evening with Jackie Kennedy," it makes possible the ironic self-characterization so crucial to *The Armies of the Night*. Indeed, Mailer's humor is almost as important here. "Ten Thousand Words a Minute" offers a symbolic reading of the Patterson-Liston fight in which Liston is Faust and Patterson is the archetypal underdog, Liston is sex and Patterson is love, Liston is the hustler and Patterson is the artist, Liston is the devil and Patterson is God (*TPP*, 255). Such weighty identifications are presented in all metaphoric seriousness. Like *The Armies of the Night*, "Ten Thousand Words a Minute" can afford such extravagance because the man who speculates so largely is himself the object of dramatic irony. Mailer is revealed here in a familiar role: "Once more I had tried to become a hero, and had ended as an eccentric" (*TPP*, 265). Yet Mailer's speculations are not to be dismissed as mere quirkishness. As in his later works, Mailer wins a hearing for his ideas as the redeeming insights of a writer who will reveal everything about himself – his most ridiculous "capers" as well as his most dazzling intellectual connections.

The essay's final sections confirm that Mailer's ultimate subject is himself. Once he describes the fight and offers his ideas as to what it all "means" (what the fighters represent), Mailer would appear to be done. Yet he goes on for another 15 pages. The fight inspires a severe self-analysis in which Mailer takes upon himself part of the blame for Patterson's defeat. (Briefly, Mailer finds that he has backed Patterson in an "idle, detached fashion"; like Patterson's liberal supporters, he has failed to nourish the champion's spirit [*TPP*, 258].) As he considers the events of that week in Chicago, including his debate with William Buckley at Medinah Temple, Mailer finds that the ledgers are stacked heavily against him. He has supported Patterson too complacently, he has drunk much too much, and he has sulked over such trivialities as the account of the debate in the *New York Times*. Mailer feels something like Patterson's humiliation because he identifies with the lonely artist in Patterson: "Patterson was the champion of every lonely adolescent and every man who had been forced to live alone, every protagonist who tried to remain unique in a world whose waters washed apathy and compromise into the pores. He was the hero of all those unsung romantics who walk the street at night seeing the vision of Napoleon while their feet trip over the curb, he was part of the fortitude which could sustain those who lived for principle, those who had gone to war with themselves and ended with discipline" (*TPP*, 241-42). Mailer has failed both Patterson and himself, for his week in Chicago has been ruled by the world's apathy, compromise, and lack of discipline.

Mailer's disruption of Liston's press conference, the essay's final episode, reveals Mailer as yet another unsung romantic who has Napoleonic visions while tripping over curbs. The scene is saved from bathos because Mailer sees it for what it is ("Once more I had tried to become a hero, and had ended as an eccentric"). Yet it is also a fitting climax to his narrative, for here Mailer dramatizes his determination to be "some sort of center about which all that had been lost must now rally" (*TPP*, 261). The defeat of Patterson becomes for Mailer the defeat of love and art and discipline. His bravura at the press conference registers his decision to reaffirm all that the week's events and the fight itself have called into question.

Indeed, this reaffirmation is what the essay is ultimately about. By intimately describing his reactions to the fighters, Mailer makes us see that Patterson and Liston do not merely represent such forces as love and sex; finally, they represent *us*, both our heroic and our demonic possibilities. Mailer comes to understand this and to act accordingly – however "comic" his action may be. Like Mailer's other major works, "Ten Thousand Words a Minute" affirms the need for just such self-awareness and self-assertion.

Years later Mailer would involve himself in another struggle in which the opposing sides would suggest the "countered halves" of his own nature (*TPP*, 261). In his account of the 1967 March on the Pentagon, Mailer would again dramatize his conversion to one side in the struggle. Both "Ten Thousand Words a Minute" and *The Armies of the Night* are narratives about the comical yet serious education of Norman Mailer. The essay anticipates the later work in technique as well as form, for "Ten Thousand Words a Minute" depends on fictional techniques to a degree unparalleled in Mailer until *Armies*. Such devices are used selectively in "Superman Comes to the Supermarket," "In the Red Light," and "An Evening with Jackie Kennedy," and Mailer's use of himself as a persona can be seen emerging as long ago as *Advertisements for Myself*, a work in which his controversial self-portrait is a major unifying device. But in "Ten Thousand Words a Minute" Mailer's fictionlike nonfiction is fully developed. Such figures as Patterson, Liston, D'Amato, Jacobs, and the cabbie who takes Mailer to Comiskey Park are treated in a manner Mailer formally reserved for his fiction. Mailer dramatizes every scene in the essay and makes particular use of the flashback, a device normally associated with fiction. If he is "hobbled to the facts of time, place, self," Mailer artfully deploys his "facts" in a literary structure that anticipates the subjective history of *The Armies of the Night*.

The most novelistic of Mailer's essays, "Ten Thousand Words a Minute" is also the piece in which his self-reference is most conspicuous. For this reason it is not surprising that the essay still receives insufficient recognition as a minor masterpiece. Nor is it really curious that Mailer's early nonfiction is so seldom examined. As F. Scott Fitzgerald once remarked, "There are always those to whom all self-revelation is contemptible, unless it ends with a noble thanks to the gods for the Unconquerable Soul."[15] Mailer's detractors are quick to find *his* self-revelations contemptible, failing to see that in registering its effects on him Mailer illuminates the history of his time. Mailer offers his reactions to modern life as those of a representative American – unusually sensitive and intelligent, perhaps, but subject to the same contradictory emotions as the rest of us in confronting such phenomena as Barry Goldwater, Floyd Patterson, the peace movement, women's liberation, the space program, and such enigmas as Richard Milhous Nixon. As Mailer says, there is no history without nuance. What his method suggests is that the nuances of recent history can be caught only in the response of a troubled American to the events that *are* America. If he demonstrates this idea most convincingly in *The Armies of the Night,* Mailer anticipates that achievement in the essays I have grouped here as the most appealing Mailer miscellany.

Chapter Six

The Armies of the Night
The Education of Norman Mailer

Mailer once remarked that with the stabbing of his second wife he lost all chance of becoming an American Jeremiah (Brower, 100). Nothing he has said about his ambitions as a writer is more revealing. Of course, it is a bit comical to suggest that one's talents recall Jeremiah's, but those of us who sympathize with Mailer's work will forgive the hyperbole. However pretentious, Mailer's comment hints at his deeply felt desire to be something more than a respected literary figure. In 1959 Mailer announced his modest goal of creating "a revolution in the consciousness of our time" (*AFM*, 17). If he has not had that kind of impact, Mailer has persisted in his belief that the great writer and the great prophet should merge in a single figure (one who resembles Norman Mailer).

Mailer's prophetic inclinations have shaped most of his works since *Advertisements for Myself.* Increasingly suspicious of the novel's immediate "relevance," Mailer has devoted more and more of his time to nonfiction, a mode in which he can suggest not only the sources of that "plague" he sees everywhere in the land but also its possible remedies. Thus, we have been offered what sometimes seems an endless supply of Mailer nonfiction, beginning with his political essays of the early 1960s and highlighted by *The Armies of the Night* and *The Executioner's Song.* Though he lavishes the accumulated lore of a novelist on these works, Mailer's ultimate purpose is consistent with the connotations of the term *analysis.* He wants to tell us something about America, about ourselves. Mailer once referred to himself as "a poor man's version of Orson Welles" (*AOTN*, 32), but his real ambition has been to offer a modest version of the prophet himself.

Mailer comes closest to this ideal in *The Armies of the Night* (1968), a book that climaxes his decade-long concern with "the task of examining America" (CC, 99). This achievement is at once the culmination of much earlier work and the luckiest of accidents. Technically, *Armies* draws on Mailer's work in nonfiction throughout the 1960s, as I suggested in chapter 5. But if it now seems the "inevitable" climax to this earlier work, such a book was far from Mailer's mind when he was first invited to attend the 1967 March on the Pentagon. Whereas Truman Capote went looking for an event worthy of being immortalized in a "nonfiction novel," Mailer discovered his materials rather against his will. Mailer's reluctance even to attend the demonstration is great irony today, for by the end of that eventful weekend in Washington he knew that he had stumbled upon a literary treasure. The march proved once more what Mailer had been saying for years, that in the twentieth century "the real had become more fantastic than the imagined" (FOM, 141). The march was precisely Mailer's kind of material, for as he once said, "mate the absurd with the apocalyptic, and I was a captive" (AFM, 221). The absurd, the apocalyptic, and Mailer came together that October weekend in Washington, and a book was born. What began as a wasted weekend participating in "idiot mass manifestations" (AOTN, 18) ended by inspiring Mailer's most successful work.

This opinion is surprisingly widespread. *Armies* received almost uniformly excellent reviews and won both the Pulitzer Prize and the National Book Award. Today one does not have to defend the quality of this book (as one must defend the quality of *The Deer Park*, for example). Yet for all its good reviews and awards, *Armies* raises certain questions its critics tend to ignore. They acknowledge its essential wisdom, the chastened prophetic strain that here informs the work of a man who once said he wanted to create a revolution in the consciousness of our time. But Mailer's critics are all too timid in discussing the narrative strategy by which he channels his prophetic desires into meaningful form. Those who acclaim Mailer's "objective" self-portrait ignore the narrative pattern he imposes on his work by means of this portrait. Those who refer to Mailer's formal "breakthrough" deal with the book's initial, "novelistic" section as if it were formally unrelated to the second, "historical" part. Surely these are important matters. What is the narrative pattern in *Armies?* Is the book a "nonfiction novel" or a history? Indeed, is it fiction or nonfiction? If we cannot answer such questions, we are in no position to praise *Armies* as Mailer's masterpiece. And if *Armies* is a work of real distinction – if it is more than a "report" on Mailer's role in a peace demonstration – then surely something must be made of its apparently independent parts. Mailer came to write book 2 of *Armies* after fulfilling his obligation to *Harper's* by writing book 1. It would be well for his literary reputation if he had something in mind other than padding out his account of the march to the dimensions of a full-length book.[1]

In what follows, then, I want to do three things: (a) discuss the generic question, (b) describe the narrative pattern of book 1, and (c) suggest how books 1 and 2 are related. My aim is to show that *Armies* is the most powerful synthesis of Mailer's artistic and prophetic ambitions.

The Generic Question

"History as a Novel/The Novel as History" – Mailer's subtitle calls attention to one of the more obvious questions about *Armies*. What kind of animal is this book, a history or a novel? Because we bring such different expectations to works of fiction and nonfiction, I do not think this question irrelevant, as some readers argue. Before discussing the book's form, however, I want to comment on two other American works that challenge the traditional distinction between fiction and nonfiction. If we compare these books with *Armies*, I think we will better understand Mailer's formal innovations. I have in mind Hemingway's *Green Hills of Africa* and Capote's *In Cold Blood*. Like Mailer, Hemingway and Capote do more than employ *some* of the devices of fiction in the service of nonfiction; they presume to employ *all* (or nearly all) fictional devices in the creation of what Capote calls the "nonfiction novel."

This is not quite the claim that Hemingway makes for *Green Hills of Africa* (1935). In his foreword to this work Hemingway in fact draws attention to the difference between his book and "many novels": "Unlike many novels, none of the characters or incidents in this book is imaginary. . . . The writer has attempted to write an absolutely true book to see whether the shape of a country and the pattern of a month's action can, if truly presented, compete with a work of the imagination." *Green Hills of Africa* is therefore a pure example of nonfiction: "an absolutely true book." Yet the work reads much like a novel. Hemingway dramatizes his material as he would in a work of fiction, even to the point of altering the chronology of events to achieve such "fictional" effects as suspense and a narrative climax.[2] The usual defense for material included in a work of nonfiction – things happened this way – does not altogether apply to Hemingway's book. So "novelistic" does it seem that the literary conversations at the beginning impress us as digressive; quite simply, they detract from the story that is developed everywhere else in the book. These conversations may have occurred just as Hemingway describes them, yet they have no meaningful relation to anything else in the work. This seems suggestive, for if we begin to evaluate a book by its internal coherence and not its fidelity to fact, shouldn't we conclude that it is structured as fiction rather than nonfiction? If we *seem* to be reading a novel, isn't it the case that we *are* reading a novel (one that happens to be "absolutely true")?

But how unfortunate for Hemingway's reputation if we decide that *Green Hills of Africa* is a novel. Artfully structured to achieve a dramatic climax in its hero's hunt for kudu, *Green Hills of Africa* is nonetheless a powder puff of a novel. More to the point, it is not a novel at all. We see this most clearly in the book's principal characterization. "Hemingway" is the protagonist, yet he is entirely without depth as a character. We learn nothing about him when he finally gets his kudu hunt; nor have we learned much about him earlier except that he is persistent and loves to hunt. In fact, "Hemingway" is a device that allows Hemingway to work up his real – and announced – concerns: "the shape of a country and the pattern of a month's action." We learn almost nothing about "Hemingway's" past, not because Hemingway chooses to develop his hero in terms of the present but because he is committed to describing one month's activities on safari in Africa. To go into "Hemingway's" past would only distract us from the work's fundamental concerns – concerns that are documentary and not novelistic, nonfictional and not imaginary. *Green Hills of Africa* is a marvelous account of hunting in Africa. We do Hemingway no favor by insisting that it is a novel about a man named Hemingway who achieves the hunt of his life after many frustrations.

Truman Capote also wanted to produce "an absolutely true book" when he came to write *In Cold Blood* (1965). Capote goes so far as to argue that *everything* in his book is "immacuately factual": "One doesn't spend almost six years on a book, the point of which is factual accuracy, and then give way to minor distractions."[3] Capote presses this claim both in his subtitle ("A True Account of a Multiple Murder and Its Consequences") and in his acknowledgments: "All the material in this book not derived from my own observations is either taken from official records or is the result of interviews with the persons directly concerned, more often than not numerous interviews conducted over a considerable period of time." Since we *expect* a work of nonfiction to be accurate, Capote's remarks are interesting only because he also insists that his book is formally unique, a "nonfiction novel."

Capote defines the nonfiction novel as "a narrative form that employ[s] all the techniques of fictional art but [is] nevertheless immaculately factual" (Plimpton 1966, 41). Readers who believe that Capote achieves this form naturally emphasize the novelistic character of *In Cold Blood*. David Galloway, for example, praises Capote for "a careful and artful selection of details, calculated to evoke a variety of moods, to establish character, to produce suspense, and to convey a number of intricately related themes. It is in the selection of such details and in their rearrangement that the technique of the novelist is vividly present."[4] But does novelistic technique inevitably point to the form of the novel? This appears to be the crucial question – one neither Capote nor his partisans address directly. It seems to me that what Capote does hardly differs from what Hemingway wished to do in *Green Hills of Africa*. When he remarks that the "point" of his book is factual accuracy, Capote defines it as that most stolid form of historical writing, a documentary.

The novelist is free to depict only the most "authentic" persons, places, and things. Like the naturalist, he may insist that his fictional world is "lifelike," a genuine representation of the world we all know and move about in. Every detail in his book may be "true." For example, Henry Miller may well render his experiences more accurately than either Hemingway or Capote.[5] But it really does not matter whether Miller is as "accurate" or not. Because he does not *claim* that his books are immaculately factual, we read them as fictions, never thinking to condemn their author if we should find that he "distorts" events from his own life. By contrast, I think we would condemn Hemingway or Capote if we found that either seriously distorts the truth.[6]

I am suggesting that from the moment we first read Capote's subtitle we begin to assimilate his material as the evidence in his reconstruction of a true event. We do not ask that this evidence be
"probable" or arranged in some effective, climactic fashion. If it is so
arranged, we receive a more powerful impression of the evidence
without ceasing to evaluate it as such; we do not cease to read the
book as a documentary. Of course, this would not remain the case if
In Cold Blood differed from a book like *Tropic of Cancer* only in the
claim that appears on its title page. As it happens, however, this claim
is more or less accurate. We continue to read *In Cold Blood* as a
documentary because finally it *is* a documentary. The resemblance to
fictional structure in Capote's book is really quite superficial. As
Capote says, his materials were selected because they *are* the Clutter
murder case in all its solid specificity. Capote rearranges a few
events, but this rearrangement should not be confused with the
imaginative structure of a fiction. In theory, Capote cannot alter the
events or details of his story to develop character or theme; indeed,
he can do nothing that might violate the factual accuracy of his
account. The inevitable result is that character and theme, as we
know them in the novel, do not appear in *In Cold Blood.* Capote's
central characters have no more depth than Hemingway's persona.
We could argue that Capote simply fails as a nonfiction novelist, but I
think the explanation is otherwise. I do not think it accidental that
the "Henry Miller" revealed in Miller's novels is a much richer
creation than anyone in Capote's book. The events in these novels
may be real, but they are introduced because they dramatize the
many sides of Miller's controversial hero. After all, the revelation of
character is what Miller – as novelist – is principally about. The
writer who wants to document an event may well find that to
"develop" his or her characters actually runs counter to the work's
formal requirements. I believe this is true for Hemingway and Capote
in the works I am discussing.

These remarks on Hemingway and Capote may seem somewhat
gratuitous, but I hope to demonstrate their relevance to what Mailer
does in *Armies.* The comparisons suggest themselves because *Armies*
shares so many features with *Green Hills of Africa* and *In Cold
Blood.* Like those books, *Armies* is an experiment in nonfiction by a
famous writer who brings to his task the accumulated resources of a
novelist. Like Hemingway, Mailer uses himself as the protagonist of

his book. Like Capote, Mailer selects a subject that offers what Galloway calls "instant symbolism" and embodies Mailer's long-standing thematic concerns. Tony Tanner sums up what is symbolically apposite about Capote's material: "By juxtaposing and dovetailing the lives and values of the Clutters and those of the killers, Capote produces a stark image of the deep doubleness of American life."[7] Mailer also believes in this deep doubleness, as Tanner acknowledges by citing the passage in "Superman Comes to the Supermarket" in which Mailer speaks of America's "double life" (*TPP*, 38). In *Armies* Mailer finds yet another image of America's deep doubleness in the forces that confront each other during the March on the Pentagon. These armies of our divided country seem almost to have been deployed for Mailer's purposes.

Mailer's narrative techniques also recall Hemingway and Capote. Most obviously there is the full-scale use of novelistic devices, especially techniques of dramatization. Like Capote, however, Mailer also relies on public sources that allow him to cover events he did not personally witness.[8] Mailer also follows Capote in digressing from his narrative to analyze issues relevant to the event he is describing. Where Capote presents a psychoanalytic interpretation of Perry Smith, one of his two mass murderers,[9] Mailer offers an argument on why we are in Vietnam and why we should get out (*AOTN*, 181-89). The resulting blend of novelistic and nonfictional devices extends the method Mailer first developed in the shorter form of the personal essay. Capote went through a similar training for *In Cold Blood* with interviews he published in the *New Yorker* and in his book *The Muses Are Heard.*[10]

Is *Armies* a history, then? Like *Green Hills of Africa*, does it try to capture a real event with absolute truth? Like *In Cold Blood*, is its principle of selection factual accuracy? Or does *Armies* differ significantly from these two works? I believe that it does differ, though not as fiction differs from journalism. We must finally read *Armies* as a history and not as a novel, but we must also see that it is a very unusual history, quite different from what Hemingway and Capote tried to do.

Mailer's subtitle hardly makes it clear that *Armies* is a history, but in the work itself lies abundant evidence that he conceived his book this way. At the end of part 1 (book 1) Mailer sends his protagonist home from the Ambassador Theatre to his room at the Hay-Adams

Hotel. He then remarks, "Of course if this were a novel, Mailer would spend the rest of the night with a lady. But it is history, and so the Novelist is for once blissfully removed from any description of the hump-your-backs of sex" (AOTN, 52). Later, following his release from jail, Mailer says that he went home to begin "his history of the Pentagon." He characterizes this work as "history in the costume of a novel" (AOTN, 215). In addition to these passing references to Armies as a history, Mailer offers a defense of his narrative method that clearly defines Armies as a history (albeit a special version of history, closely related to the novel).

Mailer defends his method early in book 1. Here he explains why it is proper for him "to write an intimate history of an event which places its focus on a central figure who is not central to the event" – that is, himself. This procedure is justified by the nature of the March on the Pentagon, "an ambiguous event whose essential value or absurdity may not be established for ten or twenty years, or indeed ever." Mailer argues that to focus on one of the founders or designers of the march – David Dellinger, Jerry Rubin, and others – would resolve none of the ambiguity. For this we need "an eyewitness who is a participant but not a vested partisan . . . ambiguous in his own proportions, a comic hero." Given such a hero, Mailer hopes "to recapture the precise feel of the ambiguity of the event and its monumental disproportions" (AOTN, 53).

Mailer's defense of his method may or may not seem plausible. In any case, it does define his major objective in Armies: "to recapture the precise feel of the ambiguity of the event." This may be compared with Hemingway's use of himself as a vehicle to suggest what it is like to hunt in Africa. Both Mailer and Hemingway are primarily interested in the event they describe – a historian's interest, not a novelist's. Yet Mailer's definition is interesting, for it almost outlines the intentions of a novelist. To recapture the precise feel of an event is to search for nuance rather than fact – always Mailer's intention in his nonfiction – and to recapture what an event feels like requires that he create a protagonist who can register this feeling in himself and in others. Writing his history of the march, Mailer ends up developing his own character much as he would a fictional hero's.

Throughout his nonfiction Mailer presents himself as such a persona. In Miami and the Siege of Chicago he suggests the reason for doing so: "If this were essentially an account of the reporter's actions, it would be interesting to follow him through the chutes on Thursday, but we are concerned with his actions only as they illumine the event of the Republican Convention in Miami, the Democratic Convention in Chicago, and the war of the near streets" (*MSC*, 197). In *Armies* too Mailer uses himself to illuminate the event he is describing. But in *Armies* Mailer illumines the event by describing *all* of his actions during the march. The difference is quantitative; however, as Mailer is fond of saying (citing Engels), quantity affects quality. Formally, *The Armies of the Night* is closely related to *Miami and the Siege of Chicago* (as well as to the essays discussed in chapter 5). Yet it is different too, for Mailer employs his methods so exhaustively that he creates a form almost indistinguishable from the novel.

Mailer does this for the reason offered in the text: to understand the March on the Pentagon, we must grasp its essential ambiguity, the *feel* of its ambiguity. We must understand its "subjective reality." This is the phrase Tom Wolfe uses to describe what he is after in *The Electric Kool-Aid Acid Test* (1969), yet another book sometimes referred to as a nonfiction novel. In an author's note Wolfe says that he has tried "not only to tell what the Pranksters did but to recreate the mental atmosphere or subjective reality of it." What Wolfe says of his book about Ken Kesey and the Merry Pranksters Mailer might have said about *Armies*. But Mailer would never go on to say, as Wolfe does, that "all the events, details, and dialogue I have recorded are either what I saw and heard myself or were told to me by people who were there themselves or were recorded on tapes or film or in writing,"[11] for it would then be a short step to Capote's explicit claim: this work is to be judged by how accurate it is. To say the least, Mailer has small sympathy for such claims to accuracy. At the end of *Armies* he writes of events at the Pentagon after the massive crowds are gone and the few remaining demonstrators are left alone with the soldiers. He first reprints two remarkably dissimilar accounts of what happened at this time (*AOTN*, 260-62) and then comments, "It may be obvious by now that a history of the March on the Pentagon which is not unfair will never be written, any more than a history which could prove dependable in details!" (*AOTN*, 262). Mailer is indeed writing history in *Armies*, but it is a very subjective history, and the difference between subjective history and fiction is a subject on which most theorists fear to tread.

Treading softly, I would suggest at least two differences between these forms. The first is fairly obvious. Any history, no matter how subjective, is purportedly based on fact, as a fiction need not be. This notion may seem to contradict what I have just said about Mailer's attitude toward "accuracy," but the contradiction is more apparent than real. The subjective historian does not claim to be absolutely accurate in reporting "what happened"; indeed, his or her concern is to *interpret* what happened, to discover its real significance. Nonetheless, such a historian acknowledges that the work is founded on what actually occurred. Mailer acknowledges this throughout *Armies*, as when he says that he is not obliged to work up a love interest for all us readers of novels. He is not obliged to do so because his narrative is restricted to what happened during four days in October 1967. Fortunately, what happened to Mailer is interesting (if sexless) material – we would not be reading about it otherwise. Yet the "rightness" of his material does not alter the fact that Mailer denies himself the enriching possibilities of imaginary episodes by his choice of forms.

A second difference between subjective history and fiction is rather more important. These forms differ in their basic ends. The historian wishes to discover the meaning of an event. If a subjective method is used, it may render private impressions of the event or the impressions of others; it may even dramatize the entire event as the writer experienced it. But it will do so for the reason Mailer offers in the passage just quoted: to illumine the event itself. Most fictions are structured toward a very different end, one I take to be the creation of emotional effects – for instance, tragic or comic effects – appropriate to the particular fictional action. The characters in a fiction exist for the sake of such effects, not to "explain" an external phenomenon (the March on the Pentagon, say).[12] Another way of putting this is that whereas Huck Finn's story is presented for its own sake, Mailer's personal story is developed so that we may finally understand the March on the Pentagon. In this context the crucial fact about *Armies* is that it does not end with book 1, as a novel on the subject might have ended. Book 2 is relevant precisely *because Armies* is a history – that is, because its formal end is to interpret a historical event rather than to dramatize its hero's spiritual growth. Book 2 extends Mailer's avowed purpose, "to elucidate the mysterious character of that quintessentially American event" (*AOTN*,

216). As we sense well before Mailer explains its purpose, book 1
prepares for book 2. Mailer's historical intentions, advertised
throughout, lead us to expect that his highly personal account of the
march will issue finally in a subjective but general interpretation of
the event as a whole. When this in fact occurs in book 2, we should
realize that *Armies* is organized as something other than a novel.

If it is right to see that *Armies* is not a novel, it is even more
important to appreciate how the book differs from works like *Green
Hills of Africa* and *In Cold Blood.* The difference lies principally in
Mailer's treatment of his own character. Hemingway directs our
attention to his African setting and the events of his hunt by refusing
to develop himself as a "rounded" character; Capote rigorously
excludes his own role in the Clutter investigation to concentrate on
the data he has accumulated. Mailer, by contrast, emphasizes his
own reactions to the march. These internal "events" are hardly
verifiable in the manner of a documentary. In no meaningful way can
it be argued that Mailer "documents" his response to the March on
the Pentagon. Rather, he uses his reactions as the material for what
he calls his "interior" history of the demonstration (*AOTN*, 255).

Though these distinctions may seem somewhat academic, they
have the value of suggesting that book 2 of *Armies* is an integral part
of Mailer's work. Before we can fully appreciate this point, however,
we must understand what Mailer does in book 1. What distinguishes
book 1 is that Mailer fulfills his obligations as historian while writing
a narrative with the appeal of a novel. Whether or not his material is
inherently interesting, Mailer makes it seem so by clothing it in a
novelistic "costume." As suggested earlier, the shape of this costume
is seldom discussed. In a sense, of course, Mailer's form was
imposed on him by his choice of the historical mode. Yet however
"factual," the form of book 1 is not merely chronological. The events
form a narrative pattern – a plot – that is much more significant
than a record of "what happened." There is a meaning to the events
that Mailer is able to get at *because* his history is subjective. To see
how this is so, we must first turn to Mailer's portrait of Mailer.

The Structure of Book 1

"From the outset, let us bring you news of your protagonist" (*AOTN*,
3). In this, the first sentence in *Armies*, Mailer introduces his hero.

He will refer to him later as the Participant, the Historian, the Novelist, and the Existentialist. He will refer to him as "a simple of a hero" (*AOTN*, 215). Readers who come to Mailer's book by way of his legend as a self-advertising egomaniac will be puzzled to learn that Mailer is here laughing at Norman Mailer.

Mailer's decision to write about himself in the third person is oddly reminiscent of *The Education of Henry Adams*. While a full-scale comparison of *Armies* and *Education* would be misleading,[13] the similarities are interesting. D. W. Brogan summarizes *Education* in this fashion: "It is indeed, on the surface, the story of one who failed because, trained to be at home in Franklin's world, he had to live in a world transformed by the new science and the new technology."[14] Mailer's readers will recall *his* obsession with the evils of technology, his increasing conservatism as he confronts the modern technocracy. In much of his writing (*Cannibals and Christians*, say) Mailer rivals Adams as a pessimistic analyst of the machine age. In *Armies* Mailer's Pentagon is as much a symbol for this age as the dynamo was for Adams. I do not want to push this comparison too far – Henry Adams and Norman Mailer will not seem every reader's idea of soul brothers – but the likeness does suggest Mailer's increasingly conservative image of himself, rendered most fully in *Armies*. It also suggests the seeming objectivity of this image, achieved partly by use of the distancing third person and partly by an exceedingly scrupulous – and Adams-like – inquiry into the author's personality.

Mailer's personality is the figure in the carpet so far as *Armies* is concerned. This personality is as baroque as Mailer's description of it: "Now Mailer was often brusque himself, famous for that, but the architecture of his personality bore resemblance to some provincial cathedral which warring orders of the church might have designed separately over several centuries, the particular cathedral falling into the hands of one architect, then his enemy. (Mailer had not been married four times for nothing.)" (*AOTN*, 17). Indeed, Mailer is fairly merciless in pointing up his own mistakes and unworthy feelings. He tries always to view himself as others do, no matter how unflattering the result. He admits that he is "much too vain" to wear eyeglasses before professional photographers (*AOTN*, 106); he acknowledges the "hot anger" he feels because Robert Lowell is loved and he is not (*AOTN*, 45); he notes his desire for a hasty arrest at the Pentagon in order to return to New York for a dinner party (*AOTN*, 118-19); and he characterizes some of his actions in jail as those of a "mountebank" (*AOTN*, 173).

Yet our comic hero is not so much unlikable as he is contradictory. He is a "notable," a famous writer worthy of being petitioned to lend his name to the antiwar demonstrations, yet he is capable of beliefs like the following: "He had the idea – it was undeniably oversimple – that if you spent too much time on the phone in the evening, you destroyed some kind of creativity for the dawn" (*AOTN*, 4). He is "a snob of the worst sort" (*AOTN*, 14) and captive to a "wild man" in himself, referred to rather tolerantly as "the Beast" (*AOTN*, 30), yet he is a loving, even sentimental, husband and father (*AOTN*, 166-71) and is even a patriot of the first rank (*AOTN*, 47, 113). Once dedicated to revolutionary socialism, he is at heart a *grand conservateur* (*AOTN*, 18). Mailer's many contradictions are best illustrated by the confession that he is a "Left Conservative" (*AOTN*, 124). During his mayoral campaign of 1969 Mailer was fond of saying that he was running further to the left and further to the right than any of the other candidates. In *Armies* too Mailer can be seen running in many directions at once.

Nonetheless, Mailer does not expose randomly the many fine and ugly features of his character. Rather, he traces in book 1 a critical moment in the history of this complex personality as Mailer's divided self achieves at least temporary wholeness during the March on the Pentagon. Later we will see that this account is crucial to Mailer's interpretation of the march; here it is enough to say that the structure of book 1 corresponds to the stages of Mailer's spiritual experience.

Mailer's less endearing features are naturally emphasized early in book 1, where we encounter the side of his personality that will be transcended in the course of the march. Here we are introduced to Mailer's theory of evening telephone calls, his "virtual" conservatism on the subject of drugs (*AOTN*, 5), and his "neo-Victorianism" on the subject of sex (*AOTN*, 24). Here we observe his reluctant acceptance of Mitchell Goodman's invitation to attend the antiwar demonstrations in Washington. Our hero is not very heroic in his first appearance. He is more concerned about editing his latest movie and attending his Saturday-night dinner engagement than with actively protesting the war in Vietnam. Indeed, he looks forward to his weekend of "idiot mass manifestations" as in every way a lost weekend: "Mailer wished as the Washington weekend approached that the Washington weekend were done" (*AOTN*, 10). Mailer's portrait of himself as a touchy and incongruous "revolutionary-for-a-weekend" (*AOTN*, 56) is confirmed by his distaste for the "innocent" young girls and liberal academics who surround him at the buffet he attends his first night in Washington (*AOTN*, 13-16). His masterless performance as master of ceremonies at the ensuing rally completes the portrait of our much-flawed hero on the eve of the demonstrations (*AOTN*, 28-52).

But if Mailer begins *Armies* by revealing the more comical aspects of his own character, he does so in full confidence that book 1 as a whole will place these features in an artful and not-unappealing perspective. In fact, the rest of book 1 records Mailer's conversion to the cause he ostensibly came to Washington to support. Part 2 of book 1 depicts his shift from apathy to involvement, as Mailer is variously impressed by a number of demonstrators who do not conform to his stereotype of the ineffectual "liberal academic": the students representing different chapters of Resist, an antiwar organization (*AOTN*, 61-63); William Sloane Coffin, Jr., chaplain at Yale (*AOTN*, 66-67); Robert Lowell, the famous poet who addresses the demonstrators at the Department of Justice. Lowell also figures prominently in the events of part 1, in which Mailer offers a chilly account of Lowell's motives and general character. Now Mailer concedes that "all flaws considered, Lowell was still a fine, good, and honorable man, and Norman Mailer was happy to be linked in a cause with him" (*AOTN*, 74). Unmistakably, as this first day of protest comes to an end, Mailer has begun to join the "cause" himself. He even speaks to the demonstrators, advising that perhaps the time had come "when Americans, many Americans, would have to face the possibility of going to jail for their ideas" (*AOTN*, 79). It is after this speech, after this day of antiwar activities, that Mailer first commits himself to staying for the March on the Pentagon.

As Saturday arrives (part 3), it is clear that Mailer has assimilated Friday's lessons. No longer does he think of the protest as "idiot mass manifestations." Now as later he believes that the march is "that first major battle of a war which may go on for twenty years"; he even entertains the idea that "in fifty years the day may loom in our history as large as the ghosts of the Union dead" (*AOTN*, 88).

Mailer is all but liberated by the prospect of leading his newly discovered "troops," the hippies and other young people who are a
majority of the demonstrators (he is to be their general, of course).
Assured that he is engaged in noble work and capable of performing
his part without fear (*AOTN*, 113), subsequently "lifted" into a sense
of comradeship by the tribalistic music of the Fugs (*AOTN*, 125),
Mailer gives himself up to the spirit of the protest by "transgressing"
a police line and getting arrested (*AOTN*, 129-31). The act is not
obviously heroic, but it does issue from Mailer's new sense of commitment and comradeship, the growth of which he traces throughout
book 1. He can therefore describe this act – with saving humor – as
"his Rubicon" (*AOTN*, 138).

During part 3 Mailer does not portray his hero as altogether
transfigured. The great Mailer ego is still on display, as when he
decides on a quick arrest in order to obtain a quick release ("Such
men are either monumental fools or excruciatingly practical" [*AOTN*,
119]). References to one's Rubicon do not signal absolute humility.
But these reminders of Mailer's none-too-flawless personality only
emphasize by contrast the remarkable conversion he undergoes.
They take the curse off his account of how he got religion in the
country of the young and the liberal academic.

It is hardly a metaphor to say that Mailer gets religion during the
march. For Mailer, the experience is nothing less than a rite of purification. At the Lincoln Memorial he decides to observe a fast until the
march is over (*AOTN*, 106). This hint of a purification ritual is reinforced once he is arrested. Mailer notes that "he felt as if he were
being confirmed" by his arrest (*AOTN*, 138); later he says that "he
felt shriven" (*AOTN*, 158). Throughout his stay in jail Mailer feels an
exaltation we normally associate with saintliness (even in saints so
unlikely as Mailer): "and he knew by the unfamiliar variety of happiness he now felt that much indeed had happened to him" (*AOTN*,
160). He breaks his fast only when assured he has passed his "test":
"He had felt, despite every petty motive, or low calculation on how
to get back to New York for the party, a mild exaltation on which he
had traveled through the day, a sense of cohering in himself which
was he supposed the opposite of those more familiar states of alienation he could always describe so well" (*AOTN*, 162-63). When
released on Sunday morning, Mailer is sure his experience has been
liberating: "he felt one suspicion of a whole man closer to that free-

dom from dread which occupied the inner drama of his years, yes, one image closer than when he had come to Washington four days ago" (AOTN, 212-13).

Book 1 dramatizes this change in Mailer. It describes an almost-religious experience. This conviction lies behind Mailer's otherwise curious remarks upon leaving the makeshift courtroom at Occoquan, Virginia. Here Mailer says that protests such as the march may have to become more militant because "we are burning the body and blood of Christ in Vietnam. Yes, we are burning him there, and as we do, we destroy the foundation of this Republic, which is its love and trust in Christ" (AOTN, 214). Behind his statement rests Mailer's conception of America as a Christian country. For Mailer, Christianity is marked by its belief in mysteries, the greatest of which is "the bleeding heart of Christ." Vietnam reveals that America has lost its soul to "a worship of technology," for Vietnam is *the* technological war (AOTN, 188). Mystery ("the bleeding heart of Christ") has been replaced by the procedures of technology; therefore, by implication, we are burning the body and blood of Christ in Vietnam.

Mailer's statement issues from the dramatic context of not only his release from prison but also his completion of a liberating, quasi-religious experience begun in apathy but concluded in mild exaltation. It derives from a mind spiritually refreshed and inclined toward the solemnity of things religious. We will encounter this mind again, at the end of book 2, where Mailer will speak not of his own experience but of the general experience of the demonstrators. In tracing his own belated conversion Mailer therefore prepares for the more general rite of passage that is celebrated in book 2. What appears to be an egotistic emphasis on his own actions is really Mailer's attempt to persuade us that his reactions are representative. We see as he sees. We share his initial indifference to this "radical" act of civil disobedience. Then, if we are in fact persuaded, we experience with him the transforming event the march ultimately became. And having passed through this experience with Mailer, we are prepared for his retrospective analysis of the march in book 2.

The Relevance of Book 2

That is one answer, of course, to the question of how Mailer's personal story is relevant to the materials of book 2. At the beginning of book 2 Mailer takes up this question directly. Here he tells us that book 1 is "a tower fully equipped with telescopes to study – at the greatest advantage – our own horizons" (*AOTN*, 219). He makes it clear that *Armies* should not be read as a novel, for the "novel" of book 1 is a means toward an end. Book 1 – our metaphoric tower – provides the perspective we need on the massive and somewhat chaotic particulars of the march itself. It does so in at least three ways: (a) it offers intimate portraits of the various political factions involved in the march; (b) it establishes Mailer's right to speak of the march in the impersonal, authoritative tone of book 2, since it bears witness to his profound involvement in the event ("I suffered, I was there"); and (c) it provides, in Mailer's transformation from comic hero to mildly exalted initiate, a model for the experience of the demonstrators, who will be shown undergoing an analogous experience from the initial, humorous negotiations for the march to the final, transfiguring events of Saturday night at the Pentagon.

Book 2 returns to the beginning to trace the genesis and execution of the march. "Obedient to a general style of historical writing" (*AOTN*, 255), book 2 is a history of the march that focuses on its major figures, the antiwar leaders and their counterparts in the government, the students and soldiers who confront each other at the Pentagon. In 1963 Mailer could write, "The play of political ideas is flaccid here in America because opposing armies never meet. The Right, the Center, and what there is of the Left have set up encampments on separate hills. . . . No Man's Land predominates. It is a situation which calls for guerrilla raiders" (*TPP*, 25). Book 2 documents the emergence of such guerrillas. It is a history of opposing armies very much in conflict.

Mailer depicts these "armies" throughout book 1. His portraits there both illustrate and occasion his analysis of America – always the final end in Mailer's fictionlike nonfiction. Chapter 2 of part 4 offers, in the marshal and the Nazi, prototypes of that cannibalistic right wing Mailer describes so well in his account of the 1964 Republican convention, "In the Red Light." Latter-day versions of the WASP, these men suggest to Mailer the bigotry his own "army" must transform if it is to alter America. Other figures of the Right described in *Armies* are more sympathetic but no less alienated from the demonstrators who have come to Washington to protest the war. In the eyes of a turnkey, for example, Mailer discovers "narrowness, propriety, good-will, and that infernal American innocence which could not question one's leaders, for madness and the boils of a frustrated life resided beneath" (*AOTN*, 169). Mailer is equally saddened by those "clean American kids" who stare at the demonstrators, for they bring home the fact that marshals and turnkeys have children who will never gather in Washington to protest American wars (*AOTN*, 156).

Mailer's attention in *Armies* is more often devoted to figures of the Left. As his book makes clear, Mailer takes the Center and the Left of American politics to be somewhat inharmoniously united in the peace movement. The Center for Mailer is liberalism, represented by those liberal academics Mailer encounters at the pre-Ambassador buffet. Mailer feels little sympathy for these people. If they oppose the war in Vietnam, they do not oppose the technological machine behind the war – their opposition to the Johnson administration is "no more than a quarrel among engineers" (*AOTN*, 15). Mailer is temperamentally opposed to the pacifism and rationality of the liberals; they are not the guerrilla raiders he dreams of commanding. But then neither is the Old Left, the least impressive radical force in the march. For Mailer, the Old Left is but a step removed from the liberal technologues. The former's penchant for speeches ("The Great Left Pall") is more impressive than its disposition to act (*AOTN*, 98); like the liberals, its members are "the first real champions of technology land" (*AOTN*, 96). Much more interesting is the New Left. Among the young girls and hippies and SDS provocateurs Mailer discovers a true if ignorant army to engage America's marshals and technologues.[15]

Mailer is not entirely charmed by his troops of the New Left, however. They are too much like the young girls he meets at the buffet, "innocent, decent-spirited, merry, red-cheeked, idealistic, and utterly lobotomized away from the sense of sin" (*AOTN*, 14). Mailer's sense of sin is such that he has come full circle from his search for the apocalyptic orgasm ("The White Negro") to his present "neo-Victorianism." Not for nothing is he a left *conservative.* He can describe his troops as "middle-class cancer-pushers and drug-gutted flower children" (*AOTN*, 35); he can suggest that they are "bombed by the use of LSD as outrageously as the atoll of Eniwetok, Hiroshima, Nagasaki, and the scorched foliage of Vietnam" (*AOTN*, 93). Yet they are his troops still. Mailer is very much impressed by the young people he meets during the march – for example, the student leaders of Resist, and the young man at Occoquan who "gave Mailer a critique of the staging of his play *The Deer Park* which was about as incisive as his own. A remarkable boy" (*AOTN*, 164-65). Mailer does not have Charles Reich's faith in the children of flowers, but neither does he feel an alien in the country of the young.[16] He is especially taken with the political tactics of the New Left. For Mailer, the New Left is truly a *new* political phenomenon.

Mailer finds that the young radicals make an almost-absolute contrast with their older comrades: "A generation of the American young had come along different from five previous generations of the middle class. The new generation believed in technology more than any before it, but the generation also believed in LSD, in witches, in tribal knowledge, in orgy, and revolution. It had no respect whatsoever for the unassailable logic of the next step: belief was reserved for the revelatory mystery of the happening where you did not know what was going to happen next; *that was what was good about it*" (*AOTN*, 86; my emphasis). We recall Mailer's words at the Ambassador Theatre, where he advised those assembled that they were up against "an existential situation," the outcome of which was uncertain. Mailer's admiration for those who embrace such a situation is obvious. Here he goes on to say, "The New Left was drawing its political aesthetic from Cuba. The revolutionary idea which the followers of Castro had induced from their experience in the hills was that you created the revolution first and learned from it, learned of what your revolution might consist and where it might go out of the intimate truth of the way it presented itself to your experience" (*AOTN*, 87). Mailer sees such an aesthetic at work in the March on the Pentagon, which is why he finally endorses it. He has always sponsored such "existential" acts, for they challenge static political situations and force the powers involved to reveal their true natures. Thus, he once wrote that "an existential political act, the drive by Southern Negroes, led by Martin Luther King, to end segregation in restaurants in Birmingham, an act which is existential precisely because its end is unknown, has succeeded en route in discovering more of the American reality to us" (*TPP*, 26). Thus, he applauds the guerrilla tactics of the New Left, for they too reveal something of the American reality.

Unhappily, what they reveal is that "the center of America might be insane." The March on the Pentagon confirms Mailer's most pessimistic analysis of the American scene: "The country had been living with a controlled, even fiercely controlled, schizophrenia which had been deepening with the years. Perhaps the point had now been passed." Mailer defines this schizophrenia as our irreconcilable allegiance both to Christianity ("Mystery") and to technology ("the love of no Mystery whatsoever"). Because they have witnessed the effects of this condition on their elders, the young have arisen in protest (*AOTN*, 188). Our plight is therefore what it seemed to Mailer as early as 1962: a tragic impasse in which "we diverge as countrymen further and further away from one another, like a space ship broken apart in flight which now drifts mournfully in isolated orbits, satellites to each other, planets none, communication faint" (*TPP*, 98). The March on the Pentagon is a "symbolic battle" in which no one is killed (*AOTN*, 199), but what it symbolizes is so agonizing that it constantly reminds Mailer of the Civil War (*AOTN*, 88-89, 91, 93, 113, 126, 263).

Mailer's purpose in *Armies* is to discover the meaning of one episode in this second Civil War. Though he is drawn to the demonstrators, his title implies that he must deal with armies equally ignorant. (The title comes, of course, from Matthew Arnold's "Dover Beach": "And we are here as on a darkling plain / Swept with confused alarms of struggle and flight, / Where ignorant armies clash by night.") In a sense, both armies should be seen as "villains" (*AOTN*, 93). Indeed, Mailer fears that "nihilism might be the only answer to totalitarianism" (*AOTN*, 176). Thus, we see that Mailer's ignorant armies – nihilism and totalitarianism, respectively – embody very unattractive alternatives. Mailer adds that his "final allegiance" is with the villains who are hippies (*AOTN*, 93), but his reading of the embattled armies inspires little enthusiasm for his choice. If the March on the Pentagon is nothing more than a symbolic battle between unappealing forces, it seems unlikely to issue in anything resembling catharsis.

Yet the march does produce a catharsis. It has this effect on Mailer himself, as we have seen, and it has this effect on the "best" of the demonstrators. What Mailer charts in book 2 is the conversion of nihilism into purposeful rebellion, which he refers to as a rite of passage. Fittingly, this rite is enacted at the very end of *Armies*, where it climaxes not only the demonstration but Mailer's narrative as well.

When he comes to describe the confrontation between the sons of the middle class (the demonstrators) and the sons of the working class (the soldiers), Mailer's history of the march undergoes a definite shift in tone. The first half of book 2 is full of the humor of embattled armies that negotiate when and where they will confront each other, what routes the demonstrators may take and what territory they may occupy. This section of book 2 is therefore analogous to the first part of book 1, in which Mailer's misadventures are recorded with a similar eye for the ridiculous. But just as Mailer's experience intensifies – and with it the tone of the book – so the humor of book 2 dissolves once Mailer turns to the events of Saturday night after the masses have departed and the most dedicated demonstrators are left alone with the soldiers. Mailer devotes 20 pages to these events, and they are among the most impressive pages he has ever written. Here we listen to the voice not of the bourbon-inspired master of ceremonies but of the much-humbled veteran of the march who cautions that we are burning the body and blood of Christ in Vietnam.

What emerges is Mailer's interpretation of the march. In Mailer's view the demonstrators are visited with grace as they sit face to face with the soldiers: "some hint of a glorious future may have hung in the air, some refrain from all the great American rites of passage when men and women manacled themselves to a lost and painful principle and survived a day, a night, a week, a month, a year." These "tender, drug-vitiated jargon-mired children" (*AOTN,* 280) endure a night that begins in "joy" but includes the terror of military attack. Those who remain to the end are subtly transformed: "they were forever different in the morning than they had been before the night, which is the meaning of a rite of passage, one has voyaged through a channel of shipwreck and temptation. . . . [S]ome part of the man has been born again, and is better" (*AOTN,* 280-81). Where Mailer has come through his experience "one suspicion of a whole man closer to that freedom from dread which occupied the inner drama of his years," these flower children and fledgling revolutionaries are forever different in the morning from how they had been before the night. The particular experience of book 1 is generalized in book 2. The knot of nihilism is untied, if not "forever," then at least for the moment. This is the "mystery" Mailer discovers in the March on the Pentagon, first in his own experience and then in the

collective experience of the demonstrators. Transcending the count
of bodies, the tactical success or failure of the demonstration, is the
spiritual renewal attested to by the now-impersonal narrative voice
of *Armies.*

Perhaps the most important contribution of book 1 is that it
makes this voice possible as the achieved result of the experience
recorded there. Norman Mailer – dwarf alter ego of Lyndon Johnson
himself (*AOTN*, 49) – can therefore plausibly end his book with the
moving image of "naked Quakers on the cold floor of a dark isola-
tion cell in D.C. jail" and with a question almost worthy of Jeremiah:
"Did they pray, these Quakers, for forgiveness of the nation? Did
they pray with tears in their eyes in those blind cells with visions of a
long column of Vietnamese dead, Vietnamese walking a long column
of flame, eyes on fire, nose on fire, mouth speaking flame" (*AOTN*,
287). Finally, Mailer can offer nothing less than his own prayer for
America: "Deliver us from our curse. For we must end on the road to
that mystery where courage, death, and the dream of love give
promise of sleep" (*AOTN*, 288). Mailer's narrative leaves us on that
road, for having presented a vivid and brilliantly annotated account
of our condition as a people, Mailer concludes with the images of
young demonstrators undergoing their rite of passage and Quakers
praying for the forgiveness of sins: images bearing witness to courage
and the dream of love in the face of our death as God's chosen
country.

"False Prophecy"?

In this coda I want to comment on two challenging and related
objections to the conclusion of *Armies.* The first involves Mailer's
language – his intense, hyperbolic rhetoric. The final page (and
chapter) has been attacked by many readers, including such reliable
critics as Wayne Booth and James Phelan.[17] Booth himself offers a
mixed evaluation of the final passage, but he tells of a graduate student at the University of Chicago who, having been moved when he
first read it, was embarrassed by this section in 1978. I believe this
student's reaction shares much with Robert Solotaroff's attack on the
"false prophecy" offered in Mailer's final pages and indeed throughout book 2 (Solotaroff, 233). Writing in 1974, Solotaroff sums up his
objections in a single stern sentence: "However much the rich prose

of the last thirty pages of Book Two works to lift Mailer's hopes above the barren ground of wild optimism, the events of the last five years bring the collective implications of the long night right back to that barren ground" (Solotaroff, 237). For both Booth's graduate student and Solotaroff, Mailer's "reading" of the radical young has not stood the test of time (in Solotaroff's case, a five-year test). Where is SDS today (or in 1974, or 1978)? Just what did this rite of passage *produce*?

J. Michael Lennon answers Solotaroff in part by noting that the march and similar peace efforts hastened the end of the war.[18] The point is well taken in an era in which virtually everything about the 1960s seems open to a "new" (and profoundly cynical) interpretation. But I would add a second, even more relevant point. The rite of passage Mailer describes is an individual, not a collective, experience. Mailer does not say that events such as the march have made the New Left a political force for the future. Rather, he speaks of the individual metamorphoses experienced (or so he imagines) by many of the more persistent demonstrators. Asking what these people went on to *do* is rather like worrying the question of what Thoreau did after leaving Walden, or whether Yossarian ever got to Sweden. Indeed, one might as well ask what happened to Mailer himself after the march. As it happens, we know what Mailer did: he went home to write *The Armies of the Night* and to report on the 1968 political conventions. Did his personal transformation "take"? To focus on such questions, however tempting, is to confuse the symbolic and the literal. It is rather like supposing that the real object of the march was to take over the Pentagon.

Solotaroff is right when he remarks the failure of the New Left. But of course Mailer himself identifies the New Left's inadequacies. In any case, the essence of Mailer's "prophecy" is his claim that spiritual rejuvenation is available to anyone willing to persist in a cause. This is romanticism, not false prophecy. It is very much the stuff of the 1960s, embraced here by a contradictory but ultimately eager convert. Mailer's eagerness is romantic, yes, but I take it to be touching as well. Better Mailer's faith in the young – *some* of the young – than the tepid, more "mature" perspectives of the past 20-plus years. Better the Mailer who left Washington than the Mailer who first arrived.

Chapter Seven

After *Armies*

Mailer's More Recent Nonfiction

Mailer's literary career has had almost as many ups and downs as his well-publicized personal life. The early stages of this career are by now almost legendary: early success with *The Naked and the Dead*; decline and fall with *Barbary Shore* and *The Deer Park*; self-announced resurrection with *Advertisements for Myself*; a 10-year period in which Mailer "wasted" his novelistic talents on grubby journalism, only to justify his apparent vagrancy by writing *The Armies of the Night*, one of the more distinguished works of the 1960s. My concern in this chapter is not to reexamine these earlier "periods" but to begin to evaluate Mailer's next phase as a writer of nonfiction, what I would half-seriously call his post-*Armies* period. Extending from 1968 to 1978, this period curiously resembles the 10-year gap between Mailer's third novel, *The Deer Park*, and his fourth, *An American Dream*, for Mailer again went a full decade without producing a novel while publishing so much journalism that even Mailer specialists have trouble keeping track of it all. Given that no fewer than 13 volumes appeared during this decade, the period would seem to be an even more productive one than Mailer's first respite from novel writing – until one notices that a few of the more recent books (*The Idol and the Octopus, Some Honorable Men*) are in fact Mailer's earlier writings reassembled; that Mailer's fourth miscellany (*Existential Errands*) is distinctly unworthy of its three predecessors; that the two fight accounts (*King of the Hill, The Fight*) are inferior to "Ten Thousand Words a Minute"; and that the two major examples of Mailer's "engaged" reportage (*Miami and the Siege of Chicago, Of a Fire on the Moon*) are unequal to their model, *The Armies of the Night*. Indeed, anyone who looks closely enough will notice that the Mailer of this period even published a "book" expounding the philosophical assumptions behind graffiti.[1]

All of which suggests that we may have a new Mailer "period" in the work done between 1968 and 1978, but if so, it is a period calling for discreet silence, not critical evaluation.

Benign neglect will not do, however – Mailer is too important a writer and his more recent works, good and bad alike, are far too interesting to be ignored. My discussion attempts to establish three points: (a) that *Miami and the Siege of Chicago* (1968) and *Of a Fire on the Moon* (1970), so successful in their parts, ultimately fail for reasons not yet fully understood; (b) that *The Prisoner of Sex* (1971) and *Marilyn* (1973), though hardly major performances, are much better than is usually thought; and (c) that Mailer's most distinguished work in this period was done in the unlikely genre of literary criticism. In general, then, I hope to explain, not simply assert, the limitations of Mailer's more recent works and to establish what in this body of writing deserves a more sympathetic response than it has yet received.

Miami, Chicago, and the Moon: The Age of Aquarius

Jimmy Baldwin once entertained the readers of *Esquire* with a sweet and generously written piece called *The Black Boy Looks at the White Boy* in which he talked a great deal about himself and a little bit about me, a proportion I thought well-taken since he is on the best of terms with Baldwin and digs next to nothing about this white boy. As a method, I think it has its merits.

– Norman Mailer, *The Presidential Papers*

Mailer remarked on the method of Baldwin's essay in 1962, and everything he has written since confirms that he understands very well the "merits" of Baldwin's approach. Indeed, the preceding two chapters trace the evolution of this method from Mailer's earliest essays to *The Armies of the Night*. With the publication of *Armies*, however, Mailer did not abandon his commitment to a subjective form of historical writing. To the contrary, Mailer's many books prior to *The Executioner's Song* (1979) all suggest that, for him at least, a work of nonfiction will have conviction only if its author occupies whatever stage he happens to be describing. Yet the extent of Mailer's authorial presence varies greatly in his more recent works. Only in *Miami and the Siege of Chicago* and *Of a Fire on the Moon* do we find a method truly comparable to that of *Armies*. It is natural,

then, to judge these two books in light of Mailer's earlier
achievement. Such a comparison should underscore both the virtues
and the very real limitations of these later works.

The virtues are those of a supremely interesting journalism.
Miami and the Siege of Chicago offers the most vivid and
comprehensive account of the 1968 nominating conventions, while
Of a Fire on the Moon is a remarkable reconstruction of the *Apollo
11* moon shot. Each book is studded with descriptions and
characterizations any novelist, let alone any journalist, would envy.
The history and architecture of Miami Beach, Nelson Rockefeller's
arrival in Miami, the stockyards of Chicago, the enigmatic candidacy
of Eugene McCarthy, the police attack on demonstrators outside
Chicago's Hilton Hotel – these and other phenomena described in
Miami and the Siege of Chicago allow Mailer to exercise that
"phenomenal talent for recording the precise look and feel of
things" first praised by Norman Podhoretz more than 30 years ago
(Podhoretz, 371). Indeed, Mailer's portrait of McCarthy is the equal
of any character study in his novels. Although Mailer has always been
at his reportorial best in dealing with political conventions – as
witnessed by his essays on the 1960 Democratic National Convention
("Superman Comes to the Supermarket"), the 1964 Republican
National Convention ("In the Red Light"), and the 1972 nominating
conventions (*St. George and the Godfather*) – *Miami and the Siege
of Chicago* is his most compelling treatment of the people and
movements that constitute contemporary politics. And from a
journalistic perspective, *Of a Fire on the Moon* is an even more
stunning achievement, especially in those sections which describe
the Vehicle Assembly Building at Cape Kennedy, the blast-off of
Saturn-Apollo, and the craters of the moon.

The virtues of these books lay not merely in their descriptions
however. Even more impressive are those speculative passages
inspired by Mailer's observations. At certain points in both works we
hear the unmistakable cadence of Mailer at his prophetic best. Mailer
has many other voices, of course – some shrill, some egomania-
cal – but this particular voice is heard whenever his shrewdness and
lyrical intensity are happily joined. In *Of a Fire on the Moon* it is
heard most clearly in the concluding chapter, "A Burial by the Sea,"
in which Mailer manages to blend reflections on the end of his
fourth marriage with thoughts on our exploration of space to form a

deeply moving meditation on the state of America at the end of the
1960s. In *Miami and the Siege of Chicago* it emerges at many points
in the narrative, most notably when Mailer watches the Republican
leadership file into their grand gala and is moved to reflect on the
nature and fate of America's WASPs:

> Yet he felt himself unaccountably filled with a mild sorrow. He did not detest
> these people, he did not feel so superior as to pity them, it was rather he felt a
> sad sorrowful respect. In their immaculate cleanliness, in the somewhat
> antiseptic odors of their astringent toilet water and perfume, in the
> abnegation of their walks, in the heavy sturdy moves so many demonstrated of
> bodies in life's harness, there was the muted tragedy of the Wasp – they were
> not on earth to enjoy or even perhaps to love so very much, they were here to
> serve, and serve they had in public functions and public charities (while
> recipients of their charity might vomit in rage and laugh in scorn), served on
> opera committees, and served in long hours of duty at the piano, served as the
> sentinel in concert halls and the pews on the aisle in church, at the desk in
> schools, had served for culture, served for finance, served for salvation, served
> for America – and so much of America did not wish them to serve any longer,
> and so many of them doubted themselves, doubted that the force of their faith
> could illumine their path in these new modern horror-head times. On and on,
> they came through the door, the clean, the well-bred, the extraordinarily
> prosperous, and for the most astonishing part, the almost entirely proper. . . .
> [N]ow they were subdued, now they were modest, now they were looking for
> a leader to bring America back to them, their lost America, Jesus-land. (*MSC*,
> 35-36)

I quote at such length to give a fair example of Mailer's
meditative technique at its best. Surely it is at moments like these, if
ever, that we sympathize with Mailer's celebrated contention that he
is "the best writer in America" (*AOTN*, 22).

But no one ever based this claim on a reading of *Miami and the
Siege of Chicago* and *Of a Fire on the Moon* as wholes, and so it is
necessary to ask why these books seem less successful than *The
Armies of the Night*. It is not, I think, because *Armies* surpasses the
later works in the quality of its reportage or the intensity of its
meditative passages; if this is true, it is true only in degree, and
relatively slight degree at that. Nor is it because *Armies* provides
Mailer with inherently richer material, as so many discussions
suggest. In fact, the March on the Pentagon was probably less
significant historically than either the political conventions of 1968
or the mission of *Apollo 11*. To be fair, those who point to the

"richness" of Mailer's material are thinking of the actions undertaken by Mailer as participant rather than the march itself. Thus, Robert Solotaroff explains Mailer's relative failure in "Nixon in Miami" by saying, "The Republican convention offered the reporter no opportunity for dramatic action and so few for dramatic thought that except for a small crisis involving his feelings about Negroes, the most his inner drama could offer hung upon his ruminating about whether Nixon had really changed" (Solotaroff, 238). But if we adopt this view, what are we to say about "The Siege of Chicago," in which Mailer's opportunities for dramatic action are legion but his published account also fails to match the level of *Armies*? I do not mean to deny the problems Mailer faced in dramatizing the somewhat intractable materials of the Nixon convention or, even more obviously, the *Apollo 11* moon shot. Yet I cannot see that these problems are inherently greater than those Mailer dealt with in writing about the March on the Pentagon. It is simply that with *Armies* Mailer *solved* his problems.

I have already argued that Mailer did this by employing numerous fictional techniques to illuminate his subject. This may not seem an interpretive key, for these devices are also used in the later works, but the most crucial fictional technique is precisely what is missing in *Miami and the Siege of Chicago* and *Of a Fire on the Moon:* the conscious shaping of the given materials to form a dramatic action. It is no accident that *Armies* moves from "pugnacious personal comedy to prophetic witness and litany,"[2] for only through some such movement could Mailer present his conclusions about the march with that prophetic authority he has sought throughout his career. As noted in chapter 6, Mailer earns this authority by depicting in book 1 the somewhat comical initiation undergone by his hero, "Norman Mailer," who then returns in the form of a chastened, "objective" narrator for the historical treatment of the March on the Pentagon in book 2. This rather elaborate procedure hardly recalls the average journalist, who tends to stick doggedly to the chronological order of events, however unclimactic that may be. But it is the key to the book's extraordinary effect, especially in the concluding chapters. And while it is true that Mailer also deviates from strict chronological development in his later works, he does so for relatively minor, local effects, not in the service of a pervasive rhetorical strategy. What Jack Richardson says about the author of *Miami and the Siege of Chicago* could also be said of the man who wrote *Of a Fire on the Moon:* "He becomes less and less concerned with maintaining a literary center . . . and allows the sequences from Miami to Chicago to unfold for the most part unchallenged by his imagination."[3]

Richardson's criticism is most relevant to "Nixon in Miami," for this section of *Miami and the Siege of Chicago* is almost literally a report on the 1968 Republican convention. Occasionally Mailer alters the chronology of events to permit continuous treatment of Nixon's or Rockefeller's presence at the convention, but for the most part he gives us a 70-page description of the convention's daily proceedings. This method is in contrast not only to his strategy in *Armies* but also to his practice in such essays as "In the Red Light," in which the events of a political convention become the stages in a personal drama. "In the Red Light" dramatizes Mailer's internal debate with America's warring social forces, particularly those represented by the Goldwaterites. Through such debate Mailer arrives at a clarified vision of the country, the end he always seeks and the principle that determines which events are to be represented. In "Nixon in Miami" we get a radically reduced version of this strategy. Again Mailer introduces himself into his narrative, this time as "the reporter"; again he offers his impressions as an eyewitness; again he dramatizes his attempt to comprehend the convention's "meaning." As Solotaroff suggests, however, there is not much to dramatize. In Miami, Mailer tells us, "the reporter had moved through the convention quietly, as anonymously as possible, wan, depressed, troubled" (*MSC,* 14). This modest movement fails to provide the personal drama that unifies *Armies* and the earlier convention pieces, and so Mailer settles for describing, event after event, what passed before his eyes as he made his anonymous way through the heart of Republican politics. Mailer is curious about the possibility of a "new Nixon," but his engagement with this issue hardly structures his account. At the end Mailer does not know "if the candidate were real as a man, or whole as a machine, lonely in his sad eminence or megalomaniacal" (*MSC,* 82), and his retrospective treatment of the convention offers few hints that might allow the reader to achieve a more definitive insight.

The problem with "Nixon in Miami" is structural, for the lack of a "literary center" reduces the work to the level of superior journalism. A subtler form of the same problem arises with Mailer's treatment of the 1968 Democratic convention. After an introductory description of Chicago, Mailer devotes the first 40 pages of "The Siege of Chicago" to the political forces at work in the convention, an account climaxed by his report on the debate among Eugene McCarthy, George McGovern, and Hubert Humphrey before the California delegation. Mailer then moves outside the convention hall to what he calls the real "event" of the convention (*MSC*, 131), the confrontation between Mayor Daley's police and the demonstrators who have come to protest Lyndon Johnson's war policies. Mailer devotes 50 pages to describing the demonstrators, their first engagements with the police, and finally the infamous police attack outside the Hilton Hotel on the third day of the convention. At this point, fully 90 pages into "The Siege of Chicago," Mailer shifts to his personal role in the convention. Thereafter he depicts his own activities, including his several speeches to the demonstrators, his efforts to organize a protest march of unhappy delegates, and his contretemps with the National Guard on the last night of the convention. To present his three narrative "movements" Mailer must of course move back and forth over the chronological events of the convention, thus emphasizing that he is consciously shaping his narrative. But toward what end?

Mailer concludes "The Siege of Chicago" with his own "story," so it would seem that he means to emphasize his personal reactions to the convention. Yet he tells us that "we are concerned here with his actions only as they illumine the event of the Republican Convention in Miami, the Democratic Convention in Chicago, and the war of the near streets" (*MSC*, 197). Curiously, this passage describes the persona's role in *Armies* but fails to square with Mailer's practice in the work he is actually characterizing. If the reporter's actions are to illumine the Democratic convention in Chicago, why are they presented only toward the end, where they receive the emphasis that goes with climactic placement? Do they "illumine" the convention or do they in fact provide a quite different focus? Mailer's procedure here reverses his strategy in *Armies* and reverts to what he did so successfully in the last 15 pages of "Ten Thousand Words a Minute." In the essay, however, Mailer's personal story is developed throughout the work, not just at the end. The last 40 pages of "The Siege of Chicago" read too much like a separate narrative within the work as a whole. Indeed, the real problem is that "The Siege of Chicago" reads very much like *three* separate narratives, all related by time and place but insufficiently united by an encompassing narrative structure.

This criticism assumes that Mailer's account of his own activities fails to illuminate the convention's meaning. If such illumination was intended, Mailer is far too reticent in making the necessary connections. I would suggest that Mailer faced an artistic dilemma here and throughout the book. Early in "Nixon in Miami" Mailer remarks that the American political scene is dominated by "Left-wing demons, white and Black, working to inflame the conservative heart of America, while Right-wing devils exacerbated Blacks and drove the mind of the New Left and liberal middle class into prides of hopeless position" (*MSC*, 15). It is clear that Mailer finds himself squarely in the middle, threatened on both sides by these unattractive political extremes. But, of course, this is precisely the position he was in a year earlier, during the March on the Pentagon. *The Armies of the Night* dramatizes Mailer's efforts to adjudicate between the ignorant armies of the Left and the Right; indeed, it dramatizes the internal debate of a left conservative who is drawn to both sides in the battle. Was Mailer to describe this struggle again, just one year later? Such repetition would horrify Mailer more than any other literary sin, for he takes pride in never repeating himself.[4] On the other hand, Mailer's long-standing distaste for "straight" reportage – plus the vicissitudes of his ego – seems to dictate his presence on the reported scene. We thus get that relatively anonymous figure, "the reporter." This persona is not to be regretted altogether, for without him we would lack such splendid moments as Mailer's conversations with Eugene McCarthy. But Mailer's perfunctory development of his own activities deprives his work of an organizing principle significantly different from that of "pure" journalism.

It is possible that I have misconstrued Mailer's dilemma. I have suggested that Mailer could have focused *Miami and the Siege of Chicago* in the same manner as *The Armies of the Night*, but this option may have seemed closed to him. Mailer structured *Armies* around what I have called his "internal debate" because this debate was finally resolved. When he came to see the final moments of the March on the Pentagon as a true rite de passage for the demonstrators, Mailer was able to present his participation in the march as leading to a richly climactic insight. Perhaps the reason he presents no such dramatic moment in *Miami and the Siege of Chicago* is that no such resolution occurred. Mailer sides with the demonstrators, as he finally does in *Armies*, but is disinclined to see their confrontation with the police in the same light as the occupation of the Pentagon. Mailer's brilliant account of the police attack outside the Hilton Hotel occurs 50 pages before the end of the book and offers no final clarification. Although we can only speculate as to why Mailer responded so differently to the events in Washington and Chicago, I think the answer lies in that growing personal conservatism noted in chapter 5. This growth was well advanced by 1967, as we see in Mailer's hostility toward the liberals and New Leftists who make up one of the "armies" in *The Armies of the Night*. At that time, however, Mailer's radical spirit was sufficiently intact to overcome his sometimes querulous, sometimes shrewd objections to the demonstrators. This factor made possible the resolution already noticed, both in Mailer's personal feelings and in the book he went on to write. One year later, however, the balance has shifted, Mailer's left conservatism is very conservative indeed, and our author can only record with sorrow and journalistic detachment "the war of the near streets."

Mailer describes this "war" with great skill, but it is the skill of a gifted journalist who is more or less content to let the facts speak for themselves. In Mailer's next book this characteristic is even more pronounced. Indeed, the problems of *Of a Fire on the Moon* and *Miami and the Siege of Chicago* are so similar that I will restrict my remarks to Mailer's failure to transcend the narrative structure of a report – in this case, a report almost 500 pages long!

Of a Fire on the Moon is formally divided into three parts. Part 1, "Aquarius," presents Mailer's eyewitness account of the final preparations for *Apollo 11* and the awesome blast-off; part 2, "Apollo," describes the mission in voluminous and technical detail, from its inception to the recovery of its astronauts; and part 3, "The Age of Aquarius," returns to Mailer's coverage of the mission via television – at the same time that his fourth marriage is deteriorating – and concludes with his thoughts on the significance of it all. This structure seems to resemble that of Mailer's better essays, in which he begins and ends with his own relation to an event described in the middle. The resemblance, however, is ultimately superficial. In an essay like "Ten Thousand Words a Minute," for example, the concluding section resolves both personal and more general issues raised by Mailer's participation in the reported event. Thus, we experience what Frank Kermode calls a "sense of an ending" on both the essay's dramatic and its intellectual levels.[5] By contrast, part 3 of *Of a Fire on the Moon* returns us to an essentially unchanged observer who is perplexed by the same unanswered questions he brought to the mission in part 1. Mailer again structures his work around his role as reporter, but the dramatic implications are never realized because literally there is no dramatic movement.

Mailer refers to himself here as Aquarius, a persona he will characterize in *St. George and the Godfather* as "modest and half-invisible."[6] Aquarius is a man who has "learned to live with questions" (*FOM*, 4); he is sufficiently detached from "the imperial demands of his ego" to become "an acolyte to technology" (*FOM*, 6, 56) and to describe an event advertised as the triumph of twentieth-century science. Indeed, he is so adept at living with questions, so detached from the demands of his ego, that for the most part he is *entirely* invisible. Certainly nothing happens to him that Mailer can use to focus his account of the moon shot. We might therefore expect *Of a Fire on the Moon* to be quite modest in its proportions. Instead, Mailer fills the middle section of his typical structure with no fewer than 300 pages on the mechanics of *Apollo 11* – perhaps the longest description of a single event in literary history. It is as if Mailer would somehow conceal that he has nothing to dramatize by expanding to heroic proportions what is usually a subordinate section in his essays. A similar strategy seems at work in Mailer's endless reiteration of *the* question posed by *Apollo 11:* does our effort in space serve God or the devil? Richard Poirier suggests that Mailer's more recent works use the unresolved dualisms in such questions as a kind of literary crutch.[7] It is fitting that *Of a Fire on the Moon* is his first example, for Mailer's many variations on this question seem calculated to substitute for the dramatic insights experienced by other, less invisible personae in his earlier works.[8]

Mailer's dilemma here recalls his problem in *Miami and the Siege of Chicago*. Either his personal experience of the event in question led to a climactic insight or it did not – in either case, Mailer is in a losing position: without a climactic insight, he has to make do with the tactics of superior journalism; with such an insight, he has to confront the unappealing prospect of repeating the successful narrative strategy of *Armies* ("Once a philosopher, twice a pervert," as Mailer has so often quoted Voltaire). *Miami and the Siege of Chicago* and *Of a Fire on the Moon* therefore suggest the limitations of Mailer's subjective approach to nonfiction insofar as reporting historical events is concerned. These limitations suggest that to continue with this approach in the 1970s Mailer had to find other materials on which to apply it. I believe *The Prisoner of Sex* and *Marilyn* are the literary results of just such a search.[9]

Prisoners of Sex: Mailer and Monroe

The Prisoner of Sex and *Marilyn* have much in common. Each is centrally concerned with women, a subject Mailer had never before placed at the heart of his work. Each was received with great critical chagrin. Indeed, each was a kind of cause célèbre; the initial publication of *The Prisoner of Sex* in the May 1971 issue of *Harper's* led to the dismissal of the magazine's editor, Willie Morris, while the appearance of *Marilyn* provoked many accusations that Mailer had defiled the memories of Marilyn Monroe and the Kennedys, Jack and Bobby. The two works are also related in more literary ways. Each represents Mailer's attempt to find a different use for those nonfictional techniques he developed during the 1960s. In *The Prisoner of Sex* Mailer employs these techniques in the service of an extended philosophical essay; in *Marilyn* he uses them to enrich a formal biography. Neither effort is altogether successful, but each represents a modest success we would never anticipate from the massive literary gossip that accompanied its publication.

Mailer's success in *The Prisoner of Sex* is so modest it has escaped the notice of even sympathetic readers. Among unsympathetic readers, the only issue has been whether Mailer's persona or his thought is more objectionable. Brigid Brophy's description of the book as "an appreciative meditation by Norman Mailer on Norman Mailer" calls attention to the fact that Mailer once again introduces a self-portrait into his nonfiction.[10] Because *The Prisoner of Sex* does not report a historical event and has all the trappings of a philosophical essay, we might first ask why "Mailer" is in the work at all.

The role of Mailer's persona is really quite familiar. Mailer again
thrusts himself forward as a representative figure, though here he
represents only the male half of the population. Mailer refers to
himself as the PW, which stands for Prisoner of Wedlock (a four-time
loser!) or Prizewinner. He explains that these are "polar concepts to
be regarded at opposite ends of his ego" (*POS*, 9), but they can also
be seen as his credentials for undertaking a philosophical
examination of women in general and women's liberation in
particular. As one who has known the intimate trials of marriage and
the masculine world of work, Mailer is prepared to represent the
male point of view on our most recent version of the war between
the sexes. He offers his qualifications in section 1; proceeds to
examine literary manifestations of feminine unrest in section 2;
conducts an extended attack on his feminine counterpart, Kate
Millett, in section 3; and concludes with a meditation on masculinity
and femininity in section 4. This structure suggests that hostile
readers are right to see the book as an elaborate self-defense; it
should also be said, however, that Mailer's self-portrait focuses what
might otherwise have been a hopelessly abstract philosophical
inquiry. (Given Mailer's views, it is still sufficiently abstract, even
mystical, in its published form.)

Still, Mailer achieves this focus at great cost. It is one thing to be
an eccentric but representative American – Mailer's role in such
works as "Ten Thousand Words a Minute," "In the Red Light," and
The Armies of the Night. It is quite another to be a representative
male chauvinist. This role is too confining, too partisan, to illuminate
the issue in question. Mailer's role is such that we finish *The
Prisoner of Sex* knowing a good deal more about his idiosyncratic
view of the world than about women's liberation. This problem is
compounded by Mailer's decision to treat Kate Millett as a
representative feminist. Nothing in *The Prisoner of Sex* is more
effective than Mailer's attack on Millett's treatment of Henry Miller,
D. H. Lawrence, and Jean Genet (not to mention Norman Mailer) in
her book *Sexual Politics*,[11] but the most sympathetic reader must
finally wonder whether Kate Millett is an adequate opponent. Read
out of context, the third section of *The Prisoner of Sex* is a superb
example of Mailer's gift for literary criticism; read in context, it has
the look of a personal quarrel gratuitously elevated to the level of an
exemplary debate between male and female. Indeed, Mailer's

"victory" over Millett is even counterproductive, as one of Mailer's despised technocrats might say, for it gives rise to the suspicion that Mailer has avoided the more difficult task of confronting a truly formidable feminist.

These criticisms are valid, I think, insofar as *The Prisoner of Sex* aspires to be an objective critique of feminism, specifically women's liberation. In fact, however, Mailer's pretensions in this direction are only intermittently pursued. Mailer's persona ultimately represents nothing more inclusive than his own instinctive biases. The result is a much more personal, less ambitious work than we expect from Mailer. The positive side to this is that judged by these more modest standards *The Prisoner of Sex* is relatively successful: well written, often humorous, agreeably structured around its author's response to the women's movement. The negative side is that Mailer's personal views cannot be argued away as ironic self-characterization. Here these views are the immediate occasion for Mailer's essay, the full burden of what he wants to communicate. For many readers, this is a heavy burden indeed.

Mailer's views on women have been attacked by any number of critics, perhaps most successfully by Jean Radford (Radford 155-59). I do not wish to defend Mailer's views, but I think it fair to add that they are more complex than is usually acknowledged. Mailer does believe that men and women are inherently different, that "man is alienated from the nature which brought him forth, he is not like women in possession of an inner space which gives her link to the future" (*POS*, 111). For Mailer, man defines himself by what he *does;* woman, by what she *is.* Thus, he can say that "nobody was born a man; you earned manhood provided you were good enough, bold enough" (*AOTN*, 25). Mailer resents the feminist's "dull assumption that the sexual force of a man was the luck of his birth, rather than his finest moral product" (*POS*, 45). Of course, he is quite willing to assume that a woman's sexual force – derived from her "inner space" – is precisely the luck of her birth, not her finest moral product. The contradiction is glaring, but it is rooted in Mailer's insistence on the biological foundation to all human realities, even those we tend to think of as conventional or moral. As Radford points out, this all too closely resembles the view that men and women are inherently different because God made them that way (Radford, 157).

Nonetheless, Mailer's distrust of women's liberation is not simply based on chauvinistic clichés. Mailer also fears that feminist ideas are "artfully designed to advance the fortunes of the oncoming technology of the state" (POS, 50). Mailer has in mind feminist advocacy of test-tube babies, or indeed any attempt to alleviate the burdens of childbearing and child care by technological means. He can be accused of acute paranoia in his attitude toward modern science – he would have us suffer headaches rather than use aspirin – but this is hardly a simple form of male chauvinism.

To continue this dissection of Mailer's views on women would be cruel and unusual punishment, however – the best that can be said about *The Prisoner of Sex* is that it is much better than its critics insist.[12] It is *Marilyn* that deserves serious reconsideration. The excellence of Mailer's biography of Marilyn Monroe has been all but overlooked in the hoopla attending its publication and the subsequent charge of plagiarism by Maurice Zolotow, one of Mailer's sources.[13] *Marilyn* is perhaps the most curious of Mailer's relative successes, for it is his one book that succeeds by rejecting the grandiose ambitions that characterize his other works. That it avoids crippling excesses, that it is almost surely the best written of Mailer's works since *Armies* – these points needs to be reaffirmed in the wake of the book's short-lived notoriety.

It may seem perverse to argue that one of *Marilyn*'s virtues is its modesty, for Mailer begins by asserting Monroe's exemplary status. Her suicide is cited as one of those "deaths and spiritual disasters" that epitomize the 1960s (M, 16); she is said to represent an entire generation: "In her ambition, so Faustian, and in her ignorance of culture's dimensions, in her liberation and her tyrannical desires, her noble democratic longings intimately contradicted by the widening pool of her narcissism (where every friend and slave must bathe), we can see the magnified mirror of ourselves, our exaggerated and now all but defeated generation" (M, 17). Indeed, Mailer refers to Monroe as "the last of the myths to thrive in the long evening of the American dream" (M, 16). Such a prologue must create apocalyptic expectations in readers who know nothing of Mailer's other works; readers familiar with those works will anticipate a book in the same vein as "Ten Thousand Words a Minute," in which Floyd Patterson and Sonny Liston represent the Lord and Satan, respectively, or "Superman Comes to the Supermarket," in which Jack Kennedy is cast as the American hero incarnate. Surprisingly, however, Mailer's book sticks very much to its first announced goal – to pursue "the identity of a lovely if seldom simple woman" (*M*, 9). Whether Mailer captures that identity is arguable, but at least he never abandons the flesh-and-blood Monroe in pursuit of some grander, more inclusive hypothesis about contemporary America. Mailer's concern for the "real" Monroe is such that even the reviewer for *Ms.* praised "the passionate effort of mind and feeling which he applies . . . to really knowing what it must feel like to be a woman."[14]

I do not mean to suggest that Mailer restricts his role to purveying facts. Mailer once remarked that "he could not engage in a creative act without a set of major theses to support him" (*EE*, 98), and *Marilyn* is filled with major and minor theses: about Monroe, of course, but also about film, acting, Hollywood, Joe DiMaggio, Arthur Miller, and the other men in Monroe's life. At one point Mailer even pushes forward a notion he first advanced in a discussion of his own ventures into filmmaking: *"Film is a phenomenon whose resemblance to death has been ignored too long"* (*EE*, 134; *M*, 177). But this unhappy preface to a dissertation on film is soon abandoned in the pursuit of Monroe's difficult identity. Indeed, the most infamous of Mailer's theses – that Monroe may have been killed by right-wingers in the government who sought to embarrass Bobby Kennedy – is a tentatively presented, all-but-insignificant detail in the work as a whole. For the most part, Mailer's theses are limited to crucial matters in Monroe's life. Because they derive from the facts of that life, they are immediately relevant to Mailer's goal of writing "a novel biography" (*M*, 15).

Mailer's intentions as a "novel biographer" are not so pretentious as the phrase might suggest. Certainly he does not want to create fictions where facts once reigned; one of his continuing concerns is to distinguish the facts of Monroe's life from what he calls "factoids" ("facts which have no existence before appearing in a magazine or newspaper"; *M*, 18). As a novel biographer Mailer seeks to comprehend the reliable facts concerning Monroe in order to present "a literary hypothesis of a *possible* Marilyn Monroe who might actually have lived and fit most of the facts available" (*M*, 20). He wants to write a version of "psycho-history" (*M*, 19) in which Monroe's complex character is explained to his own satisfaction and that of his more sympathetic readers. This approach involves Mailer in a good many speculations, as when he tells us that "there is no way to comprehend Monroe unless we assume that her deepest experience in life was the act of playing in a superb role" (*M*, 130). But this particular surmise grows out of Monroe's well-documented concern for her acting career and illustrates the kind of speculative freedom we grant other, less controversial biographers as a matter of course.

Mailer begins by remarking that Monroe is always presented as either "an angelic and sensitive victim or a murderous emotional cripple" (*M*, 23). It seems clear to him that she was both; his book is an attempt to discover the "literary hypothesis" that will do justice to her all-but-schizophrenic character. Mailer departs from previous biographers by searching for his hypothesis in Monroe's films as well as her personal life. The major conclusion he draws from the films is that Monroe was a great actress, a great *artist*, whose theatrical ambitions were as responsible for her subsequent tragedy as was her dismal childhood. This is so for two reasons: (a) the men in her life were insensitive to her talent and (b) she cultivated her great ambition with almost no sense of an "inner identity" (*M*, 126). Lacking such a sense, inevitably exploited by those who could not understand her, Monroe was doomed to a series of self-destructive acts that anticipated her suicide. Most of *Marilyn* is devoted to justifying these claims. Mailer works carefully through the available information on Monroe's affairs and marriages and other pieces of evidence that support his crucial contention that Monroe, for all her egotism, lacked a solid sense of identity. Ultimately, Mailer's success or failure depends on whether he satisfies the most common demand we make on biographers: that their evidence support their accompanying conjectures.

It is a matter of opinion, of course, as to whether Mailer succeeds. I argue that he tries to succeed by means entirely consistent with the biographer's task, and I would add that if Mailer does not "capture" Monroe, he comes closer than anyone else. I have in mind Mailer's impressive treatment of Monroe's films, especially his lengthy analysis of *The Misfits*, for these discussions suggest that Mailer's hypothesis is superior precisely because it incorporates the artistic side of Monroe's character. It also derives from Mailer's painstaking consideration of Monroe's men, who are etched so persuasively that they seem like the most compelling

characters in a realistic novel. Again and again Mailer brings
Monroe's relationships to life, as when he remarks of Joe DiMaggio,
"He will found a dynasty with her if she desires it, but he does not
see their love as a tender wading pool of shared interests and tasting
each other's concoctions in the kitchen" (*M*, 100). Yes, we come to
feel, this is a marriage that prepares a certain kind of personality for
suicide. There are scores of such passages in *Marilyn*, each based on
information to be found in other biographies but transformed by
Mailer's intensely sympathetic yet considered reflection.

Like *The Prisoner of Sex*, *Marilyn* succeeds by pursuing certain
limited ends with a kind of professional purity. The book is informed
by Mailer's belief that only another artist can comprehend Monroe:
"Set a thief to catch a thief, and put an artist on an artist" (*M*, 20).
This proposition is one we will encounter again, in the even more
impressive context of Mailer's literary criticism.

Mailer as Literary Critic

There is something incongruous – even depressing – about the fact
that Mailer's most successful work from 1969 to 1978 was literary
criticism. I may be exaggerating the incongruity, for Mailer has been
publishing literary criticism since the 1950s, but to argue that
Mailer's best work in the 1970s is to be found in a few literary essays
is to acknowledge the relatively minor dimensions of this period.
Still, we must follow Mailer's career wherever it leads us, and it
remains a stubborn fact that Mailer's more recent criticism poses
none of the aesthetic problems that mark even such interesting
books as *Miami and the Siege of Chicago* and *Of a Fire on the
Moon*. For the most part, its limitations are those of the form Mailer
is employing. Perhaps it is significant that the same thing can be said
of *Marilyn*, for these are the works of the 1970s furthest removed
from the "engaged" reportage Mailer first perfected in the 1960s.
Forced to retreat from the successful strategies of his earlier works,
Mailer achieved a limited success in such traditional forms as
biography and the literary essay.

From the first, Mailer's literary criticism reveals a decided
interest in the writer as opposed to the writer's works. Mailer
cherishes no desire to be included among the newer New Critics:
"There is a kind of critic who writes only about the dead. He sees

the great writers of the past as simple men. They are born with a great talent, they exercise it, and they die. Such critics see the mastery in the work; they neglect the subtle failures of the most courageous intent, and the dramatic hours when the man took the leap to become a great writer" (*CC*, 108). As these remarks suggest, Mailer usually assesses a writer's *character* rather than "the mastery in the work." He believes that "the writer, particularly the American writer, is not usually – if he is interesting – the quiet master of his craft; he is rather a being who ventured into the jungle of his unconscious to bring back a sense of order or a sense of chaos" (*CC*, 108). Mailer is fascinated by the writer's excursion into this "jungle" – after all, he has made such a journey himself – and finds literary criticism a meaningful activity only when he is dealing with the artist and/or the creative process. In Mailer's early survey of his contemporaries, "Evaluations – Quick and Expensive Comments on the Talent in the Room" (*AFM*, 463-73), the result is little more than character assassination. Here James Jones is attacked for his "blind vanity" (*AFM*, 463), J. D. Salinger is rejected as "no more than the greatest mind ever to stay in prep school" (*AFM*, 467), and Chandler Brossard is summed up as "a mean pricky guy who's been around" (*AFM*, 469). But Mailer's method can lead to much better results. Among the earlier essays "The Dynamic of American Letters" and "Some Children of the Goddess" (both reprinted in *Cannibals and Christians*) are first-rate critiques. More recently Mailer has provided excellent analyses of the New York intelligentsia and Norman Podhoretz's *Making It* (*EE*, 171-97), the psychological struggles of D. H. Lawrence (*POS*, 134-60), and the "gargantuan talents and vices" of Henry Miller.[15] Indeed, Mailer has written several times on Miller, and it is this body of work (brought together in *Genius and Lust*) that illustrates his critical intelligence at its best.[16]

Reviewers of *Genius and Lust* suggest that the book represents a subtle form of self-aggrandizement. Because Mailer's Henry Miller resembles no one so much as Norman Mailer, this argument goes, Mailer's inflated claims for Miller are claims for his own work. This rather unkind theory is based on a genuine biographical connection between critic and subject. Both Mailer and Miller grew up in Brooklyn and devoted their early years to escaping from the vise of middle-class culture; both achieved fame as literary "outlaws" best known for their use of obscene materials; both experienced the pain of four marriages ending in divorce. (Indeed, each first married a woman named Beatrice!) It is certainly clear that Mailer identifies with Miller. How else are we to account for his remarkable claim that Miller's achievement equals or surpasses that of Melville, Faulkner, Hemingway, and Fitzgerald ("one has to take the English language back to Marlowe and Shakespeare before encountering a wealth of imagery equal in intensity"; *GL*, 4)? But to remark that Mailer sees himself in Henry Miller fails to tell us much about his critical analysis of Miller and his works. Here we have another example of an artist set to catch another artist. Questions of identification aside, does Mailer "catch" anything about Henry Miller that is worth keeping?

Mailer presents a powerful case for Miller as a first-rate talent (though his ranking of Miller is no doubt an indulgence). The case is persuasive because Mailer does not shrink from Miller's faults; to the contrary, Mailer believes "it is impossible to talk of a great artist without speaking of failure" (*GL*, xii), the great artist's failure to achieve his inevitably grandiose intentions. Mailer speaks often and eloquently of Miller's failures: the fact that "at his worst, he sounds like a small-town newspaper editorial" (*GL*, 6); the revealing truth that "he could be poetic about anything and everything except fucking with love" (*GL*, xiii); the absence of fully created women in his books, especially in his 1,600-page magnum opus, *The Rosy Crucifixion*. Mailer understands the justice in Miller's description of himself as a man "filled with wisdom and nonsense" (*GL*, xi). He captures the nonsense in Miller as no one else ever has, perhaps because he places it in the context of Miller's wisdom.

This wisdom has little to do with Miller's tendency to philosophize, which Mailer rightly deplores as diverting attention from Miller's real gifts. In Mailer's view these gifts are essentially those of a superior realist. Miller's genius is for describing areas of human experience, predominantly sexual ones, untouched by previous writers; his literary salvation is to understand "that no account of an unpleasant event could survive its evasions" (*GL*, 96), that the writer who would engage life's underside must do so wholeheartedly, with something like Miller's gusto, or the attempt will flounder. Mailer is very good at evoking this aspect of Miller – the massive selections from Miller's works are intended to represent it – but he is even more impressive in tracing its sources in Miller's life. The best passages in *Genius and Lust* are true to

Mailer's biographical orientation as a critic, describing as they do
Miller's struggles with his Germanic background (personified in his
mother), his Brooklyn-inspired contempt for tender sex and women,
his only partly successful efforts to overcome this training, his
amazing decision at the age of 40 to devote the rest of his life to
writing unpublishable books, and the gradual emergence of his
unique literary posture despite the handicaps of overwhelming
poverty and a high school education. Mailer's prolonged treatment
of Miller's life illumines the artist as well as the man, for we are
finally made to understand both the size of Miller's achievement and
its inevitable limitations. This side of Richard Ellmann, few other
critics have achieved happier results with the biographical method.

It must be admitted that the later sections of *Genius and Lust*
are unequal to the earlier ones. Mailer's long essay on Miller is
divided into nine introductions to the selections from Miller's books;
as the later selections grow shorter and less interesting (thus
mirroring the course of Miller's career), Mailer's discussions become
hardly more than assembled notes on the later Miller. Even in
discussing Miller's less valuable works, however, Mailer illuminates
Miller's ouevre. Mailer sees most of the later books as the limited but
honorable efforts of a man who will not repeat his early successes:
"If he had remained the protagonist by which he first presented
himself in *Tropic of Cancer* – the man with iron in his phallus, acid
in his mind, and some kind of incomparable relentless freedom in his
heart, that paradox of tough misery and keen happiness, that
connoisseur of the spectrum of odors between good sewers and bad
sewers, that noble rat gnawing on existence and impossible to kill,
then he could indeed have been a legend, a species of Parisian
Bogart or American Belmondo. Everybody would have wanted to
meet this poet-gangster, barbarian-genius" (*GL*, 12). But this is
precisely what Miller could not do and remain true to his complex
personality. And so he went on to write very different works in his
later years: literary criticism, reportage, sentimental travel books,
hymns to America, jeremiads against America. Mailer argues that the
variety of these works must be traced back to the nature of their
author, and even those of us skeptical about the critical method
involved must find the argument compelling.

We must also recognize the striking parallel between Miller's
later works (as Mailer describes them) and Mailer's productions

since 1968. In some ways the parallel is not a happy one, for Mailer's pursuit of new forms has also met with either failure or partial success. Nonetheless, it is important that we honor Mailer's willingness to experiment, to wear many hats (some too large, some too small), for this makes possible his successes as well as his failures. Besides, the books discussed in this chapter are only relative "failures"; if they do not satisfy us entirely, it is because Mailer established such high standards in his earlier works. In their distinctive ways these books contribute to that ever-growing body of work that makes Mailer the most important writer of nonfiction in the postwar period.[17]

Chapter Eight

The Executioner's Song

Mailer's Sad Comedy

I am one of those people that probably shouldn't exist.
> – Gary Gilmore, in *The Executioner's Song*

This is an absolutely astonishing book.
> – Joan Didion, "I Want to Go Ahead and Do It"

The time is right, I think, to reconsider the merits of *The Executioner's Song* (1979), Mailer's famous "true life novel" (the book's oxymoronic subtitle). Though the work received an extremely favorable reception from reviewers (more favorable than any of Mailer's other books save *The Naked and the Dead, The Armies of the Night*, and, curiously enough, *Existential Errands*),[1] *The Executioner's Song* remains an enigma in the history of Mailer's critical reputation. Since 1979 most essays on the book have been friendly, but they have all dealt with limited topics – Mailer's presence or nonpresence within the text, Gary Gilmore's "character," the validity of Mailer's claim to have written a true-life novel. It almost seems as if the book's sheer size has discouraged even its advocates from addressing such basic issues as the work's overall structure and informing themes. What are we to make of the final 500 pages, in which Mailer focuses on the intense legal and media activity that marked Gilmore's last three months? How should we assess the relationship between books 1 and 2, almost equally long but often thought to be of radically unequal narrative interest (the first book surpassing the second)? Perhaps most crucial, what are we to think of Gilmore? Is he a Maileresque hero, "fighting the whole liberal establishment for the right to choose his own death and expiation," as Robert Begiebing argues?[2] Or is he no more than a violent punk, as many readers no doubt suppose? Finally, what are we to make of

Mailer's claim that his subject is "American Virtue," as he once considered titling the book?[3] This claim should lead us to reconsider Mailer's thematic intentions in general, intentions all too often downplayed because Mailer himself is so conspicuously "absent" from this huge book. Such a review should allow us to see that *The Executioner's Song* is Mailer's most ambitious attempt to "explain" America (*CC*, 99), his fundamental purpose in all his nonfiction but especially the series of books he published in the 1970s.

This reconsideration will allow me to address the concerns suggested by the two epigraphs that open this chapter. How are we to take such statements as Gilmore's severe self-judgment? Do they point to an exemplary self-understanding (and self-transformation) achieved during Gilmore's final days, or do they simply express an obvious truth that calls Mailer's whole enterprise into question? Is this book "astonishing" in any meaningful literary sense? I want to engage these questions while offering a thoroughgoing assessment of Mailer's accomplishment. First, however, I think we should reengage generic questions that Mailer's works have posed throughout his career as a journalist and/or nonfiction novelist. As I argued earlier in relation to *The Armies of the Night*, we must first understand what kind of book Mailer has written before we can presume to judge its relative success or failure.

Novels and True-Life Novels: The Question of Genre

There is no fiction or nonfiction as we commonly understand the distinction: there is only narrative.

— E. L. Doctorow, quoted in *Newsweek*

I love the idea of a novel; to me a novel is better than a reality. I mean as good as [*The Executioner's Song*] may become . . . it can never be as good as a novel.

— Norman Mailer, in *Conversations with Norman Mailer*

Two days after Gary Gilmore's execution on 17 January 1977 – the first execution in the United States in almost 10 years – Larry Schiller invited Mailer to write the exclusive story Schiller had managed to secure during the preceding three months. When Mailer accepted Schiller's proposal, he must have been relatively unconcerned about the generic or formal nature of his task. His first instinct was to do "a major essay,"[4] perhaps 20,000 words in length (Lennon 1988, 26) – a piece very much on the scale of "Ten Thousand Words a Minute," his essay on the first Patterson-Liston fight. His plan was to write "an essay on the nature of capital punishment, on what to do with our prisons, on why people murder, on karma, on a dozen different things" (Lennon 1988, 229). Though some would argue that he went ahead and did all this in more than 1,000 pages, most readers would agree that the final product bears little resemblance to this initial concept. Whereas he first hoped to do his "major essay" in 6 months, Mailer eventually spent 18 months and made six or seven trips to Utah, two or three to Oregon, and one to Marion, Illinois. Indeed, he ended up conducting about 100 interviews and working his way through some 16,000 pages of transcripts.[5]

Mailer's many paeans to the novel suggest that he disagrees with E. L. Doctorow's belief that there is no distinction between fiction and nonfiction. This point is of some consequence, for, as we shall see, many of Mailer's commentators share Doctorow's view and ascribe it to Mailer as well. Mailer's actual views are at best complex and at worst contradictory. In the afterword to *The Executioner's Song* he says that he has done his best to offer "a factual account" (*ES*, 1020). The chronology of events has been thoroughly researched, for "one understood one's characters better when the chronology was correct" (*ES*, 1020). The true-life story of Gary Gilmore's final nine months is told "as if it were a novel" (*ES*, 1022), but, of course, this construction implies that the book is something other than a novel. What it *is*, however, depends very much on one's literary definitions. As was the case with *Armies*, Mailer makes little pretense to strict documentary accuracy. Although the book represents a major effort to get the facts straight, "this does not mean it has come a great deal closer to the truth than the recollections of the witnesses" (*ES*, 1020) – and the witnesses here are probably no more reliable than those cited in the second half of *Armies* (*AOTN*, 260-62). Where participants offer different versions of the same event, Mailer has chosen "the version that seemed most likely" (*ES*, 1020). Gilmore's interviews and letters have been slightly edited; the old prison rhyme with which the book begins and ends was written by Mailer himself for his 1968 film *Maidstone;* and the reflections of one character in one scene were first formulated on a later and quite

different occasion from the one dramatized (*ES*, 1021). These literary
"adjustments" may seem to betray Mailer's novelizing, but in fact
Mailer sees them as distortions all but inevitable in the writing of history (a view John Hersey deplores with some eloquence).[6] When he
calls his book a "novel," Mailer is thinking not of how the facts are
distorted but of how they are presented.

Indeed, Mailer seems to agree with Tom Wolfe and Truman
Capote that the extensive use of dramatic techniques is what really
defines the nonfiction novel. Like Wolfe, Mailer develops an
extended narrative in which all four of the New Journalism's defining
features are prominent: (a) the frequent use of dramatic scenes; (b)
fully recorded dialogue; (c) consistent attention to "status details";
and (d) the complex use of point of view to depict events as they
unfold.[7] Like Capote, Mailer offers "a narrative form that employ[s]
all the techniques of fictional art but [is] nevertheless immaculately
factual" (Plimpton 1966, 41) (though Mailer would no doubt delete
Capote's audacious adverb). Thus Mailer's claim, repeated in interview after interview, that *The Executioner's Song* is a novel in which
everything is as true as he could make it.

It would be easy to conclude that Mailer is a bit fuzzy about his
own generic claims. Sometimes he says his book can never be as
good as a novel, or talks about what it would be like "if I'd written it
as a novel" (Lennon 1988, 234), and sometimes he directly labels it a
novel (most famously in his subtitle). The real nature of his experiment is best revealed, I think, by comparing it with Capote's *In Cold
Blood*, the book most often cited in relationship to *The Executioner's Song*. The comparison is almost irresistible, for the two
books deal with very similar subjects in what seems the same literary
form. In each case the author describes a notorious murder case
climaxed by the execution of the killer(s), the murderers and their
victims are rendered in fulsome detail drawn from numerous historical documents presumed to be authentic, and the "plot" alludes
briefly to the murderers' pasts while focusing on the crime itself and
the events leading up to the execution(s). Both Capote and Mailer
devote a great many pages to the character and especially the
motives of their killers, whose explanations for what they did are
ultimately endorsed by each author. (Indeed, both "explanations"
involve a crucial displacement: Perry Smith says, "[The Clutters]
never hurt me. . . . Maybe it's just that the Clutters were the ones

who had to pay for it [the accumulated resentments of his past] [Capote, 339]; Gilmore says, "I killed Jenkins [*sic*] and Bushnell because I did not want to kill Nicole" [*ES*, 672]. The only significant difference is that Gilmore points to a more immediate source of tension.) Each writer offers an exhaustive account of murder and its consequences (as Capote's subtitle puts it), dramatizing at great length what is usually summarized and then made the subject of editorial commentary.

As it happens, Capote rejects almost violently the notion that *In Cold Blood* resembles *The Executioner's Song*, a book for which he expresses nothing but scorn. (By contrast, Mailer has praised *In Cold Blood* as "a wonderful book" and "a very good novel.")[8] Capote's objections are in part personal – he can't respect Mailer's book because Mailer, unlike Capote, did not do 100 percent of the research on which his book is based (Grobel, 113) – but they are also literary: he does not like Mailer's attitude toward his characters, his point of view, or his style (Grobel, 113). Whatever they think of the book, most recent critics agree that *The Executioner's Song* is a very different kind of work. Each writer might seem to employ what Chris Anderson calls "the rhetoric of silence" (Anderson, 57), in which direct authorial commentary is eschewed for a strictly dramatic representation, but Capote is usually seen as intruding by means of conspicuous artistic manipulation. Whereas Mailer embraces a kind of perspectivism by employing no fewer than 100 Jamesian "centers of consciousness" in telling his story, Capote prefers omniscient narration and is reluctant to enter his characters' minds.[9] Capote's desire is to direct us toward what he frankly calls the "right" interpretation (*Plimpton* 1966, 41).

Of course, Capote has come under great fire for the nature of this "control." Phillip K. Tompkins argues that Capote's manipulations amount to outright distortion, even fabrication, as Perry Smith ("an obscene, semiliterate and cold-blooded killer") is transformed into the real hero of Capote's narrative.[10] Tompkins offers excellent evidence that Capote all but invents entire episodes, and Jack De Bellis effectively supports Tompkins's claims by revealing how many details – including facts – were changed in the 10 weeks between the initial appearance of *In Cold Blood* in The *New Yorker* and its subsequent publication by Random House.[11] Even if his critics are wrong about his distortions, however, Capote is happy to accept their judgment that he shapes the narrative to reinforce his own interpretation of the Clutter murder case. Some of the more relevant textual features include the regular alternation of sections dealing with the killers and their victims-to-be; the authorial comments whereby Capote points up the impending catastrophe (Mr. Clutter heads home for the day's work "unaware that it would be his last"; Capote, 13); the almost-complete suppression of Capote's role in the later events; and the relative brevity of Capote's narrative, which condenses 8,000 pages of material into a book one-third the length of *The Executioner's Song.*

For better or worse, Mailer is usually seen as less selective, less insistent on his own views, and more inclined to *amass* his case than to shape it toward a single conclusion. Indeed, almost all discussions of *The Executioner's Song* begin by noting Mailer's stunning impersonality. Where once he offered "unabashedly subjective accounts of public events,"[12] now he seems to have become an Olympian artist à la Joyce: "Gone from *The Executioner's Song* are the familiar, patent Mailerisms – the baroque syntax, the hectoring tone, the outrageous epigrams, the startling bravura imagery, the political/metaphysical digressions, the self-conscious presence of the author in every line."[13] As Mailer himself has put it, Mailer seems to be "nothing but a conveyor belt" to disperse his fascinating material.[14] While many reviewers were delighted with this artistic about-face (as if Mailer had finally rejected his notorious indulgences), others felt that Mailer had gone too far and left his readers "unguided by the author and unconfronted with a meaningful shape of experience."[15] Friends or foes, all readers seem to agree that *The Executioner's Song* represents a radical departure in Mailer's career.

The Executioner's Song is not really such an unprecedented experiment, however. Mailer remarks the parallels with his very first novel, *The Naked and the Dead,* and J. Michael Lennon points out that Mailer became less and less interested in his own role in public events throughout the 1970s (Lennon n.d., 28). (Indeed, Mailer comments on this trend in such works as *Miami and the Siege of Chicago, Of a Fire on the Moon,* and *The Fight.*) Moreover, Mailer has offered quite specific reasons for adopting a severe narrative manner: to write about Gilmore in Mailer's own style would have risked the accusation of inflating Gilmore rhetorically; the nature of the story required a faster narrative movement than many of Mailer's earlier books ("I wanted my book to *move*"); Mailer felt unusually humble in the face of his mysterious materials and did not think he had the "right" to generalize; and the material itself was "gold," if he had enough sense not to "gild" it (Lennon 1988, 270). We might ask whether these reasons adequately account for Mailer's narrative choices, but in any case *The Executioner's Song* is hardly the rudderless text so often invoked by Mailer's critics. Mailer once said that "to write was to judge" (*FOM*, 436), and this remark applies to *The Executioner's Song* as much as to Mailer's other works. What distinguishes his judgments here is that they are more tentative than in the past, not that they have disappeared altogether. They are not the judgments we associate with the books from *The Armies of the Night* through *The Fight*, because we do not get the formal conclusions toward which the earlier narratives move (through whatever serpentine stages). These judgments are real enough, however, and differentiate *The Executioner's Song* from those "novels" Mailer consistently honors in his literary criticism.

Yet the formal distinction between novel and history is more precarious now than it was when Mailer wrote *The Armies of the Night*. In 1967 Mailer characterized *Armies* as "history in the costume of a novel" (*AOTN*, 215), an apt and precise definition, and several years earlier he described *In Cold Blood* as a "documentary" (*CC*, 101). As we have seen, however, the author of *The Executioner's Song* speaks of *In Cold Blood* as "a very good novel" and is willing to label his own work a kind of novel, that is, "a true life novel." This shift may represent nothing more than literary politics, and it certainly involves Mailer's obvious fondness for the novel as *the* modern literary form – as if works like *The Executioner's Song* (or even *In Cold Blood*) could not be major if they were not novels. But it also involves Mailer's intuition that, formally speaking, *The Executioner's Song* goes well beyond what Mailer did in works like *Armies*. In part the difference involves excising the historical apparatus still visible in *Armies:* authorial commentary, whole chapters written as essays ("Why Are We in Vietnam?"), formulated conclusions at the end of the narrative. In part, however, the difference derives from Mailer's crucial decision to tell his story through the eyes of 100 different participants. The aesthetic results of this decision seem to have persuaded Mailer that his book is indeed a novel, though not the *kind* of novel he had in mind when he praised the form in the past.

Mailer has always derided journalism and other forms of non-fiction because they require straightforward conclusions: "It's hard to think of a good book of nonfiction whose waters are not clear" (Lennon 1988, 244). Such "clarity" is never Mailer's literary destination, and especially not in *The Executioner's Song,* a book in which he stresses the mysteries of life more than in any earlier work. Here, of course, it is the mystery of real life that is stressed, for Mailer insists on his fidelity to what happened in terms that recall Capote's claims if not his practice. This mystery is rendered in hundreds of subjective accounts either transcribed or dramatized. Paradoxically, this radical perspectivism makes possible what Mailer calls "an objective picture of American society" (Lennon 1988, 238). I take Mailer to mean that the *nature* of American society is discovered even if its mysteries remain mysteries – indeed, mystery is often what is discovered. The formal result is "a social drama" (Lennon 1988, 238) that recalls the nineteenth-century novel but avoids made-up episodes and the sort of "tampering" to which Capote's critics object.

Should such a structure be called a novel? Obviously, the answer depends on what we mean by the label. When Mailer says that a novel is better than reality, he is thinking of an imagined fictional world he can alter as he pleases. By this standard *The Executioner's Song* is clearly not a novel. Unlike *In Cold Blood,* however, Mailer's book does not seem to be a documentary either. Doctorow would say that it is simply a *narrative,* but I think this is untrue both to Mailer's profound respect for the imaginative depths of the novel and to the innumerable real-life details that make up the texture of his book, for what distinguishes *The Executioner's Song* – what makes it almost sui generis – is its remarkable combination of the real and the novelistic. The two come together here because the real, for Mailer, is precisely the hundreds of subjective accounts from which he builds his story. Unlike Capote, Mailer does not wish to construct *the* interpretation of events by presenting the facts that support this reading. Instead, he offers what is made to *seem* like all the facts, all the "versions" or interpretations of the events he is describing. And by presenting each event from the point of view of a participant, he ensures that the texture of each episode resembles that of a novel. The dramatic method employed here is such that we gain little by denying the book's claim to be fiction.

Yet there is also something misleading about the book's being honored with the Pulitzer Prize in fiction, for this is a *true-life* novel, very much to be distinguished from the novels Mailer grew up admiring so much. As such, it is subject to many of the same restrictions I noted earlier in such works as *Green Hills of Africa, In Cold Blood,* and *The Armies of the Night.* That the accuracy of his book has not been challenged[16] is not only to Mailer's credit but essential to the book's artistic rationale, for the "social drama" Mailer renders here is neither symbolic nor metaphoric but the thing itself. Such is Mailer's claim, at any rate, and such is the remarkably difficult "contract" he tries to fulfill by arranging hundreds of brief narratives in such a way as to interest us in their reality even as he uncovers their most fascinating – and "novelistic" – mysteries. Indeed, I believe we should judge Mailer's book by the terms of his subtitle or what I am calling his contract. The events and dialogue depicted must be as true to Mailer's sources as he can make them, yet they must also be presented so as to elicit the effects we usually associate with the novel. Anything less would call into question either the immense research underlying *The Executioner's Song* or Mailer's decision to dramatize every aspect of the story.

The task I describe obviously goes way beyond the transcription of reality or even the artistic "shaping" practiced by Capote, for even as Mailer fashions his narrative as subtly and decisively as Capote fashioned his, Mailer must preserve the illusion that his text is nothing but life itself, uncoerced by any one controlling "vision." He must eat his cake but somehow keep it too by employing structure and style to highlight what he thinks most suggestive in his massive materials, even as he persuades us that the book as a whole and not just a particular episode is "most likely" – perhaps *the* most likely of all Mailer's tales, fictional or nonfictional, imagined or transcribed. To justify these somewhat abstract generalizations, I turn now to the narrative structure of what often seems the most unstructured of Mailer's books.

The Structure of *The Executioner's Song*

It's as if he has set a camera down in the middle of the event, in the tradition
of Warhol and cinéma vérité, and simply recorded all that passed the camera's
eye.
                                                        – Chris Anderson, *Style as Argument*

When Chris Anderson says that *The Executioner's Song* resembles
Warhol's more extravagant experiments, he is referring to his impression on first reading Mailer's book; according to Anderson, a second
reading reveals the author's shaping hand in ways that recall
Capote's in *In Cold Blood* (Anderson, 122). Anderson's comment is
all too representative, however. It does take some time to appreciate
that there is a "shaping consciousness" at work, as John Hellmann
puts it (Hellmann 19, 57). For example, a number of critics have
pointed to Mailer's habit of concluding narrative sections with telling
comments phrased in his own voice, as when he compares Gilmore's
trip home after being released from prison with the westward journey of Brenda Nicol's great-grandfather many years earlier (*ES*, 22).
The passage in question "connects" a dedicated Mormon pioneer
and the all-too-aimless Gilmore, a fine irony made available by the
author and not one of his characters. And there are many other such
moments, often, as noted, at the end of sections. But it is easy to
exaggerate Mailer's "presence" in the book as a whole – a few
summarizing remarks do not go far in a book of more than 1,000
pages. Thus, Anderson's allusion to Warhol; thus, Richard Stern's
amusing comment: "Mailer's absence is so pronounced that it domi-
nates the book like an empty chair at a family dinner."[17] To locate
Mailer, I would suggest, we need to look not at explicit formulations
but at the narrative structure itself.

Book 1 of *The Executioner's Song* is titled "Western Voices," and
we do overhear many different western voices during the 500 pages
devoted to Gary Gilmore's three-and-a-half months of freedom in
Provo, Utah (after he spends 18 of his previous 22 years in prison
and before he murders two men for no apparent reason). These
many western figures, however, primarily observe and comment on
Gilmore, who remains the unmistakable focal point of book 1. By
presenting Gilmore from so many points of view, Mailer provides
what seems as broad and objective a portrait as possible. Nonethe-

less, the details selected highlight certain features of Gilmore's character, as a brief review of part 1, "Gary," should confirm.

The first 15 pages offer a number of quite sympathetic moments or details concerning Gilmore's past. In these first pages his cousin, Brenda Nicol, remembers a seven-year-old Gary helping her during "a good family get-together" (*ES*, 17); the unattractive details of Gary's reform-school days in Portland are left out of the narrative; Brenda's sister, Toni, testifies to the impact of Gary's drawings, especially those which depict "children with great sad eyes" (*ES*, 19); one of Gilmore's letters is quoted in which he says of prison, "It's like another planet" (*ES*, 20), a haunting simile reinforced a bit later when he remarks that he seldom saw stars while in prison (*ES*, 55); Brenda is surprised when he comes out of prison "marked up much more than she had expected" (*ES*, 27); the pathetic austerity of his one tote bag, his inability to stop "gawking" at beautiful girls, and his ignorance of the fact that one can try on clothes before buying them all point up his abysmal past (*ES*, 33, 36); and Gary's sensitive interplay with the small children of friends is noted twice (*ES*, 44, 46). Later in part 1, when Gilmore meets Nicole Baker, those who know him are amazed at his positive transformation (*ES*, 73). These early pages consistently present Gilmore as a kind of waif, good at heart but deprived of the normal opportunities to express his goodness. Almost immediately, however, evidence from several sources begins to define Gilmore as what Mailer calls a "habit-ridden petty monster," "trapped" within his apparently unshakable selfishness (Lennon 1988, 256). During his first date in Provo Gilmore demands sex, refuses to listen when told he must *earn* things, and raises his fist against a woman who has done nothing to him (*ES*, 41); only a few weeks later he repeats this performance with a second date, finally breaking the windshield of her car when she refuses to sleep with him (*ES*, 66). In the midst of many conversations Gilmore launches into grim prison stories about beating a convict with a hammer (*ES*, 44-45), photographing a convict performing fellatio on himself (*ES*, 48-49), killing "this black dude . . . a *bad* nigger" (*ES*, 65), and tattooing a friend with little phalluses (*ES*, 76-77); indeed, this ominous repertoire of prison tales is trotted out whenever Gilmore makes a new acquaintance in book 1. Soon we observe Gilmore lying to his sympathetic parole officer (*ES*, 62) and shouting obscenities at a movie screen (*ES*, 67-69). Thus, Mailer establishes at once the extraordinary difficulty of defining Gilmore's essence or even how one should respond to him.

This complex portrait is embellished throughout the remaining six parts of book 1. As developed in part 2 ("Nicole") and part 3 ("Gary and Nicole"), Gilmore's affair with Nicole deepens our sense of both his pathos and his viciousness. Mailer's treatment of their first days together is very sympathetic. He takes seriously their belief in reincarnation and presents without irony their separate assertions that they knew each other "from another time" (*ES*, 83, 88). He shows Gilmore playing the engaging youthful lover despite the fact he is 35 and Nicole 19: Gilmore labels Nicole his "elf" (*ES*, 93-94), carves their names on an apple tree (*ES*, 94), and tells her "that he hoped no unnecessary tragedies would ever befall them" (*ES*, 97). With Nicole he seems much more in control of himself, as when he tells her that the whole point of living is "facing yourself" (*ES*, 88). Yet Gilmore still seems compulsively violent: he forces Nicole into all-night sexual engagements to combat his impotence (*ES*, 89), clips off the speakers in a drive-in (*ES*, 113), hits Nicole at least twice (*ES*, 158, 162-63), throws a tape deck at a security guard (*ES*, 164), and gets drunk soon after promising to give up drinking (*ES*, 200-201). His frequent reflections on reincarnation betray his basic childishness, for at this point his faith is little more than a pleasant fantasy: "After death, he said, he was going to start all over again. Have the kind of life he always wished he had" (*ES*, 197). And so it is no surprise when Gilmore cannot sustain his relationship with Nicole, who leaves him toward the end of part 3. Indeed, the depressing histories presented in part 2 offer almost no hope that Gilmore and Nicole can reverse the pattern of failure that informs both lives.

The first three parts of book 1 create sympathy for Gilmore even as they document his "monstrous" character. This opening movement is crucial to the work's overall effect, for beginning with part 4, "The Gas Station and the Motel," Mailer is obliged to record Gilmore's ghastly performance in murdering for $100 one night and $125 the next. The almost-shockingly-flat account of the Jensen and Bushnell murders is followed by Gilmore's pathetic effort to make love to Nicole's 15-year-old sister, April (*ES*, 238); his absurdly amateurish lies to the police (*ES*, 263, 277-81); his repulsive boasting about the 70 to 100 "successful" robberies he committed as a kid (*ES*, 292) and the murder of Bushnell (*ES*, 356); and his extremely evasive stance at the subsequent trial, where he claims that he had no control over himself when he committed the murders (*ES*, 381), that it was *fated* for him to kill Bushnell (*ES*, 435-36). In part 5 ("The Shadows of the Dream"), part 6 ("The Trial of Gary M. Gilmore"), and part 7 ("Death Row") we see Gilmore at a much greater distance, back in jail and no longer the somewhat sympathetic figure of the early sections. During Mailer's clinical account of the murders and Gilmore's subsequent arrest, trial, and sentencing, our "hero" often seems little more than the "recidivist" John Hersey takes him to be (Hersey, 13). There is precious little to corroborate the initial hints that Gilmore is partly the victim of a system that imprisons a man for almost his entire adult life for relatively petty crimes. By the end of book 1, however, a strangely positive side to Gilmore does emerge, one that will become a major subject in book 2.

I refer here partly to Gilmore's relative stability when he once again becomes a convict. Early in his jail stint in Provo Gilmore tells a fellow convict, "I am in my element now" (*ES*, 357), and the final sections of book 1 tend to confirm this claim rather than to undercut it as another instance of Gilmore's cheap self-inflation. But I also refer to the odd capacity Gilmore seems to develop to judge his life with apparent objectivity. Soon after his arrest he tells an officer, "I can't keep up with life" (*ES*, 293), as accurate a comment on his frenetic three and a half months in Provo as anyone is able to offer. A bit later he writes a long letter to Nicole in which he says he cannot be the devil, because he loves Nicole and the devil cannot love. "But I might be further from God than I am from the devil," he adds. "It seems that I know evil more intimately than I know goodness" (*ES*, 305). This remarkable letter is followed by others equally fascinating, letters in which he praises Nicole's fearlessness ("Fear is an ugly thing"; *ES*, 327), speaks of the unendurable pain he felt when he thought he had lost Nicole (*ES*, 328), celebrates their two months together while referring again to the thousands of years they may have known each other (*ES*, 329), and affirms courage as the ultimate virtue (*ES*, 345). Perhaps the most important letter is the one in which he tells Nicole, "I believe we always have a choice" (*ES*, 344).

Gilmore's choice now is to die rather than allow his soul to deteriorate further in this life. This logic leads him to reject any appeal of the death penalty, a decision that soon makes him nationally famous and confirms Mailer's portrait of Gilmore as profoundly ambiguous.

This man who acts like a barbarian at one moment and quotes Emerson at another is a "mystery," Mailer has said, "malignant at his worst and heroic at his best" ("PW Interviews: Norman Mailer," 9). Book 1 does not verify Gilmore's heroism, but it does project a man whose complications are as vivid as his unforgettable malignancy. Although Gilmore as habit-ridden monster is the key to book 1, we are made to ask whether that is all there is to say about the man. Book 2, of course, will offer many more words, as Mailer pursues the mystery of Gary Gilmore through another 500 pages.

Before turning to the lawyers and media figures who dominate book 2, I should say something more about the many relatives, friends, acquaintances, and victims who share the stage with Gilmore in book 1. These people are observers who contribute to the composite picture of Gary Gilmore, but they also help Mailer achieve the broad social panorama he admires in writers as different as Tolstoy and Dreiser. Indeed, Mailer has chided himself for doing so little with the secondary characters in his previous novels, a "flaw" he hoped to correct in *The Executioner's Song* (Lennon 1988, 260). Here Mailer develops virtually every "minor" character and permits each to speak in something like his or her own voice, however much the several idioms blend into the flat, colloquial style for which the book is famous. Mailer's defense of his unadorned prose might apply to the minor characters themselves: "one's style is only a tool to use on a dig" (Lennon 1988, 266). Like the style by which we know them, the secondary characters are supposed to contribute to the book's larger formal ends.

One such end is to "examine" the American reality exposed by the strange saga of Gary Gilmore. Joan Didion sees Mailer as capturing two crucial features of western America. The first is "that emptiness at the center of the Western experience, a nihilism antithetical not only to literature but to most other forms of human endeavor."[18] The second is an inability to direct our own lives, a failing so pervasive that all the characters seem to share in "a fatalistic drift, a tension, an overwhelming and passive rush toward the inevitable events that will end in Gary Gilmore's death" (Didion, 81). I believe that Didion's insights are exaggerated, but they do point up suggestive connections between Gilmore and the people who surround him. Bessie Gilmore, Brenda Nicol, Vern Damico, Kathryne Baker and her daughters Nicole and April – all are "trapped" in their futile efforts to find a life worth living. Indeed, almost every woman in the book first marries at 15 or 16 and eventually marries at least three or four times, and the men seem equally caught up in the "fatalistic drift" Didion notices. Although Didion does not do justice to the admirable stability of people like Brenda Nicol and Vern Damico, the wasted and wasteful lives of those around Gilmore suggest that his own fate is only an exaggerated instance of the moral emptiness Didion hears in the book's western voices.

In this respect as in others, Nicole Baker is the second most important character. Mailer has called her "a bona fide American heroine" (Lennon 1988, 270), but most readers will think she is instead the quintessential American victim. Promiscuous at 11, institutionalized at 13, married at 14 and again at 15, Nicole suffers three broken marriages before she is 20. "Sex had never been new to Nicole," we are told (*ES*, 143), and it is more than plausible when she runs off with an older man because "she didn't care where she was going" (*ES*, 117-18). Yet Nicole has virtues to match her troubling irresponsibility. As Gilmore sees, she is fearless and fiercely loyal. These are the very qualities he counts on when he manipulates her toward a suicide pact. In his many letters from jail he pleads with Nicole not to make love with other men (*ES*, 350), to give up sex altogether (*ES*, 403-4), and to join him on the other side in death (*ES*, 472). At the end of book 1 he leads her into a double-suicide attempt that epitomizes both his romanticism and his selfishness, even as it climaxes Mailer's portrait of Nicole as an endearing victim. Later Nicole will be denied the "clean" resolution of death, will emerge from yet another institution to tell Larry Schiller (and Mailer) the story of her love for Gary Gilmore, and will finally drift off to Oregon to new lovers if not a new life. Nicole's story is a familiar one among her family and friends: years of acute aimlessness followed by an utterly hopeless commitment. Surely it is no accident that Nicole comes to love Gilmore most fiercely when he is cut off from her forever. For the Nicoles of this world (and perhaps this means for all of us), there is no consummation except in an imagined future.

The stories of Nicole and the other witnesses point to one of Mailer's most crucial decisions in structuring book 1. Rather than trace Gilmore's grim history from reform school through his term in Marion, Illinois, Mailer chooses to focus on Gilmore's last months in Provo in 1976. The reasons for this arrangement no doubt include

Mailer's desire to achieve greater dramatic unity and to emphasize Gilmore's "mystery" instead of the familiar stages of American crime and punishment. But another important reason is to allow Mailer to flesh out the human context in which Gilmore plays his final role or sings his final song, as the title would have it.[19] This context is dominated by the same hateful "habits" that take more spectacular forms in Gilmore. Yet the human resources displayed in book 1 should not be dismissed quite as easily as Didion's formulation would suggest. Here we get example after example of human folly, western-style, but also many instances of what Mailer calls "American virtue," the American's dogged determination to do his or her best in the worst of circumstances. The range of such portraits is extraordinary, from Gilmore's mother Bessie, to Brenda Nicol, to the Damicos, to the irrepressible Nicole. One of the earliest reviewers called *The Executioner's Song* "a remarkably compassionate work,"[20] and the truth in this judgment should remind us that book 1, like Mailer's portrait of Gilmore, is structured to highlight the human frailties as well as the abominations of American life.

It might seem that book 2 offers a less sympathetic, more satiric history of Gilmore's last months. The very title of part 1, "In the Reign of Good King Boaz," signals a new kind of irony. Here lawyers and the press are omnipresent, and one 82-page section, "Exclusive Rights," is devoted to virtually nothing but Larry Schiller's and David Susskind's efforts to corner the Gilmore market, so to speak, by securing exclusive rights to his story. Packs of reporters are everywhere, confirming Mailer's worst fears about the press. The many lawyers introduced are often distinguished by one bizarre detail or another, as when Earl Dorius, Utah's assistant attorney general, is *excited* at the prospect of an execution and proceeds to work himself into a near-breakdown to ensure that the state of Utah gets its execution on 17 January (*ES*, 500), or when Dennis Boaz, Gilmore's second lawyer, supports his client's desire to be executed until it occurs to him that Gary would prefer to live if he could have connubial visits from Nicole (*ES*, 590-91), perhaps in Mexico (*ES*, 611)! Gilmore's final lawyers, Bob Moody and Ron Stanger, are a good deal less eccentric, but they too partake in the grim legal struggle in which the state of Utah pursues its pound of flesh and the ACLU and other liberal groups fight stubbornly to save a man who does not want to be saved. The ironies here are obvious and may even seem undramatic. In the film version of *The Executioner's Song* (1982), scenarist Mailer and director Schiller chose to leave out most of the materials of book 2, as if they were less relevant than the more "immediate" events of book 1.

My own view is that book 2 is at least as interesting as book 1, a remarkable feat when one considers that the protagonist is all but unavailable and the heroine is locked up throughout. Once again Mailer gets great mileage from his so-called minor figures, a few of whom (for instance, Boaz, Schiller, and Barry Farrell) are among his most memorable characters. Of real interest for their own sake, they also provide perspective on Gilmore. For example, the producer David Susskind and his prospective scenarist, Stanley Greenberg, help define the moral nature of Gilmore's decision to die. Greenberg supposes that Gilmore must be "out of his head" to want to die (*ES*, 587), thus expressing the liberal position on life and death that Mailer has been attacking at least since *Cannibals and Christians*. Both Susskind and Greenberg come to think of the Gilmore saga as "no longer a story about the breakdown of the criminal justice system"; for them, it becomes "a farce . . . bizarre and sick" (*ES*, 613). For Mailer, one suspects, it was never a story about the breakdown of the criminal justice system, though it was always a story well beyond the rational categories of the Susskinds and Greenbergs.

Other minor characters contribute in large or small ways to the sympathetic portrayal of Gilmore in book 2. Gary's brother Mikal is at first reluctant to allow his brother to die and participates in legal actions to prevent it. When he finally talks with Gary, however, Mikal is won over by his brother's seriousness and depth of feeling. Mikal acknowledges the force of Gary's character by withdrawing his opposition to the execution and by embracing Gary at their final meeting. As they part, Gary first kisses Mikal and then utters perhaps the most haunting words in this very long book: "See you in the darkness" (*ES*, 840). A cellmate of Gilmore's named Gibbs also effectively testifies in Gary's behalf. A police informer, Gibbs refers to Gilmore as the most courageous convict he has ever seen (*ES*, 759). And Gilmore's relatives, especially Vern Damico and Toni Gurney, find themselves moving ever closer to Gilmore as he approaches death, thus confirming the man's odd appeal. Toni's relationship with Gilmore is especially moving. She first visits him the day before he is to be executed and is overwhelmed by his gentle affection (*ES*,

874-75). Later that day, after her own birthday party, she returns to the party Gilmore has been permitted at the prison and again experiences Gary's new warmth (*ES*, 884-86). Toni is sufficiently moved to try to attend Gary's execution (*ES*, 929). This sequence blends with many other small but affecting moments to verify the change sensed by many people during Gilmore's final weeks.

Mailer uses Barry Farrell and Larry Schiller to temper the more sentimental implications of book 2, but ultimately these veteran journalists also testify to Gilmore's surprising depth. The title of book 2, "Eastern Voices," seems to refer to all those safely established in the social system, whether in the East or the West: lawyers, reporters, producers, assistant attorney generals, and so on. Farrell and Schiller are such voices. Each brings a heavy load of urban skepticism to the Gilmore assignment, hating Salt Lake City, as Farrell does, and believing there is no "center" to this story, nothing of real human resonance (*ES*, 577). When both men come to see Gilmore in a very different light, Mailer is able to bring his book to something like a genuine climax.

Farrell is at first confident that nothing sets Gilmore apart but his willingness to die. If Gilmore is not executed, Farrell suggests, he will become indistinguishable from the hundreds of others condemned to die but never executed (*ES*, 611). As he works with Gilmore's responses to hundreds of questions, however, Farrell notices that Gilmore "was now setting out to present the particular view of himself he wanted people to keep" (*ES*, 711). Later Farrell responds profoundly to Gilmore's tapes: "Barry was crying and laughing and felt half triumphant that the man could talk with such clarity" (*ES*, 804). Farrell still thinks that Gilmore "had a total contempt for life" (*ES*, 805), but this makes it all the more impressive when Gilmore responds so "humanely" to the massive attention of his last months (*ES*, 805). Farrell is stunned at Gilmore's apparent complexity. In the transcripts Farrell spots "twenty-seven poses," 27 different Gilmores ("racist Gary and Country-and-Western Gary, poetic Gary, artist manqué Gary, macho Gary"; *ES*, 806). Farrell begins to pursue the single Gary who presumably stands behind these multiple poses, but he is "seized with depression at how few were the answers" to his inquiry (*ES*, 811). Though there is an "evil genius" in Gilmore's planning Nicole's suicide, much else in Gilmore's life suggests sheer ignorance (*ES*, 812); though Gilmore's relations with his mother,

Bessie, seem a potential key, the answers to many related questions provide no "hope of a breakthrough" (*ES*, 827; 844). Continuing to ponder Gilmore's transcripts just before the execution, Farrell turns to yet another possible solution to the Gilmore mystery: Gilmore's fascination with small children. But this "answer" is also unsatisfactory: "It was too insubstantial. In fact, it was sheer speculation. . . . [B]eware of understanding the man too quickly!" (*ES*, 855). Beware indeed. Farrell's final comment on Gilmore takes us back to the passage from André Gide ("Please do not understand me too quickly") Mailer first used as his epigraph to *The Deer Park*. Farrell's conclusion should caution us against reductive readings, psychological efforts to pluck out Gilmore's mystery. Indeed, Gilmore's complexity should impress us as much as it does Farrell, whose prolonged efforts to understand Gilmore are, of course, akin to Mailer's.

Larry Schiller's role is in part like Farrell's. Schiller also looks for the human side to Gilmore, the "sympathetic character" buried inside the cold-blooded killer (*ES*, 629), because Schiller cannot imagine making a successful book or film unless he first makes this discovery. Like Farrell, Schiller begins with many doubts and ends up convinced of Gilmore's essential seriousness, especially on such matters as life after death (*ES*, 670-71). Schiller shares with Farrell the scenarist's desire to grasp his subject, to "reduce Gary's mystery, attach him to conditions, locate him in history" (Chevigny, 191). Together Farrell and Schiller prove that it is impossible to achieve this "reduction" no matter how many materials are scrutinized. Schiller's role is larger than Farrell's, however, for it also includes Schiller's personal drama. Both Farrell and Schiller make interesting discoveries about Gary Gilmore, but Schiller makes such discoveries about himself as well.

In book 2 Schiller's importance surpasses Nicole's and rivals Gilmore's. Much of book 2 is organized around Schiller's efforts to sign up the principals in the Gilmore story and to get information from Gilmore before the execution. This intricate, frustrating process educates Schiller about Gilmore but also constitutes a belated rite de passage for Schiller, who becomes "part of the story," as he himself notes (*ES*, 694). Before coming to Utah Schiller has achieved "a terrible reputation" (*ES*, 581) as a journalist. The last man to interview Jack Ruby, the author of "a quick and rotten book" about Susan Atkins (*ES*, 585), Schiller describes himself as a "communicator" (*ES*,

585) but is laughed at by people who take him to be a hustler or, worse, "a carrion bird" (*ES*, 698). Even his fiancée labels him a "manipulator" (*ES*, 620). With the Gilmore story Schiller struggles to be a good businessman as well as a good journalist (*ES*, 620-21); however, he often seems to lose this fight as he worries about whether there are any "sympathetic characters" in the plot he has purchased, works out alternative scenarios depending on whether or not Gilmore is executed, and schemes to get at Nicole, the love interest in this "democratic Romeo and Juliet," as Boaz describes the Gilmore tale (*ES*, 611).

Yet Schiller turns out to be much more than a carrion bird. He deals more honestly with everyone involved than most of us would have done; he suffers acute physical and emotional stress in deciding how far to go in exploiting his material; and he ends up committing himself to doing the best he can for the story rather than his bank account, even rejecting an offer of $250,000 from the *New York Post* (*ES*, 833). In his afterword Mailer says that Schiller "stood for his portrait, and drew maps to his faults" during their interviews (*ES*, 1022). As Mailer says elsewhere, Schiller "wanted the best book that could be gotten out of what had become the biggest event in his own life, and so he did not spare himself, he offered himself."[21] As a result, Schiller's faults and his final integrity in confronting them are deeply embedded in Mailer's text.[22]

Schiller's role in *The Executioner's Song* is a bit like Mailer's in *The Armies of the Night*. I have referred to Schiller's experience as a rite of passage, and, of course, that is the nature of Mailer's experience during the March on the Pentagon. In each case a man of mixed motives, even a mild cynicism, comes to believe in what he is doing and to act more honorably than we would have thought possible when introduced to him. Schiller is only one of many important characters in this large book, so he is not as central as Mailer is in *Armies*. As we shall see, however, his story very much resembles Mailer's in bringing out the book's more positive implications. The point to be made here is that Schiller's late-blooming integrity confirms Mailer's portrait of Gilmore as a man of unsuspected depth. The more we come to believe in Larry Schiller, the more we believe in his conception of Gary Gilmore.

This is not to say that Mailer's Gilmore is saintly. In fact, Mailer has noted his distaste for Gilmore: "When I started *The Execu-*

tioner's Song, I thought I would like him more than I did" (Lennon 1988, 348). In book 2 as much as in book 1, Mailer does ample justice to what is unattractive, even hateful in Gilmore. As Mailer says, Gilmore was "a bad man, a dull man, a mediocre man" (Lennon 1988, 349). Gilmore's intense racism is evident throughout book 2[23]; he never expresses any real contrition for his crimes[24]; he is a man with "surprising veins of compassion or real feeling" but also "large areas that were absolutely unfeeling" (Lennon 1988, 237); his diatribes against "publicity-hunting lawyers" are amusing but foul (*ES,* 797), exhibiting the "little mean streak" Gilmore is still exposing just before his death (*ES,* 878); and to the nurses who treat him after his first suicide attempt he is simply "spiteful, revengeful, obscene" (*ES,* 597). Joseph Wenke points out that after his arrest Gilmore becomes "more and more demonically manipulative as his futile, despairing, and incredibly selfish desire to possess Nicole assumes control of his being" (Wenke, 207). Indeed, Gilmore is still demanding celibacy of Nicole in his last letter (*ES,* 914), just as he is still asking his lawyers to help him to escape after supposedly resigning himself to a death that is best for his soul (*ES,* 879-80, 886-87).

Yet Mailer's Gilmore is a man with "a capacity to grow" – for Mailer, the most crucial heroic quality (Lennon 1988, 256). Mailer agrees with Boaz, Farrell, and Schiller that Gilmore is "serious about dying with dignity" (*ES,* 517). For Gilmore, this means recognizing "the need to take responsibility for our deeds" (*ES,* 543) and acknowledging that we can choose death as well as life. In an interview Gilmore says, "In death you can choose in a way that you can't choose in life" (*ES,* 673), an assertion that reveals not only Gilmore's great difficulty in making choices in life but also the seriousness of his belief in karma. Gilmore's earlier remarks on karma and reincarnation may seem juvenile, but his later statements impress Mailer (as well as such witnesses as Farrell and Schiller) that Gilmore achieves a genuine philosophical conviction. Thus, Gilmore is able to say, when asked if there is anything worse than taking someone's life, "Well, you could alter somebody's life so that the quality of it wouldn't be what it could've been. . . . I think to make somebody go on living in a lessened state of existence, I think that could be worse than killing 'em" (*ES,* 808-9). Mailer obviously sympathizes with this view, just as he shares Gilmore's belief that "the meaning of the events in any given life can't be comprehended entirely by what one's done in one

life" (Mailer's definition of karma; Lennon 1988, 258). Gilmore's
desire to die rather than to continue to deteriorate appeals to Mailer
not only as an act of self-definition but also as morally valid; as Mailer
says in an interview, "we have profound choices to make in life, and
one of them may be the deep and terrible choice most of us avoid
between dying now and 'saving one's soul' . . . in order, conceivably,
to be reincarnated" (Lennon 1988, 263). Thus, Mailer describes
Gilmore's belief in karma as "profound" (Lennon 1988, 263) and
highlights Gilmore's growing ability to analyze his own moral condition, as when Gilmore says, "I was always capable of murder. . . .
There's a side of me that I don't like. I can become totally devoid of
feelings for others, unemotional. I know I'm doing something grossly
fucking wrong. I can still go ahead and do it" (*ES*, 906). No one in
The Executioner's Song offers a more persuasive psychological pro-
file of Gilmore than Gilmore himself.

Gilmore's capacity to "grow" is impressive, then, but it does not
lead Mailer to forget Gilmore's viciousness. Instead, it leads him to
conclude that it is hard to draw conclusions. Mailer says that as he
learned more and more about Gilmore he "knew less and less"
(Lennon 1988, 229). His efforts to define Gilmore are no more
successful than Farrell's or Schiller's, unless it is a success to realize
that Gilmore is finally "too complex" to label (Lennon 1988, 349).
Mailer's Gilmore challenges civilized society's "firm premise that we
have one life and one life only and that if we waste this one life there
is nothing worse we can do" (Lennon 1988, 257), but his sordid acts
and unalterable meanness call into question the coherence of his
personality. For Mailer, this makes Gilmore "another major American
protagonist," someone who "comprehends a deep contradiction in
this country and lives his life in the crack of that contradiction" (PW
Interviews: Norman Mailer," 8-9). But this means Gilmore is only
partly "a modern man in search of his soul, wondering whether he
might be closer to God or Devil, wanting to make himself whole,
willing to pay his debts until he is right and clean and able to 'stand
in the sight of God,' " as Begiebing would have it (Begiebing 1980,
189), for Gilmore is also a habit-ridden monster whose essence is
contradictory, if indeed he *has* a definable essence.

This balanced assessment of Gilmore is the key to the work's
structure. Book 1 tends to highlight Gilmore's violence and book 2
his capacity to "grow," but each presents Gilmore's strengths and

weaknesses through the eyes of many witnesses who try to understand this profoundly enigmatic figure. The very mode of representation stresses the many perspectives on Gilmore, who is the one significant character never seen from "within." In addition, the book's sheer size underlines the many facts any theory about Gilmore must finally encompass. Whether witnessing Gilmore's grimmest acts (as in book 1) or pondering his most intelligent self-assessments (as in book 2), we are all but overwhelmed by the difficulty of reducing the material or the man to manageable dimensions. While some have felt that Mailer aggrandizes Gilmore by presenting his affair with Nicole in "tragic tones" denied to Gilmore's victims,[25] Mailer's handling of Gilmore's last hours illustrates the more complicated effect of his narrative method.

Toward the end Mailer continues to present Gilmore as he is seen by others in relatively detailed accounts of Gilmore's last-night party (*ES*, 875-88), the execution (*ES*, 945-63), the autopsy (*ES*, 980-84), the memorial service held in Gilmore's behalf (*ES*, 988-93), and the dispersal of Gilmore's ashes after cremation (*ES*, 993-94). In these final sections, however, the views of the several witnesses blend into a common awe at Gilmore's cool acceptance of his fate. This effect is most pronounced during the execution scene, in which Mailer shifts the point of view 20 times among seven characters yet seems to present an event perceived in much the same way by everyone present. The effect is awesome – indeed, the scene is perhaps the most powerful in all Mailer's writing – but not in such a way as to exonerate or glorify Gilmore. Gilmore's courage is acknowledged here much as his monstrousness is acknowledged in the depiction of the Jensen and Bushnell murders. Mailer's comment on the autopsy scene also points to the nature of his narrative interests: "That's why I took the execution right through the autopsy – because that was something that I wanted the reader to feel. That's what it means when we kill a man. That even this man who wanted to die and succeeded in getting society to execute him, that even when he was killed, we still feel this horrible shock and loss" (Lennon 1988, 247). We feel shock and loss despite what we know of Gilmore's selfishness and despite our now-intimate knowledge of what he has done. In part we respond because of what we have come to know of Gilmore as lover, Gilmore as poet, Gilmore as philosopher, and especially Gilmore as self-critic. In part we respond

because, all his faults fully acknowledged, Gilmore remains com-
plexly human. Like the book itself, our response is a complicated one
that we can only try to dissect, as I have just done. To try to get at
the meaning of such responses, as I am about to do, is an effort that
Mailer makes a part of his very subject in this massive, painful, but
fully articulated masterpiece.

The Meaning of *The Executioner's Song*

He appealed to me because he embodied many of the themes I've been living
with all my life long.

> – Norman Mailer, in *Conversations with Norman Mailer*

I used to hate America for what it was doing to all of us. Now I hate all of us
for what we're doing to America.

> – Norman Mailer, quoted in *Publishers Weekly*

There are of course many meanings in *The Executioner's Song*, but
the one to which I refer at the end of the previous section has been
especially popular among Mailer's more recent critics. Noting
Mailer's challenge to traditional generic definitions and his insistence
on Gilmore's ultimately impenetrable "mystery,"[26] these critics argue
that Mailer's theme is "the necessity of fiction for the apprehension
of complex reality" (Hellmann, 56-57), "the fictionality of all narrative" (McCord, 66), or the view that "all history is in the end
fiction."[27] Mailer's sympathy with such views is both real and long-
standing. As long ago as his 1954 essay on David Riesman, Mailer
referred to the need for a sociological "fiction" to make sense of
American life (*AFM*, 196); at the end of *The Armies of the Night* he
makes fun of journalistic pretenses to complete accuracy; and in his
afterword to *The Executioner's Song* he acknowledges the editorial
contributions (however minor) that went into the making of his
book. I suspect that Mailer would agree with Phyllis McCord that *The
Executioner's Song* demonstrates the subjective nature of all truth
(McCord, 71). But it is harder to accept the notion that this is
Mailer's *principal* theme, central to everything he does in this huge
book. To accept such an idea is to place Mailer among the metafic-
tionists – something I cannot imagine doing without major qualifications.

Mailer's social interests in this book are simply too obvious to push aside as illustrating the fictionality of all narrative. Though Mailer dramatizes the difficulty of achieving even an unsure grasp of his material, his task is nonetheless to examine the American reality embedded in this material. We should recall that Mailer felt his material was "gold" if he "had enough sense not to gild it" (Lennon 1988, 270). I think we must ask what gemlike themes inform *The Executioner's Song.*

The possible answers to this question begin with Mailer's characterization of Gilmore. For many readers, Gilmore is a reconceived, more artistic version of the hipster first glorified in Mailer's "The White Negro" (1957). For one such critic, Gilmore is "the figure of the artist of the self, defining and redefining his personality, controlling events and other characters, projecting a world."[28] For another, Gilmore walks in shackles between guards but "looks freer than they, and people visiting him suspect *they* are the ones in prison" (Chevigny, 191). I have already suggested that these are very selective views of Gilmore, half-truths at best. Gilmore is no more adequately described as a hipster than Marion Faye is in *The Deer Park.* Neither the fictional Marion nor the real Gilmore commits himself to "that uncharted journey into the rebellious imperatives of the self" by which Mailer identifies the hipster (*AFM,* 304). This is especially true if we recall that the hipster's "journey" is a sensual one, quite literally an adventure of the senses. As I argue in chapter 3, Marion's "black heroic safari" (*TDP,* 328) is a matter of will and intellect, and Gilmore's actions prior to his final arrest are so aimless that they can hardly be called a quest for anything. Even Gilmore's efforts to die with dignity derive from his will and spirit, not his senses. To think of Gilmore as a sexual rebel is to see at once how little he resembles Mailer's late-1950s ideal.[29]

I suggest we might better see Gilmore as Mailer sees him: a man who lives his life in the crack of a deep American contradiction. To one side of this crack is the nihilistic emptiness Didion emphasizes, the "estrangement" Wenke rightly sees in most of the younger people in book 1 (though I would add older women, such as Brenda Nicol and Kathryne Baker, each of whom marries four times).[30] Gilmore's mistreatment of several women permits Mailer to present a seemingly endless chain of victimized women, young and old. Didion hears resignation in their voices, the belief that they cannot influence

events (Didion, 81). Perhaps the most memorable voice is that of
Kathy Maynard, the young woman who discovers Nicole after her
suicide attempt. In an interview Kathy describes her own life in the
flattest tone imaginable: married at 16 for no particular reason;
witness to her 17-year-old husband's suicide with a hunting knife;
married again two weeks later to a man she met at her husband's
funeral; stranded at 17 with two small children, no husband, and no
particular sense of what she will be doing next week (*ES*, 563-67).
Mailer has said that this interview is the one transcript he did not
even abridge, for it was "a found object" he could not improve
(Lennon 1988, 269). One might describe Kathy as stoical – Didion's
term for all the book's women – but stoicism implies recognition of
the horrors one is resigned to and Kathy seems merely oblivious. Her
brief tale should remind us of the real desert that surrounds these
small Utah towns and the metaphoric desert to which Didion alludes.

Kathy Maynard's story is one side of *The Executioner's Song* in
miniature, but there are many other memorable examples. My own
favorite involves Nicole's mother, Kathryne Baker. When Gilmore
retrieves a gun from Kathryne just before he kills Jensen, Kathryne
realizes she does not even know his last name (*ES*, 222) – this, after
Gilmore has lived with Nicole for two months. At such moments the
book's Westerners appear to be what Wenke calls them, "the beat
legatees of the spiritually and politically exhausted hipsters, hippies,
and left radicals whom Mailer derides at the conclusion of *Of a Fire
on the Moon*" (Wenke 203). But they are in fact a much broader
cross-section of the American social order, represented by the
conventional Mormons who become Gilmore's "new jailers"
(Lennon 1988, 237) (and his victims, for both Jensen and Bushnell
are Mormon), the Utah lawyers who prosecute and defend Gilmore,
and the many lower-class and lower-middle-class figures whose lives
resemble Nicole's but who could not define a "left radical." What
they share is a less extreme version of Kathy Maynard's tolerance for
the intolerable.

Gilmore is the figure in the book who seems to rebel against this
aimless society, just as he is the one who scorns the liberal establishment that takes him up as a "cause" in book 2 – thus, the
common view of Gilmore as a Maileresque hero. The partial truth to
this view is suggested by Mailer's statement that Gilmore embodied
themes Mailer had lived with all his life, among them the heroic indi-

vidual's passionate (and often-destructive) attempt to reject the deadly social environment endured so stoically by the book's western women. This attempt can also be seen in Gilmore's rejection of life in prison, his "dignified" preference for whatever succeeds this life. Indeed, Gilmore's concern for the hereafter is another of the themes to which Mailer no doubt refers, for the religious dimensions of Gilmore's thought correspond to Mailer's oft-expressed convictions or intuitions. Yet Gilmore is no less estranged than the people who surround him in prison or Provo, no less self-destructive, no less frozen in those "habits" to which Mailer relentlessly draws our attention. In his last days Gilmore may have achieved some perspective on his own compulsions and aspired to something more dignified, but he is also the primary example in the book of someone who cannot endure life as it is experienced by all the other characters, from Kathy Maynard to Larry Schiller. Gilmore is a mystery and not a model, a man who embodies Mailer's themes but not his solutions.

I do not mean to imply that Mailer offers answers to the overwhelming problems his characters confront. But *The Executioner's Song* is much less pessimistic than many of its admirers suggest. Mailer says that one of the lessons he learned is that the system is "fairer" than he had supposed (Lennon 1988, 239): "The ways things work in America are not necessarily as sinister as I always assumed. There may not be this grand paranoid network after all" ("PW Interviews: Norman Mailer," 8). This discovery lies behind Mailer's remark that he used to hate America for what it was doing to all of us but now hates us for what we are doing to America. Behind Mailer's hatred for America lay the paranoid's assumption that "they" are in conspiracy against an innocent citizenry; behind hatred for us is the romantic's faith that we know not what we do. Mailer's beliefs might be compared with the transcendental notion that we always pursue the good but don't know what the good is – see Emerson's "The American Scholar" and Thoreau's *Walden* as primary texts.[31] Thus our aimlessness or compulsive materialism, our mindless conformity or violent resistance; thus the world represented in extremis by Gary Gilmore.

As Mailer says, however, this world seems to be fairer and less sinister than he had always supposed. Indeed, the unifying theme in Gilmore's story is what Mailer calls "American virtue." In Mailer's view, everyone involved here wished to do "the right thing" and went to some trouble to act accordingly. This dedication to principle is the other side of the American contradiction embodied in Gilmore. Rocklike conservatives seeking the death penalty, dedicated liberals seeking to avoid a state execution, lawyers on all sides, friends of Gilmore, friends of his victims, men such as Barry Farrell and Larry Schiller – all did their best as they understood the best. Schiller is perhaps the most notable example, but only because his "best" involves personal growth – virtue in its most positive form. Many other examples of American virtue are grim reminders of why Mailer "hates" us for what we are doing to America. Like Gilmore, however, these other Americans are captured in the richly detailed (if depressing) context of their dull habits and assumptions, a context elaborately built up page by page as Mailer offers the most compelling "social drama" (Lennon 1988, 238, 259) in his long career.

If we read this book as Mailer conceived it, we must feel compassion for nearly everyone – for Kathy Maynard as well as Larry Schiller, for Earl Dorius as well as Kathryne Baker, for the youthful April Baker as well as the elderly Bessie Gilmore. Finally there must also be compassion for Gary Gilmore, just as there must be "hate" for what Gilmore and the rest of us are doing to one another. The least judgmental of Mailer's works, *The Executioner's Song* is also the book in which Mailer's love for America is most impressively in evidence. Mailer has said that he learned from the Gilmore saga that society might be not evil but, rather, "a sad comedy" (Lennon 1988, 240). This phrase also applies to the "astonishing" book he wrote in the wake of this discovery.

Chapter Nine

Mailer as Storyteller
The Novels of the 1980s

> Since Norman was always too ready to serve as matrimonial agent to the mating of large ideas, and prone to offer weighty metaphors without constructing a seat, he tried these days to be careful.
>
> – Norman Mailer, *The Fight*

Mailer's novels of the 1980s, *Ancient Evenings* (1983) and *Tough Guys Don't Dance* (1984), might seem to have nothing in common. *Ancient Evenings* is a densely written, 700-page novel about ancient Egypt; *Tough Guys Don't Dance* is a comparatively sparse, 200-page detective novel. *Ancient Evenings* was designed as Mailer's magnum opus and written over 10 years; *Tough Guys Don't Dance* was designed to fulfill a contract and written in about two months.[1] Mailer's detractors would probably say the two books have nothing in common but their bad reviews and narrative excesses – in *Ancient Evenings,* what Harold Bloom calls "Mailer's narrative exuberance in heaping up sodomistic rapes"[2]; in *Tough Guys,* the trail of bodies Mailer leaves at the rate of about one per 30 pages. Nonetheless, I mean to argue that the two novels share many of Mailer's continuing concerns, themes seen throughout his career but never more clearly than in these books. I also see each novel as illustrating Mailer's desire to ground his large ideas and weighty metaphors in a novelistic "seat" that is essentially dramatic rather than didactic or fabulistic. More clearly than Mailer's novels of the 1960s, *Ancient Evenings* and *Tough Guys Don't Dance* bespeak their author's desire to be a storyteller once again rather than a contemporary Jeremiah.

I suspect that people willing to give these books an attentive reading will grant their common themes. It will be harder, though, to acknowledge the narrative similarities to which I point. Indeed, it is difficult to imagine two books that read more differently. *Tough*

179

Guys Don't Dance is what we call a fast read, resembling in this as in
so many ways its precursors in the detective or mystery genre. The
book clearly reflects Mailer's interest in rereading Raymond Chandler
to sample Chandler's "narrative drive" (*P*, 133). By contrast, *Ancient
Evenings* is one of the slowest reads imaginable, a book in which, as
Bloom notes, "there is a lot less story than any summary would indi-
cate" (Bloom, 195). Mailer himself marvels at how García Márquez
creates whole lives in 10 pages: "In ten pages, I have all I can do to
get around one bend in the Nile" (*P*, 157). But there are good reasons for the respective abruptness and density of these two books,
reasons that start with Mailer's desire to create a highly stylized, even
melodramatic action in his American novel and to "immerse" his
reader in the magical murk of ancient Egypt (Lennon 1988, 305).
This is again to suggest that in its own way each book embodies
Mailer's wish to rediscover the pleasures of fictional narrative after
not writing an undisputed novel since 1967.

    Ancient Evenings and *Tough Guys Don't Dance* also share the
first-person narrative point of view Mailer has adopted in each novel
since his first, *The Naked and the Dead*. Mailer's point of view in
each of these late novels reinforces his principal themes, and so this
final chapter on Mailer's fiction should allow us to test Mailer's claim
that "the most powerful leverage in fiction comes from point of
view" (*AFM*, 221). In such technical matters as well as such common
themes as resurrection (literal as well as metaphoric), *Ancient
Evenings* and *Tough Guys Don't Dance* point to the continuities in
Mailer's career even as their remarkably different subject matters
discourage us from linking them.

The Themes of *Ancient Evenings*

Why are we in Egypt? Where else could we be? Mailer's dialectics of sex and
death have found their inevitable context.

           – Harold Bloom, *Modern Critical Views: Norman Mailer*

The horror of modern life is that there is no horror.

           – Norman Mailer, *Pontifications*

Mailer has told us a good deal about the origins of *Ancient Evenings*.
In one interview he notes that his work on the book goes back to the
early 1970s, when he first perused 10 volumes of Egyptian hiero-

glyphics at the New York Public Library and began to read a two-volume hieroglyphic dictionary by E. A. Wallis Budge (Lennon 1988, 303). Even more interesting are Mailer's views about the connection, or lack thereof, between his Egyptian materials and modern life. According to Mailer, his book proposes no metaphor between ancient Egypt and America (Lennon 1988, 300); indeed, it contains no Judeo-Christian ideas, nothing about "today" (Lennon 1988, 327-28). "I wanted to immerse the reader in the feeling that he or she was in ancient Egypt," Mailer explains (Lennon 1988, 305), and this literary goal required that he disdain any allegorical connections between life in ancient Egypt and life in twentieth-century America. Thus, as J. Michael Lennon points out, *Ancient Evenings* includes no reference to such modern intellectual staples as "Judaic monotheism, Christian compassion, Faustian progress, romantic love, and Freudian guilt" (Lennon 1986a, 18).

For Mailer's more sympathetic critics, this means that *Ancient Evenings* describes "a culture free of the rationalist assumptions made by Descartes in the seventeenth century."[3] The culture in question is that of Egypt in 1200-1000 B.C., an era supposedly "untrammeled by the ethical neuroses created by Greek rationalism and Christian contempt for the body" (Kuberski, 233). This is a period in which, as one critic puts it, there is "no clear division between the sacred and the secular" (Begiebing 1989, 99) – a period in which heaven (and its gods) replicates earth (and its men and women),[4] in which a magical, "unscientific" worldview prevails,[5] in which "carnal religiosity" suffuses everything and everyone (godlike men as well as manlike gods) (Lennon 1986a, 18). Such a period is sufficiently Maileresque to justify Bloom's sweeping claim that Mailer's dialectics of sex and death have found their inevitable context.

It follows, of course, that Mailer's very un-Judeo-Christian ideas are everywhere in *Ancient Evenings*, "naturalized," as Richard Poirier says, within the elaborately detailed portrait of this ancient but appealing civilization (appealing, that is, to anyone who shares Mailer's most distinctive beliefs).[6] The general themes are "power, wealth, sex and death," as Mailer himself notes (Lennon 1988, 301), but the specific topics include such Maileresque favorites as magic, karma, reincarnation, evolving and not all-powerful gods, and the belief that "death and life are a continuum, and not merely absurd"

(Begiebing 1989, 101). Though I think Mailer is right to deny any allegorical connection between his Egypt and more modern cultures, it is also true that Mailer turned to his version of ancient Egypt as a landscape that stressed what for him are the very essentials of life (and death). The setting of *Ancient Evenings* allows Mailer to dramatize a vision of life he once attributed to Bantu philosophy: "Bantu philosophy . . . saw humans as forces, not beings. . . . By such logic, men or women were more than the result of their heredity and experience. . . . So a man was not only himself, but the karma of all the generations past that still lived in him, not only a human with his own psyche but a part of the resonance, sympathetic or unsympathetic, of every root and thing (and witch) about him" (*TF*, 38).

Ancient Evenings embodies Mailer's mature beliefs, then, not just his more notorious notions about such subjects as feces. (Though it *does* include the latter as well; see, for example, Ptah-nem-hotep's thoughts on his stool [*AE*, 222-23], or Menenhetet II's reflections on the distinct odors of a king [*AE*, 259].) Such a belief is Mailer's conviction that God is not omnipotent but, rather, "a warring element in a divided universe . . . like us only more so" (*P*, 2, 75). This sort of Manichaeanism squares almost too neatly with the ancient Egyptian conception of the gods, dramatized most fully in chapter 2, Mailer's much-praised version of the Osiris story, in which the violent and obscene conflict between Horus and Set is rendered with a kind of anthropomorphic zest (*AE*, 45-89). Other crucial beliefs include Mailer's increasingly serious concern with karma and reincarnation. In *The Executioner's Song* Gary Gilmore's belief in such ideas marks him as more than just a cheap hood. In *Ancient Evenings* these ideas are crucial to the plot itself. Menenhetet II's fear of a "second death" (*AE*, 32), the extinction of his soul, derives from his karmic conception of life, and Menenhetet I's three reincarnations and four lives define the very boundaries of Mailer's story. (Though we should note Lennon's reminder that sexually transmitted reincarnation and mental telepathy are Mailer's concoctions, not ancient Egyptian beliefs.)[7] Indeed, these plot elements permit Mailer to reengage his most persistent notions – that the state of one's soul at the time of physical death is crucial to a very real afterlife; that overcoming fear is the key to life, for "one cannot gain a great deal unless one is willing to dare losing all" (*AE*, 65-66); that fear is the one force in life sufficient to defeat the powers of magic (*AE*, 85), otherwise a potent factor throughout Mailer's book and life itself as he understands it (as suggested by previous books such as *An American Dream*, the passage from Yeats that stands as the epigraph to *Ancient Evenings*, and Mailer's repeated claim that *Ancient Evenings* betrays "an immense preoccupation with magic as such" [Lennon 1988, 326]); and that resurrection is a literal prospect and not just the spiritual metaphor employed by earlier American writers whose interest in things Egyptian has been thoroughly traced by John T. Irwin.[8]

Ancient Evenings also embodies some of Mailer's more basic, less arcane ideas. Mailer once referred to his own brand of existentialism as "a mysticism of the flesh" (*AFM*, 292), and the four lives of Menenhetet I, with all their "carnal religiosity," amply illustrate this paradoxical phrase. The several lives of Menenhetet I and those closest to him suggest that life is indeed a struggle in which sex is the primary index to one's condition, as Mailer never tires of insisting. They confirm as well Mailer's conviction that courage is the essential virtue (directly asserted here at the end of Menenhetet I's fourth life [*AE*, 709]); that life with all its travails is still basically good and not absurd (*TPP*, 139), just as men and women are "roughly more good than evil" (*AFM*, 336) despite their seemingly ineradicable flaws; and that "primitive" life as depicted here is to be preferred to a modern civilization in which the central horror is that there is no horror, no sense of evil and therefore no real sense of goodness. As Robert Begiebing says, *Ancient Evenings* is the book in which Mailer asserts unequivocally the connections he has always posited between courage and power, magic and power, and sexuality and power – in short, the book in which human resources are exposed (and glorified) more graphically than in any previous text (Begiebing 1989, 96).

It might therefore seem that *Ancient Evenings* is a book in which Mailer explores the Lawrentian contrast between "vitality" and "entropy" (Begiebing 1989, 88), achieving precisely the Lawrentian status of prophet/preacher attributed to him by Harold Bloom in an early review (Bloom, 194). But *Ancient Evenings* is not the kind of quasi-allegory Bloom takes it to be, and its themes are finally more complicated than the comparison with Lawrence would suggest. Like Lawrence, Mailer often protests that the romantic spirit is drying up as things get smaller and smaller (*AFM*, 382); like Lawrence, Mailer celebrates the human form divine, going so far as to argue that "all cosmic achievement is attainable within the human frame . . . if we lead lives witty enough and skillful enough, bold enough and, finally, illumined enough" (*P*, 48). Indeed, Mailer's analysis of Lawrence in *The Prisoner of Sex* is one of his finest critical performances and surely reveals Mailer's affinities with the English novelist. Finally, however, the action of *Ancient Evenings* moves away from the confident prophetic stance Bloom means to invoke by comparing Mailer with Lawrence, and the novel's most important themes are problematic to the point of a very un-Lawrencian ambiguity.

At issue here is Mailer's ability to resist (at his best) the temptation to simplify his own fictional materials. I have no doubt that a large part of Mailer would agree with Lennon that Mailer's purpose in *Ancient Evenings* is "to rejuvenate the human species by showing it how life can be lived on the edge of dread and thereby intensified" (Lennon 1986b, 180). But what if life lived on this edge topples over into failure and even the sort of spiritual death Menenhetet II fears? What if *Ancient Evenings* illustrates "the difficulty – even impossibility – of knowing, finally, whether we act for noble or base purposes, whether we are more fundamentally guilty and evil or innocent and good"? Begiebing takes this to be Mailer's "major theme," the one that recurs in his most important fictions (Begiebing 1989, 105), and I think the claim is sufficiently just to give us pause as we begin to celebrate the "magical," almost literally dreadful terrain of Mailer's Egyptian novel.

Thematically speaking, *Ancient Evenings* is like Mailer's earlier novels only more so. Here there is even greater stress on the connections between sex and power, the need to confront and overcome fear, and life's overwhelming richness when engaged with sufficient intensity. Yet there is also greater stress on the amoral nature of power, the terrible consequences of failing to master one's fears or circumstances, and life's awful emptiness when one's best efforts are finally insufficient. To look closely at the novel's action is to see *all* of these ideas at work in a fiction that ultimately eschews a too-easy contrast between past and present and refuses to celebrate uncritically the barbaric splendors of a less effete civilization. To look closely is to see Mailer working once again toward a resolution in which the most strenuous efforts to master life are at best partly successful and at worst unavailing.

The themes of *Ancient Evenings* are a rich but complex subject, then, for they climax the philosophical preoccupations of almost 40 years even as they illustrate Mailer's reservations about the unqualified acceptance of any "approach" to life (including his own). The novel's action thus avoids the cruder effects of didactic fiction in general and earlier novels like *Barbary Shore* and *An American Dream* in particular. Unfortunately, this action betrays other problems we would not anticipate from Mailer's praise for the book's elaborate "architecture" (Lennon 1988, 328). If the novel's themes reward the closest study, its narrative structure cannot withstand the most elementary review. Mailer's impulse toward storytelling provides his book with an ample, even splendid "seat," but the flaws in this story are such that *Ancient Evenings* can finally be considered no more than a partial success.

The Structure of *Ancient Evenings*

If you read *Ancient Evenings* for the story, you will hang yourself.
— Harold Bloom, *Modern Critical Views: Norman Mailer*

It is the passion of Osiris . . . to conquer chaos.
— Norman Mailer, *Ancient Evenings*

I imagine that Mailer would reject any attempt to judge *Ancient Evenings* by strict formal or structural criteria. He has often spoken condescendingly about what he calls "craft," reducing the concern for such matters to an artisan's concern for his bag of tricks.[9] In this spirit he has even said that he does not feel close to *The Executioner's Song* because the book is "an exercise in craft" (*P*, 175). Thus, when Mailer acknowledges his weaknesses with story or plot, he means not to condemn his work but, rather, to point to its excellences elsewhere (as Bloom does in advising us against reading *Ancient Evenings* for the "story").[10] "Whatever I've accomplished certainly does not depend on my virtuosity with plot," Mailer notes (Plimpton 1967, 265), and we can be sure Mailer means to emphasize his achievements and not his limitations.

Yet Mailer is not really so contemptuous of structural issues as he sometimes appears to be. He even harbors "a fondness for order," as he once confessed (*P*, 26), and this predilection is on display when he argues that *Ancient Evenings* has "the most complete architecture of any book I've written" (Lennon 1988, 328). He may joke about needing 10 pages to get around one bend in the Nile, but he in fact believes that his book's length is "necessary," that its "slowness is important to give a sense of the pace" (Lennon 1988, 299). Mailer's concern for matters of proportion or harmony is thematically crucial to the novel itself, for his sympathies are rather obviously with Maat, the god of "balance," and Osiris, whose passion is to conquer chaos. Even as Mailer would point us toward his novel's many excellent parts – those sections in which he captures the feel or spirit of his Egyptian materials – he aspires toward uniting these parts into a luminous whole, "the nearest I was ever going to come to the possibility of writing a great book" (Lennon 1988, 299). By Mailer's own standards, then, the problems I see in his novel's structure are serious.

I should hasten to say that these problems are not ones of strict verisimilitude or literary realism, for I agree with Begiebing that here Mailer is "finally freed as much from the restrictions of fictional realism as from twentieth-century rationalism and scientism" (Begiebing 1989, 98). Nor is the principal problem simply a matter of Mailer's episodic narrative method, sufficiently dominant that the book has been described as "a series of embedded tales" (Begiebing 1989, 10). After all, many of the world's greatest narratives are far more episodic than Mailer's novel, in which Menenhetet I's career(s) and Menenhetet II's quest for spiritual survival provide a more than sufficient backbone for such an elaborate fiction. Nor, finally, is Mailer's problem the relative inferiority of certain episodes, though even Mailer's strongest advocates have their candidates for the least successful part. (Poirier's choice is Honey-Ball's scenes of spellbinding [Poirier 1986, 83], whereas Bloom takes the entire "Book of Queens" to be the worst 130 pages Mailer ever wrote [Bloom, 196-97].) The weakness of certain sections is more than offset by the excellence of whole episodes or even chapters, in particular the stunning beginning (*AE*, 1-41), the tale of Egypt's warring gods (*AE*, 45-89), Menenhetet I's remarkable account of the Battle of Kadesh (*AE*, 250-371), and the almost-equally-stunning conclusion (*AE*, 697-709). Mailer's problem is, rather, that the arrangement of these narrative blocks fails to do justice to matters of major narrative concern.

Ancient Evenings begins just after the death of its narrator,
Menenhetet II, who now awaits his fateful journey through the Land
of the Dead (or Khert-Neter). Poirier points out that a knowledge of
one's deeds is necessary to pass out of the Land of the Dead, and so
Menenhetet II's amnesia provides an excellent narrative rationale for
the stories told to him by his great-grandfather, Menenhetet I, who
first provides a relatively succinct account of the legendary Egyptian
gods (chapter 2) and then offers more elaborate tales from his first
life under the first great Egyptian pharaoh, Ramses II. (These tales
actually come to us from Menenhetet II, who first hears them one
seemingly endless night with his mother, his supposed father, and
the present pharaoh, Ptah-nem-hotep.) The resulting narrative proportions are distinctly odd, however. Though the book begins and
ends with Menenhetet II and his quest for a life after death rather
than spiritual extinction, the bulk of the narrative focuses on his
mentor, Menenhetet I. This maneuver recalls the relationships in
earlier novels like *Barbary Shore* and *The Deer Park*, in which the
lives of older men offer profound models for the younger narrators.
Here too the life (or lives) of Menenhetet I might function as a structural complement to that of the younger Menenhetet II. In fact, however, Mailer's treatment of the older man's story raises as many
questions as it answers.

Perhaps the most obvious point to be made is that Menenhetet I
spends 400 pages on his first life (500, if one counts the nearly 100
pages devoted to introducing the visit to Ptah-nem-hotep on the
Night of the Pig, a carnivalesque occasion that sanctions the audacious storytelling to follow). Then he (and Mailer) rush through his
second, third, and fourth incarnations in fewer than 50 pages! Bloom
must have been thinking of these proportions when he remarked
that the narrative betrays "every sign of truncation," as if it should
be much longer than it is (Bloom, 194). I think we must wonder
about the narrative results. Mailer's more treasured themes – karma,
reincarnation, the individual's spiritual progress – depend heavily
on Menenhetet I's movement through four lives, a movement that
involves steady decline, even degeneration, as Menenhetet I
becomes an increasingly commonplace figure, descending from his
first-life roles as Ramses II's chief general and sexual rival to such
later roles as a high priest who improperly serves the rich, an

immensely wealthy man, and finally a political contender whose sedi-
tious plans fail utterly just before he dies of an apparent heart attack
without providing for a fourth reincarnation and fifth life. But what
can be made of these hastily rendered second, third, and fourth
lives? What narrative force can they have against the hundreds of
pages detailing Menenhetet I's daring, Julian Sorel-like rise from
complete obscurity to the right hand of a pharaoh? Perhaps most to
the point, how seriously can we take the theme of degeneration that
seems implicit in Menenhetet I's last three lives? I think it is no surprise that, among the serious commentators, only Begieling deals at
any length with the pattern of failure informing the stories of both
Menenhetet I and Menenhetet II, for the novel's failures become a
noteworthy *pattern* only if we take seriously Menenhetet I's later
incarnations, something the narrative proportions all but discourage
us from doing. I would add that Mailer's decision to treat Menenhetet II's premature failure and death as briefly as possible casts
Menenhetet II's story into a mold as curious as his great-grandfather's.

The narrative proportions suggest that the essence of Mailer's
story is to be found in the saga of Menenhetet I's rise and fall as what
F. Scott Fitzgerald liked to call a personage. But even if we waive our
questions as to what we are to make of Menenhetet I's later lives or
their connection with Menenhetet II, we must still face the lack of
narrative progression within the story of Menenhetet I's first life.
Here the novel's episodic character does seem a liability. Mailer's
existential aesthetics lead him to decry narrative patterns in which
we can foretell the end, for such "connections" deny life's essential
unpredictability (*P*, 84). Thus, Mailer argues that each part or chapter of *Ancient Evenings* has "a separate existence," that parts 1 and
2, for example, in no way prepare us for part 6 (Lennon 1988, 328).
Because these comments occur in the same passage in which Mailer
speaks of his novel's "complete architecture," I think we must question Mailer's architectural theories. Apparently Mailer aspires here to
an almost-pure version of the imitative fallacy, a version in which he
embroiders discrete chapters as fully as possible for their own sake,
not that of later narrative developments, and the resulting structure
is all too true to Mailer's existential philosophy.

The rigor with which Mailer pursues this aesthetic allows him to
avoid the more mechanical or conventional features of his earlier

novels, but there are obvious drawbacks. The most important is Mailer's failure to establish with any real dramatic impact the climax or conclusion to Menenhetet I's story (as distinct from the conceptual understanding we may arrive at by pondering this story or relating it to that of Menenhetet II). In fact, however, almost everything in the narrative is adversely affected. Consider the novel's notorious treatment of sodomy. A reader as sympathetic as Bloom interprets this treatment as positive, whereas it seems to me the one feature of Mailer's work adequately described in Judith Fetterley's otherwise perverse critique: "Male homosexuality is not seen as an equal sexual relation between two men but rather as a situation in which one man is used as a woman by another man."[11] Such is the case throughout *Ancient Evenings,* a novel in which Menenhetet I first is victimized (that is, raped) by Ramses II, then takes out his anger on another by raping him in similar style, and finally suffers a second sexual affront from Ramses II, whose brutal treatment inspires the rebellious impulses that lead to Menenhetet I's first death. Presumably, Bloom could misread the relevant scenes only because they are interspersed throughout a narrative in which dramatic cause and effect are deliberately eschewed, so that earlier parts imperfectly explain later ones. The aesthetic result somewhat resembles the cosmic chaos that Osiris desired to conquer by means of a divine "order." We might wish that Mailer's fondness for order inspired him to impose a more coherent (if less lifelike) pattern on his own fictional cosmos.

From Mailer's point of view, such coherence is unlikely to ever turn up in one of his novels. Many years ago Mailer felt that he could never write a novel in the third person until he developed a coherent view of life.[12] Presumably, he felt restricted to a narrative perspective in which nothing is claimed to be "real" except what the individual narrator observes or feels – thus, the first-person point of view in each novel from *Barbary Shore* through *Why Are We in Vietnam?* In speaking of *Ancient Evenings,* however, Mailer says, "Maybe I'm bragging, but I think I have a coherent philosophy" (*P,* 170). This comment makes it all the more telling that *Ancient Evenings* is once again written in the first person. It would appear that what Mailer once saw as evidence of an incoherent view of things is now the very substance or proof of what he calls a coherent philosophy. At any rate, Mailer is reluctant to present experience from a point of

view that transcends the individual's immediate (if limited) perspective. He may have conceived *Ancient Evenings* as "a culmination of
his heroes' struggles to gain independent moral stature," as
Begiebing argues (Begiebing 1989, 88), but his narrative point of
view insists on the painful, line-by-line record of the struggle toward
such stature and not its achievement. Like Melville's Ishmael, Mailer
and his heroes seek the unfathomable phantom of life. Like Melville,
Mailer arrives at the mature belief that their struggle is an end in
itself in a world Melville defined all too well.[13]

This is to suggest that the story Mailer tells is one of failure. Like
the novel's more sensitive interpreters, I do not see how the stories
of Menenhetet I and Menenhetet II offer anything except a remarkably bleak vision of "human vanity, waste, and degeneration"
(Begiebing 1989, 104). If it sometimes seems that "the purpose of
Ancient Evenings is to make the mythical reappear in culture"
(Leigh, 174), the novel's action and narrative perspective insist that
efforts to embody the mythical – no matter how heroic – cannot
easily transcend life's encompassing "chaos." The godlike order of
Osiris must always elude us in life (no matter how many incarnations
we are privileged to experience). Thus the transcendent possibilities
invoked at the end of this very long narrative concern the Land of
the Dead and an afterlife we are in no position to judge or even to
characterize. This will not stop us from telling tales of the gods, as
Menenhetet I does here; nor will it restrain our efforts to achieve the
admirable if untranscendent moral independence Mailer's heroes
always pursue, perhaps never more persistently than here. But it
does point to the rich paradoxes that inform all of Mailer's better
works. Even as we impose our will on the world (or appear to do
so), we must acknowledge the great price we must pay for our temporary mastery. Even as we conquer the fears that must be overcome
if we are to grow, we must see that these fears help define us as
human. Its disproportions and anticlimactic structure notwithstanding, the action of *Ancient Evenings* embodies just such difficult
insights. To read *Ancient Evenings* for its story is therefore less fatal
than Bloom suggests. Indeed, it should lead us to agree with Mailer
that this novel is his most audacious (if not his most accomplished)
performance.[14]

Tough Guys Don't Dance and the Detective Tradition

Whether they liked or detested *Ancient Evenings*, many readers were surprised that Mailer had devoted so many years of his professional life to the subject of ancient Egypt. By contrast, Mailer has been threatening to explore the setting of his next novel, *Tough Guys Don't Dance*, since the late 1950s. "Advertisements for Myself on the Way Out" (1959), the prologue to his since-abandoned eight-volume novel, is set in Provincetown.[15] Provincetown provides the title for Mailer's 1962 essay on Jackie Kennedy, "An Interview with Jackie Kennedy, or, the Wild West of the East."[16] (In *Tough Guys Don't Dance* Alvin Regency twice refers to Provincetown as "the Wild West of the East"; *TGDD*, 32, 36-37.) In *Of a Fire on the Moon* (1970) Mailer writes at length about his experiences in Provincetown and describes a novel he planned in 1967 "about a gang of illumined and drug-accelerated American guerrillas who lived in the wilds of a dune or a range and descended on Provincetown to kill" (*FOM*, 461). The novel Mailer finally published in 1984 is a very different project, a murder mystery completed in two months to fulfill one of Mailer's contractual obligations. The extremely hostile critical reaction suggests that the time spent on the book and the form chosen are equally to blame for another of Mailer's disastrous experiments.[17]

Mailer himself refers to *Tough Guys* as "one of my favorites" (Lennon 1988, 335), and I find Mailer's critical judgment again superior to his critics'. Certainly there is little correlation between the time Mailer spends writing something and the quality of the finished product. Mailer wrote *The Armies of the Night* in two months and *Why Are We in Vietnam?* in four months, in each case writing to fulfill a contract much as Faulkner did when he wrote *As I Lay Dying* in four months.[18] The obvious contrast is with *Ancient Evenings*, to which Mailer devoted 10 years, and I must wonder whether *Tough Guys* is not the better book. Nor is Mailer's novel to be despised because it employs the conventions of detective fiction. As John Cawelti points out, many major literary works achieve their effects by playing against the expected or formulaic,[19] and so it is in *Tough Guys*, a novel in which Mailer successfully synthesizes the conventions of classical detective fiction, the American hard-boiled detective novel, and film noir. The literary result may be "Mailer's least ambitious novel," as Joseph Wenke suggests (Wenke, 229), but it is also a novel in which Mailer manages to emulate the "narrative drive" he admires in Raymond Chandler while embodying themes less successfully developed in earlier novels such as *An American Dream.*

Tough Guys Don't Dance and Classical Detective Fiction

"I love design," [Wardley] said. "That may be what it's all about."
                                   – Norman Mailer, *Tough Guys Don't Dance*

Mailer's "murder mystery" may seem so thoroughly hard-boiled as to preclude any serious connections with the detective school identified with Agatha Christie, Dorothy Sayers, John Dickson Carr, and Ellery Queen. Indeed, Mailer might seem to share Chandler's contempt for the classical detective's "futzing around with timetables and bits of charred paper and who trampled the jolly old flowering arbutus under the library window."[20] Surely Mailer would agree that "the fellow who can write you a vivid and colorful prose simply won't be bothered with the coolie labor of breaking down unbreakable alibis" (Chandler, 225). No one's style is more vivid and colorful than Mailer's, and there is as little time spent on breaking down alibis in *Tough Guys* as in any of Chandler's novels. Nonetheless, Mailer does manage to make good use of one or two classical conventions, thus justifying his own use of the phrase "mystery novel" (*P*, 188).

The first point to be made is that Mailer does make use of "the novelistic machinery of the whodunit," as Wenke calls it (Wenke, 232). Mailer's plot is worthy of an Elizabethan revenge tragedy, filled with violent deaths and strange reversals, but the narrative pattern is recognizably that of a murder investigation. At the end of chapter 1 Mailer's narrator-protagonist, Tim Madden, awakens to find blood on the seat of his car, and the rest of the book charts his efforts to explain what lies behind this stain. Soon Madden is looking to explain the deaths of Jessica Pond, a woman he met the night before, and Patty Lareine, his estranged wife; indeed, his goal is to discover whether he is responsible for either murder. (Like so many of Mailer's heroes, Madden suffers from temporary amnesia, in this case the product of excessive drinking.) Eventually, by means of his inquiries, Madden finds out how each woman died. His investigation is not strewn with clues; nor does he offer an elaborate explanation of his "solution" to the crimes. Nonetheless, his efforts allow Mailer to offer a reasonable facsimile of the classical detective narrative as Cawelti defines the formula: (a) introduction of the detective; (b) crime and clues; (c) investigation; (d) announcement of the solution; (e) explanation of the solution; and (f) denouement (Cawelti, 82).

Like the best hard-boiled novelists, Mailer declines to embrace the more stylized features of the classical formula. For example, he does not provide Madden with the dozen or so suspects Agatha Christie loves to develop, and the clues by which Madden resolves his problem would engage Sherlock Holmes or Hercule Poirot for a chapter or two, not an entire novel. Madden does have his suspects, however, and periodically, in classical fashion, he reviews how plausible each one is. When he finds the first severed blonde head in the burrow where he hides his marijuana, for instance, he narrows the "list" of suspects to those who knew of his burrow in nearby Truro (*TGDD*, 70). And when he visits the home of police chief Alvin Regency and Madeleine Falco (formerly Madden's mistress and now Regency's wife), Madden takes special note of Regency's framed military photographs, his elaborate gun collection, and Madeleine's admiring description of Regency as a man who beheaded a Vietcong with one stroke of a machete (*TGDD*, 107-9). Indeed, Mailer's play with such clues is not unworthy of a Christie or a Margery Allingham, for it turns out that Regency decapitated one of the dead women but not the other and actually murdered neither one. Mailer makes such limited use of the classical formula's suspects and clues, however, we might wonder why he even bothers to invoke the classical pattern.

I think there are two good reasons for Mailer's decision. The first is that it allows him to cast Madden in the role of detective. Unlike the classical prototypes, Madden is anything but the gifted amateur detective when he finds himself involved in a murder case. Indeed, Madden at first flounders about as most of us would do, recalling Mailer's determination to write a mystery with a hero only slightly braver than the rest of us (Lennon 1988, 330) but also reflecting the lack of direction or purpose in Madden's life prior to this crisis. Nothing in Madden's experience prepares him to take charge of his life as he must finally do to enact the detective's part successfully. Now a fledgling but unsuccessful writer, formerly a bartender, Madden is approaching 40 with no finer feature to his life than refusing to become a "punk" during a three-year stint in prison (*TGDD*, 156). Madden's deep involvement with alcohol and drugs (the source of his jail sentence) points up the failure of will Mailer believes to be all too characteristic of his generation. In Mailer's words, Madden must "strive" to be "honorable," "to regain his self-respect because he is ashamed of his life until now" (Lennon 1988, 333, 332). This effort takes the form of beginning to think like a "sleuth" about halfway through the book (*TGDD*, 99) and, more important, beginning to act like the investigator central to any detective plot. From this point of view, the key moment in the novel is Madden's decision to start looking into the people and events so bizarrely intertwined in Jessica's and Patty's deaths. Thus, as his father takes on the grisly task of deep-sixing the women's severed heads, Madden calls the airport (*TGDD*, 171), speaks with a local real estate agent (*TGDD*, 172), examines Patty's gun (*TGDD*, 174), and forces open the trunk of Regency's car to find the chief's still-bloody machete (*TGDD*, 181). At no point does Madden control events as decisively as a Holmes or a Peter Wimsey, but his active engagement with the detective's role measures his growth in what one critic calls "this story of self-regeneration" (Wenke, 230).

The second reason for Mailer to embrace the formula of classical detective fiction is his desire to engage the themes of coincidence and uncanny "design." Indeed, coincidence plays as conspicuous a role in this novel as in Christie's most convoluted tales. Repeatedly, the characters themselves remark on "the powerful signature of coincidence," as Madden calls it (*TGDD*, 197). Madeleine turns out to be married to the very man Madden must outwit to regain his self-respect and avoid arrest for murder; Madden fancifully places Patty's ex-husband, Meeks Wardley Hilby III, in the very house in Provincetown Wardley is plotting to purchase; Jessica Pond's real name is Laurel Oakwode, Madeleine is known to Madden as Laurel, and the name Madden has tattoed on his arm during the night he cannot remember is (of course) Laurel. The chain of coincidence is usually a brutal one, as no fewer than seven persons die within a week and at one point Madden discovers not one but *two* severed blond heads in his marijuana stash. "I had long been a believer in the far reach of coincidence," Madden understandably remarks, "indeed I went so far as to think one must always expect it when extraordinary or evil events occur" (*TGDD*, 118). Later Madden tells his father that people come out of their "daily static" when "big" things are about to happen (*TGDD*, 161): "Their thoughts start pulling toward one another. It's as if an impending event creates a vacuum, and we start to go toward it. Startling coincidences pile up at a crazy rate" (*TGDD*, 162). "I'm tangled up in coincidences," Madden laments (*TGDD*, 162), and the network of events he must unravel is indeed worthy of the classical detective at his most ingenious.

Do the novel's coincidences reveal anything like a meaningful design? If so, is it a "design of darkness," as in Robert Frost's famous sonnet,[21] or is it providential, as the patterns in classical detective fiction tend to be? Wardley tells us that he loves design and that the essence of life may be found in such patterns (*TGDD*, 189). Many of Mailer's earlier characters entertain similar ideas: among others, Cummings in *The Naked and the Dead*, Rojack in *An American Dream*, D. J. in *Why Are We in Vietnam?*, Gary Gilmore in *The Executioner's Song*, and Menenhetet I in *Ancient Evenings*. In Mailer's more naturalistic first novel Cummings's ideas are exposed as the grandiose illusions of a megalomaniac. In the more recent fictions, however, Mailer takes such thinking much more seriously even if he falls short of endorsing his characters' conjectures about such topics as magic and life after death. In *Tough Guys* Mailer refuses to "explain" the uncanny network of coincidences constituting his hero's world and his novel's plot, but he also declines to ratify the occult and abandon altogether more common notions of cause and effect. The seven deaths described here are anything but coincidental, for example, as one act of violence leads to another in an all-too-common human "pattern." The second blonde head is placed with the first as a deliberate act of psychological malice directed at Madden and is, of course, suggested by the first decapitation. Nor does Mailer seem to endorse the notion that all is "fate" or design here, for the very real acts of volition by Madden and his father, Dougy, expose what is going on and bring things to their admittedly troubling, even inconclusive climax. By means of his extraordinary plot, Mailer renews his insistence on the problematic nature of reality. Mailer loves design as much as Wardley does, but Mailer is a good deal less sure of its standing in the cosmos.

The novel's coincidences thus contribute to Mailer's more serious themes. This is not to excuse the more improbable features of

Mailer's plot. In *Tough Guys* good (or bad) examples include Regency's remarkably arrogant (and implausible) decision to take Jessica's body to Spider Nissen for disposal and Patty's never-explained decision to remove Jessica's severed head from Madden's burrow. Perhaps we are to accept such irrationalities as evidence of the *lack* of design that everywhere contests whatever is providential in the scheme of things. If so, this is one of the many resemblances between Mailer's fictional world and that of the hard-boiled detective novelists.

Tough Guys Don't Dance and the Hard-boiled Detective Novel

In short, the hard-boiled detective is a traditional man of virtue in an amoral and corrupt world.
                                   – John G. Cawelti, *Adventure, Mystery, and Romance*

I always wanted . . . to write a detective story with a hero a little braver – just a little – than thee or me.
                                   – Norman Mailer, in *Conversations with Norman Mailer*

The epigraphs to this section are meant to point up the contrast between Mailer's intentions and those of the major hard-boiled detective novelists. Indeed, in the passage just quoted Mailer goes on to speak of the reader's reliance on the all-but-incorruptible private detective and the risk Mailer is taking by focusing on "a man of average bravery" (Lennon 1988, 330). Important as this contrast is, however, there can be little question that *Tough Guys* reveals Mailer's affinities with the hard-boiled novelists. Dashiell Hammett and Raymond Chandler were among the writers Mailer read during World War II (Lennon 1988, 190), and as late as 1979 Mailer was rereading all of Chandler's works in one summer (*P*, 133). Whereas the classical detective writers present "mysteries made only to be solved," in Dorothy Sayers's famous phrase,[22] Hammett, Chandler, and their compatriots offer relatively realistic fictions much more to Mailer's taste. "Hammett gave murder back to the kind of people that commit it for reasons, not just to provide a corpse," Chandler noted (Chandler, 234), and Mailer's narrative interests fall into the same tradition. Chandler insisted that the serious detective story should stress "the gradual elucidation of character" (Chandler, 236). Mailer suggests that the reason writers of reputation don't do detective stories is that "the characters in the typical detective story *have* to behave for the sake of the plot"; like Chandler, Mailer refuses to sacrifice characters to plot: "I wanted a murder mystery that was recognizable as such, that had characters as complex as those in non-murder books" (Lennon 1988, 331-32). Mailer's literary relations with his hard-boiled predecessors involve many similarities, then, but also a few key differences, as we should see by reviewing their fictional worlds, detectives, and narrative structures.

The world of hard-boiled detective fiction is one in which evil is virtually pervasive. According to George Grella, "All hard-boiled novels depict a tawdry world which conceals a shabby and depressing reality beneath its painted facade."[23] This world is distinctly urban, "a place of wickedness" (Grella, 112), the home of "empty modernity, corruption, and death" (Cawelti, 141). One thinks of Hammett's Personville and San Francisco, Chandler's Los Angeles, or, more recently, Robert Parker's Boston and Sara Paretsky's Chicago. Whereas the classical detective novel offers cities and country estates temporarily besmirched by the atypical villainy of one or two individuals, the hard-boiled novel presents a social panorama in which virtually everyone seems tainted by greed, ambition, or some other modern "sin," and the novel's killer, once identified, seems no more culpable than many of the other characters and sometimes much less so. Mailer's Provincetown shares much with this depressing fictional landscape. Here too the fictional world is filled with so-called respectable sorts more corrupt than the more obvious criminals; lowlifes such as Spider Nissen must finally be credited with none of the novel's many murders, while the book's wealthiest figure (Wardley) and its highest-ranking civic representative (Regency) are responsible for much of the bloodshed and general havoc. Mailer has long stressed the common bonds between criminals and police, a theme he might have inherited from Hammett's *Red Harvest* (1929) or almost any Chandler novel, especially *Farewell, My Lovely* (1940). In *Tough Guys* the breakdown of conventional distinctions is all but absolute, as the chief of police smokes pot during an interview in his own office and a former policeman helps conceal the remains of no fewer than six murder victims. Mailer's world nonetheless differs from the hard-boiled setting described by Grella and Cawelti in two significant ways: (a) it is filled with supernatural portents Mailer takes far more seriously than anyone writing in this tradition previously and (b) it is not really urban in nature, especially as the novel is set in the November off-season, when Provincetown's thousands of tourists are missing. The evil spirits in *Tough Guys* are as American as Hammett's or Chandler's but are not confined to the so-called urban jungle.

The hard-boiled detective is all but defined by his resistance to this inhospitable world. Apparently more "common" than his classical counterpart, the "detached eccentric" like Holmes or Wimsey (Cawelti, 95), the hard-boiled detective is in fact a very uncommon figure. Cawelti notes this detective's penchant for violence, his alienation from society, his rejection of conventional values while adhering to a personal code (Cawelti, 59); Grella stresses his "keen moral sense," manifest in his insistence on a moral code, his "stoic resistance to physical suffering," and his determination to pursue what he defines as justice ("Nothing, not even love, must prevent the detective from finishing his quest"; Grella, 106-10). Chandler offered the most famous apotheosis of this figure: "[D]own these mean streets a man must go who is not himself mean, who is neither tarnished nor afraid. . . . He is the hero, he is everything. He must be a complete man and a common man and yet an unusual man. He must be, to use a rather weathered phrase, a man of honor" (Chandler, 237).

If Chandler's Philip Marlowe is sometimes less noble than this description makes him sound, Mailer's Tim Madden is considerably less heroic. Like the hard-boiled detective in Cawelti's account, Madden briefly faces "assault, capture, drugging, blackjacking, and attempted assassination as a regular feature of his investigations" (Cawelti, 143). Like this detective, Madden seeks something like "an escape from the naturalistic consciousness of determinism and meaningless death" by solving the mysteries he investigates (Cawelti, 161). But ultimately Madden is nothing like the fearless paragon celebrated by Chandler and his academic critics. What we learn of Madden's past, highlighted by episodes of wife-swapping and cocaine selling, confirms his own judgment that he was (and still is) "a collection of fragments" (*TGDD*, 91), a man very much in search of the identity he might achieve by reestablishing his self-respect. His primary response to the "problem" he awakens to is fear, the same paralyzing fear he felt when trying to climb the Provincetown Monument (*TGDD*, 60-62), the fear he experienced during a séance when Patty and Spider Nissen "saw" Patty with her head cut off (*TGDD*, 72), the fear he feels in driving slowly toward his marijuana stash (*TGDD*, 45), and again when he realizes he must return to the stash to identify the blonde head from which he instinctively fled (*TGDD*, 72, 81). Far from being the fearless ideal invoked by Chandler, Madden is all but defined by his various fears and the self-pity that accompanies them (*TGDD*, 116). Never a hero, as he acknowledges (*TGDD*, 47), Madden finally achieves something like the hard-boiled detective's fearlessness when he is confronted by Wardley's gun (*TGDD*, 191). This discovery that he is no longer afraid comes after his belated but successful efforts to investigate his situation. At this point the classical and hard-boiled conventions merge in the figure of the detective, active if not indomitable, in search of the truth if not perfect justice.

The hard-boiled detective's quest defines the narrative structure Mailer shares with Hammett and Chandler. The nature of this quest is sometimes obscured by the form's relentless violence, which is associated with unvarnished melodrama ("When in doubt," Chandler once advised the authors of tough-guy short stories, "have a man come through a door with a gun in his hand").[24] In hard-boiled novels, however, the detective and the narrative alike seek justice rather than the "solution" to the crime, and the narrative focus is the detective's effort to define what Cawelti calls "his own moral position" (Cawelti, 146). This is also the case in *Tough Guys*, a novel that proceeds much like the hard-boiled paradigm. Here too the detective's search for the answer to an initial problem leads to the discovery of other problems at least as serious, ultimately implicating most of the dramatic personae rather than a single culprit. Indeed, *Tough Guys* exhibits "the rhythm of exposure" that Cawelti sees everywhere in hard-boiled fiction (Cawelti, 147), for Madden's investigation produces discovery after discovery (or is it body after body?), until literally all the characters of any note are either dead or implicated in the death of at least one victim. The resulting structure minimizes the value (perhaps even the relevance) of a single solution to the mystery, and so it is wrongheaded of Wenke and others to complain that Mailer's solution is "anticlimactic" (Wenke, 233). The same is true in classic hard-boiled novels like Chandler's *The Big*

Sleep (1939) and especially *The Long Goodbye* (1953), in which the murderess is identified 50 pages before the novel ends. Here Mailer begins the explanation of whodunit and why in chapter 8, about 40 pages before his conclusion. Throughout this chapter, as Wardley talks at length with Madden, we learn more and more about what happened the night Madden cannot remember; then, more than 30 pages after Wardley begins to talk of the deaths of Spider Nissen and his companion Stoodie, Regency confirms that it was Patty Lareine who shot Jessica Pond, and the "explanation" of six deaths is finally complete. (We get our seventh body in the epilogue, when Madeleine kills Regency [*TGDD*, 226].) By this point, if not much earlier, we are primarily concerned with the moral position Madden manages to achieve (however precariously) amid the numerous "exposures" that highlight the narrative structure. This structure exists so that Madden can develop his "position" under conditions of great stress. Its success or failure, like that of Hammett's and Chandler's novels, turns not on its author's ingenuity but on his ability to tell a certain kind of story, one in which the narrator's investigation leads him to discover who killed whom but also – and more important – the sort of person he is capable of becoming.

I would argue that *Tough Guys* perpetuates the spirit of the hard-boiled novels even if its fictional world and detective (who is technically not even a detective) depart from traditional models. *Tough Guys feels* like a hard-boiled detective novel not only because of its pervasive violence but also because the narrative pattern is very like that of the best-known hard-boiled novels. We have already seen that the book also incorporates classical features, however, and I hope to show that the stylized world of James Cain and film noir is at work in Mailer's fictional brew as well.

Tough Guys Don't Dance and the Noir World

It's more fun to pick up a mystery novel and read it, if early in that book you decide that you and the author share a perception that no one else has.

– Norman Mailer, *Pontifications*

I do not mean to argue that Mailer and James Cain share an altogether-common "perception" of the world. So far as I know, no one has tried to connect Mailer and Cain except Tom Wolfe in his devastating review of *An American Dream* (Wolfe, 1, 10, 12-13), and the differences between the two writers are profound. Nonetheless, Mailer turns in his venture into detective fiction to ingredients long before associated with Cain and film noir.

One of Mailer's comments on Cain points to their affinities. Musing on the voice of the private detective in hard-boiled fiction, Mailer notes that "the voice of Jake Barnes in *The Sun Also Rises* could have been that of a private eye in a detective story. . . . Hemingway, James Cain, and Dashiell Hammett understood that special world in which gesture has enormous importance." "This canon of gesture," Mailer adds, "is crucial to the tough-guy murder mystery" (Lennon 1988, 330-31). Hammett did create private detectives and Hemingway might have done so; Cain and Mailer create narrator-protagonists who function like detectives even if they are not private eyes. Mailer's comment suggests that his Cain is essentially the author of *The Postman Always Rings Twice* (1934) and *Double Indemnity* (1935), the first-person narratives in which Cain evokes the world of hard-boiled fiction without resorting to literal private detectives. (Even in *Double Indemnity* it is not Walter Huff but his colleague Keyes who functions as an investigator.) Cain also provides parallels both general and specific with Mailer's fiction. A book such as *The Postman Always Rings Twice* includes literary contrivances or "coincidences" beyond even Mailer's imagination, and Cain's "narrative speed" far surpasses Chandler's or Mailer's. The scene in which Frank and Cora make love immediately after Frank kills Cora's husband and just before the police arrive must remind Mailer's readers of the notorious sexual encounter between Rojack and Ruta in *An American Dream*, perhaps most interestingly in our sense that neither author means to condemn his lovers. As Paul Skenazy notes about Cain's novel, "There is no stable moral basis, no middle ground of sympathy, from which to condemn the lovers. Frank and Cora are all one has left."[25] And so it is with Rojack and his sexual partners in *An American Dream*, and so it is with Madden and Madeleine, even at the end of the novel when Madeleine shoots Regency. In the worlds of Cain and Mailer, such acts seem all too common if not inevitable.

Cain and the noir filmmakers offer visions darker than those to be found in Hammett and Chandler, without the supremely realistic Sam Spade or the knightly Philip Marlowe to contest the evil drift of things.[26] Nor is "their black vision of despair, loneliness, and dread" tempered by the comforting conclusions of traditional melodrama.[27] Whereas melodrama attempts to resolve the most perilous problems, the noir work is much more ambiguous at the end, "leaving a sense of continuing, persisting *malaise* in its wake" (Tuska, 151). The typical noir protagonist is someone "set down in a violent and incoherent world" with which he must somehow deal, "attempting to create some order out of chaos, to make some sense of the world."[28] This effort invariably fails, however, as the noir world proves to be one in which there is "no way out," as J. P. Telotte puts it.[29] In film noir we observe "sudden upwellings of violence in a culture whose fabric seems to be unraveling" (Telotte, 2), with nothing available to repair the design. Such is the fictional world projected in Cain's best-known novels and typical films noirs such as Billy Wilder's *Double Indemnity* (1944), Anatole Litvak's *Sorry, Wrong Number* (1948), Rudolph Maté's *D.O.A.* (1949), John Huston's *The Asphalt Jungle* (1950),[30] and Orson Welles's *A Touch of Evil* (1958). (A more recent example would be Lawrence Kasdan's *Body Heat* [1981].) In all these works the tidy resolutions of classical detective fiction are virtually inverted, and even the ironic, anticlimactic "solutions" of the hard-boiled novels are made to seem wildly optimistic.

The ties between *Tough Guys* and film noir will seem especially close to those who have seen Mailer's 1987 film adaptation of his novel, for there he adopts several of film noir's most distinctive features. Film noir is almost always retrospective, for example, usually relying on flashbacks and voice-over to explain how the protagonist has arrived at his or her fated moment. Mailer's film employs this technique, beginning with Madden's reunion with his father (the last sentence of chapter 6 [*TGDD*, 152]) and going on to dramatize many episodes only briefly mentioned in the narrative (or not mentioned at all, as the film's plot differs from the book's). Film noir typically conveys the sense of "a mind meditating on the past" (Telotte, 13) and finally presents its hero as "morally ambiguous" (Tuska, 154). Mailer's film technique almost exaggerates these already-stylized features, for Ryan O'Neal's voice-over stresses Madden's sensitive reengagement with his past and the almost-sinister laughter of Madden and Madeleine at the end underlines the extremely ambiguous moral credentials of our hero and heroine. The connections between Mailer's novel and the noir world are somewhat more complex, however, for Mailer's perception of reality is not easy to categorize.

Mailer's book is filled with the kind of stylized excess we associate with noir. Compare Mailer's seven bodies with the eight children Phyllis Nordlinger helps to kill in Cain's *Double Indemnity* (a detail so grim that Wilder deleted it in the film version). And Mailer's women, especially Patty Lareine and Madeleine Falco, recall film noir's characteristic femmes fatales, played most memorably by Joan Crawford and Barbara Stanwyck. But the ambiguities of Mailer's conclusion (if not the laughter at the end of the film) should remind us that, dark as *Tough Guys* is, Mailer does not share the deterministic bent of Cain and film noir. The retrospective point of view in film noir and the confessional mode of Cain's more famous novels serve to reinforce the despairing notion that indeed there is no way out, no real alternatives to what has already happened. Mailer's decision to adopt this technique in his film is odd, for his novel tells a very different kind of story, one in which Madden's fate *and* character are in doubt until the very end. Indeed, it seems reasonable to surmise that Mailer was attracted to the mystery rather than the confession because the mystery format permitted him to leave Madden's fate as undetermined as possible. The first-person point of view, coupled with the mystery Madden seeks to penetrate, effectively stresses the series of decisions Madden must make as he gradually becomes the detective of Mailer's chosen genre(s). In the novel, then, Mailer makes occasional but limited use of flashbacks (principally those touching on Madden's marriage to Patty Lareine, his attempt to climb the Provincetown Monument, and a very select set of moments from his affair with Madeleine). Emphasis falls on Madden's efforts in the present to do something about his plight, not simply to meditate on it. Mailer's unwillingness to concede the deterministic implications in Cain and film noir is most obvious in the novel's conclusion, in which Madden roughly succeeds and Mailer seems to be devising what his critics uneasily see as a "happy" ending.[31]

I do not think the novel's ending is really a happy one, as we can see by comparing Madden's situation with Rojack's at the end of *An American Dream*. But the way in which this ending departs from Mailer's noir antecedents should again remind us that *Tough Guys* is an eclectic combination of features drawn from classical detective fiction, the hard-boiled detective novel, and film noir because none of these forms precisely mirrors Mailer's complex beliefs. The interplay of narrative features is almost always fruitful, for the emergence of the detectivelike protagonist alerts us to the fact that Mailer is not a classical determinist, yet the overwhelmingly noirlike fictional world amply fleshes out the problems Madden must face in trying to survive or, better yet, turn his life around in some believable form. As we pursue the parallels with *An American Dream,* I believe we will see that in this later book Mailer manages to combine detective traditions in a way that sustains rather than compromises his own distinctive voice and themes.

Tough Guys Don't Dance and *An American Dream*

I don't consider myself moral at all. I see myself as a man who lives in an embattled relation to morality.

— Norman Mailer, *Pontifications*

I am hardly the first to see strong parallels between *An American Dream* and *Tough Guys.* Wenke notices general parallels (Wenke, 229), Peter Balbert comments on the parallel between Rojack's walk on the parapet and Madden's attempt to climb the Provincetown Monument (Balbert, 70), and a number of other critics echo Michael Ventura's characterization of *Tough Guys* as "an overworked rehash of the critically savaged, badly underrated *An American Dream*" (Lennon 1988, 380). It is hard to see why Ventura thinks *An American Dream* is "badly underrated," as most of Mailer's critics rank the book at or near the top of his canon. It is easier to see why *Tough Guys* seems a "rehash" of the earlier novel, for there are a number of crucial similarities. In my view, however, the "rehash" is a successful reconstruction of earlier themes and characters.

The two books do share fundamental plot elements and themes. Each novel focuses on a middle-aged narrator-protagonist whose estrangement from his wealthy, domineering wife has brought him to the verge of a nervous breakdown or even suicide. In each case the wife is killed and our hero is accused of killing her (justly in *An American Dream,* unjustly in *Tough Guys*). In each novel the narrator engages in lengthy conversations with a policeman (Roberts/Regency) and enters into a sexual relationship with someone (Cherry/Madeleine) immediately after the death of his wife.

Each novel telescopes a remarkable number of violent, transforming events into a short period (less than two days in *An American Dream*, a somewhat more credible seven days in *Tough Guys*). The cathartic effect of personal violence is a common theme, expressed most conspicuously in (a) Rojack's attacks on his wife, Deborah, and Shago Martin and (b) Madden's seemingly mindless attack on Spider Nissen's car (*TGDD*, 150-52) and the remission of Dougy's cancer after he involves himself in the aftereffects of murder (*TGDD*, 179, 223, 228). The primary thematic parallel is also the principal dramatic one, as the two narrators undergo similarly life-defining experiences in which they must reject their former selves if they are even to survive. In the conditions of this survival we discover, in each case, Mailer's most fundamental beliefs about human existence.

Given these parallels, the differences between the two books and especially the two narrators are extremely revealing. In *Tough Guys* Mailer again insists on the personal voice of the man whose experiences are at issue, and the book records the sometimes subtle, sometimes conspicuous moments of confrontation as Madden faces existential decisions not unlike Rojack's. Like the book itself, however, Madden is a much more believable character whose conversion, partial as it is, compels our belief as Rojack's does not. Significantly, Madden's history is one of repeated failure, whereas Rojack's is Kennedy-like in its trajectory and even its specifics. If Rojack is a prominent national figure as a politician, author, and public personality, Madden is an ex-con who wants to be a writer but can't get published. Rojack's history fits the parabolic form of his novel, in which the American success story of rags to riches is reversed and the protagonist must learn that he was losing all the time he thought he was winning. Madden's reversals are far more modest but, perhaps for this reason, far more plausible. Similarly, the tests he must pass are rather more internalized than in *An American Dream*. Where Rojack has to strangle Deborah, sexually dominate the "evil" Ruta, do psychic battle with a series of cops and hoods, fight with Shago, and walk a parapet in the presence of his corrupt father-in-law, Madden must learn to deal with his feelings, his fears and evasions. The contrast is not absolute, for Madden also fights on one occasion and parries Regency much as Rojack duels with Roberts. But the differences are telling. The physical challenge of walking a parapet is for Rojack the climactic test of his newfound

courage; the attempt to climb the Provincetown Monument is for
Madden an earlier act of bravado that he does not repeat in his week
of crisis. Rojack's fears are objectified in the specific people who
threaten his safety throughout the novel; Madden's fears involve his
own deep reluctance to accept responsibility for his condition and
to *act*, whatever the outcome of his actions. Madden slays no drag-
ons, then, but his movement from the drifting figure we first meet to
the man who confronts Regency at the end is much more moving as
well as more believable than Rojack's evolution. Madden's
"resurrection" is less startling, but perhaps for that reason it is more
affecting. Like Mailer, Madden becomes not so much a moralist as a
man with an embattled relation to morality – a relation Mailer traces
in unusually persuasive detail.

The differences between Rojack and Madden point to a formal
difference as well. As I argue in chapter 4, *An American Dream*
constantly vacillates between the formal ends of realistic and didactic
fictions, the novel as action and the novel as apologue. *Tough Guys*
seems to me to avoid this kind of formal confusion, perhaps because
Mailer's aims are more clearly defined as well as more modest.
Madden's fears and failures are developed in the context of a more
plausible personal history and a fictional world as richly textured as
any Mailer has created. The spirits of Provincetown may be ghostly
or actual ghosts, but they are firmly rooted in Madden's psychological experience, as we would expect them to be in any novel with
realistic pretensions. Stylized as it is, the detective form provides the
necessary shape for Madden's test. The form offers the occasion,
indeed the need, for personal involvement and decisive action – for
Mailer, the essentials of a meaningful life. In tracing Madden's gradual engagement Mailer gives realistic life to a form often disparaged if
not ignored and joins Hammett, Chandler, Ross Macdonald, and
John le Carré as at least a one-time master of the realistic detective
novel.

This mastery is most evident in Mailer's conclusion. His development of Madden's story is almost always deft, and other characters, such as Wardley, Regency, and especially Dougy ("the best
thing in the book probably"; Lennon 1988, 372), testify to Mailer's
desire to create characters "as complex as those in non-murder
books" (Lennon 1988, 331-32). Other characters, however, especially the women, are somewhat sketchily handled, as Mailer only

partly transcends problems inherent in the detective format. Nor is Mailer's control of the detective apparatus without its problems, as when a character like Wardley all but magically appears to explain matters that would otherwise remain all too mysterious. Even so, at the end Mailer's basic command of his form is very much in evidence. For Madden and Madeleine, life goes on, neither happily nor unhappily. Unlike Rojack, however, they do continue to deal with their new life together in America (not the "territory" of Guatemala or Yucatán to which Rojack escapes). Their fate is neither comic nor tragic but a tragicomic mixture that seems, in context, very nearly heroic. The novel's conclusion thus eschews not only the superficial neatness of the classical resolution but also the pervasive gloom of the hard-boiled novel and especially film noir. It fits very well the concoction Mailer has made from these diverse sources and, for once, provides the kind of satisfying conclusion Mailer has sought in his fiction for more than 40 years now. Those who value this career will of course hope that Mailer continues to provide such conclusions in works even more significant than this extremely successful "murder mystery."

Chapter Ten

Mailer's Career

A Brief Review

It may seem odd to begin a review of Mailer's career by commenting on his films. Nonetheless, I think that glancing at Mailer's infatuation with film might help us see his literary career in better perspective. The problems in Mailer's films point up the contrasting strengths in his more successful books. Surprisingly, perhaps, these strengths usually involve features associated with traditional narrative.

No one would identify such features with Mailer's films. The films made by others from *The Naked and the Dead* and *An American Dream* are universally scorned as unfaithful hack works, and Mailer's own films embody an improvisational approach to film that he all but defines in opposition to literature. Speaking of his third film, *Maidstone*, Mailer notes approvingly "its lack of concern for the proportions, conventions, and sinews of literature" (*MAM*, 22). His "method," as he calls it, is "to put untried actors into situations without a script and film them with simple or available lighting" (*MAM*, 141). Such tactics produced the first three films, *Wild 90* (1967) – even by Mailer's standards "a disaster" (*MAM*, 162) – *Beyond the Law* (1967), and *Maidstone* (1968). In the 1980s Mailer twice developed films in a somewhat different mode, as both *The Executioner's Song* (1982) and *Tough Guys Don't Dance* (1987) were made from scripts (Mailer's own) and with well-known professional actors. These later, more "literary" films do not measure up to the books on which they are based, however, and so confirm the thesis that as a filmmaker Mailer is a first-rate novelist.

Mailer did not direct *The Executioner's Song*, but he did write the script and worked with the director, Larry Schiller, on the book as well as the film. I think almost everyone would agree that this is the best film with which Mailer has been involved (not counting Milos Forman's *Ragtime* [1982], in which Mailer acted), not only because the actors are first-rate professionals but because the script includes many fine moments all too rare in Mailer's improvisational films. Nonetheless, *The Executioner's Song* illustrates Mailer's unsure grasp of this medium. Faced with the daunting task of condensing more than 1,000 pages of text into a film, Mailer did many of the "obvious" things the task seemed to call for and ended up producing a good script that is nevertheless unworthy of its literary source. Mailer cut many of the "minor" characters and radically reduced the roles of people like Schiller (here rechristened Samuels). He chose to stress the events prior to Gilmore's arrest (book 1), thus effectively eliminating the story of Gary Gilmore's media "career" (book 2). The resulting script is highly focused but relatively superficial. Mailer can only hint at his subject's strange growth after Gilmore again enters the prison system; he can do almost nothing with Nicole Baker, who disappears from the film's second, shorter "half"; he can barely suggest why Gilmore becomes a national figure; and he can do little with the many characters who became crucial figures in the social drama Mailer told so powerfully in the book. Indeed, Mailer can barely hint at the representative qualities of his material, reduced as it is to the personal story of Gary Gilmore. Touching as this story is as enacted by Tommy Lee Jones and his supporting cast, *The Executioner's Song* as film is a very minor work of art when set against the expansive narrative on which it is based.

Mailer's problems with the much-maligned *Tough Guys Don't Dance* are more complicated. Although this much shorter novel might seem to lend itself to adaptation, Mailer's scenario again reveals unhappy omissions. Madden's father plays a very minor role in the film, for example, supposedly because there was no "room" for the father-son relationship (Lennon 1988, 372). There was no room, however, because Mailer chose to emphasize other, less interesting features of the book. Indeed, Mailer's choices here seem less unavoidable and more objectionable than those made in *The Executioner's Song*. I remarked earlier the odd decision to tell the story by means of extensive flashbacks and voice-over, thus converting the novel's mystery format into a version of the deterministic film noir. With this strategy, the major casualty is the story of Tim Madden's growth toward self-assertion. In the film there is no initial sequence stressing Madden's fear in response to the strange mysteries he discovers on awakening; there is no sequence of encounters with

Wardley; there is no real inquiry on Madden's part. In short, there is no story of Madden's developing response to what impinges on him; most of the action is told in retrospect, through flashbacks, and stresses what happens to Madden rather than what he chooses to do about it. The added plot elements involving a drug sale are sensational, but they tend to be more diverting than explanatory. It is hard to see any aspect of the film enhanced by Mailer's revisions.

Though the problems noted can be seen as nothing more than dubious artistic choices, I think they derive from Mailer's choice of media. Mailer's better books bespeak a gift he has been unable to translate into film: a gift for narrative. In his books Mailer has been free to tell stories of various kinds, involving large or small canvases, large or small casts of characters, and first-person narrators whose interaction with the book's materials is crucial to Mailer's narrative structures. Mailer's own comments notwithstanding, it is not just his often-lavish prose that distinguishes his books from his films – the *stories* told are more interesting, more complicated, more richly developed, and more thoroughly realized as works of art. One thinks especially of *The Naked and the Dead* and *The Deer Park*, in which Mailer develops overlapping story lines in sufficient detail to bring new life to the form of the traditional realistic novel; *The Armies of the Night*, in which he manages to tell the moving story of his own rite of passage while mixing fictional and historical modes of discourse in perhaps his most original literary form; *The Executioner's Song*, in which his scrupulous attention to the stories of 100 characters is no less impressive than his more typical (or more often remarked) attention to himself throughout his nonfiction; *Ancient Evenings*, in which he recreates a historical milieu with the overwhelming immediacy we associate with his own journalism; and *Tough Guys Don't Dance*, in which his first-person treatment reinvents and restores to significant literary heights the somewhat tattered conventions of the detective novel. Though Mailer's works betray an extraordinary thematic consistency (or repetition) from his earliest to his latest novels, the stories they tell are remarkably varied and usually the source of Mailer's greatness as a narrative artist.

It is not very fashionable to praise Mailer as a storyteller, as I did in the previous chapter and now again in this conclusion. To do so is to invoke "traditional" literary approaches supposedly irrelevant to Mailer's achievement. Laura Adams presents this point of view in its

purest form: "What the work of Poirier and others has established by
now is that traditional approaches to Mailer are inadequate. An existential criticism is needed for purposes of evaluation even more than
of interpretation of Mailer's work, and such a critical approach
would have to accept Mailer's givens as its own and judge him by his
own standards rather than insist that he conform to accepted literary
tastes and practices" (Adams, 9). Adams clearly wants to protect
Mailer from judgments based on "accepted literary tastes and practices." She assumes that Mailer must inevitably be found wanting if
judged by such old-fashioned "approaches." I can only say again
what I first said some 15 years ago: if Adams is right, so much the
worse for Mailer. I think it is perverse to argue that traditional critical
approaches are irrelevant to Mailer, as if his works were so sui
generis as to be quite outside the boundaries of normal critical analysis. In any case, I have assumed throughout this study that Mailer's
works must be judged by the same literary standards we bring to the
study of other writers.

The irony is that, judged in these terms, Mailer comes off very
well indeed. Mailer has published almost 30 original volumes, and so
it is hardly surprising that he has written a number of books that are
unsuccessful by any standard. If we cut away what is palpably
"minor" in Mailer's collected works, however, there remains a body
of writing for which relatively large claims can be made. Mailer has
written at least four important novels (*The Naked and the Dead, The
Deer Park, Ancient Evenings,* and *Tough Guys Don't Dance*), two of
the best works of nonfiction in American literary history (*The Armies
of the Night* and *The Executioner's Song,* if indeed we count *The
Executioner's Song* as a work of nonfiction), and a body of essays
that will stand comparison with the best nonfiction in this century.
Even minor works such as *Marilyn* and seriously flawed works such
as *Why Are We in Vietnam?* contribute to Mailer's imposing output of
serious and original work. Mailer's successes amply justify Lennon's
description of him as "a connoisseur of narrative forms" (Lennon
1986a, 2). It is as such a "connoisseur" that Mailer will ultimately be
remembered. I continue to believe that Mailer stands with Robert
Lowell, Saul Bellow, and Thomas Pynchon as one of the four most
important American writers in the postwar period. When the controversies about the living man have receded, it will be Mailer and not
his many critics who will have the last word.

Notes and References

Preface

1. For these figures, see, respectively, Stanley Edgar Hyman, "Norman Mailer's Yummy Rump," *New Leader*, 15 March 1965, 17; Norman Mailer, *Existential Errands* (Boston: Little, Brown, 1972), 260 (hereafter cited in text as *EE*); and Laura Adams, "Existential Aesthetics: An Interview with Norman Mailer," *Partisan Review* 42 (1975): 210.

2. *Advertisements for Myself* (New York: G. P. Putnam's Sons, 1959), 465-66; hereafter cited in text as *AFM*.

3. "What Might Have Been," *Newsweek*, 9 November 1959, 127; hereafter cited in text.

4. Robert C. Healey, "Novelists of the War: A Bunch of Dispossessed," in *Fifty Years of the American Novel: A Christian Appraisal*, ed. Harold C. Gardiner, S.J. (New York: Charles Scribner's Sons, 1951), 263.

5. Charles J. Rolo, review of *Advertisements for Myself*, *Atlantic Monthly*, December 1959, 168.

6. See Edmund Fuller, *Man in Modern Fiction* (New York: Vintage Books, 1958), 101-4, 154-62; Frederick J. Hoffman, "Norman Mailer and the Revolt of the Ego: Some Observations on Recent American Literature," *Wisconsin Studies in Contemporary Literature* 1 (Autumn 1961): 5-12; George A. Schrader, "Norman Mailer and the Despair of Defiance," *Yale Review* 51 (December 1961): 267-80; and Diana Trilling, "The Radical Moralism of Norman Mailer," *Claremont Essays* (New York: Harcourt Brace Jovanovich, 1962), 175-202.

7. This focus on Mailer's thought can lead to useful insights, of course. Robert Solotaroff's *Down Mailer's Way* (Urbana: University of Illinois Press, 1974) (hereafter cited in text) is perhaps the best study of any contemporary American writer, for example. But there is an unmistakable tendency in this kind of criticism to treat Mailer as a quasi-philosopher rather than as an imaginative writer. For other, less successful examples of this approach to Mailer, see the Adams, Gutman, Kaufmann, and Radford items in my Selected Bibliography.

8. Harvey Swados, "Must Writers Be Characters?" *Saturday Review*, 1 October 1960, 14.

9. See Eve Auchincloss and Nancy Lynch, "An Interview with Norman Mailer," *Mademoiselle*, February 1961, 76-77, 160-63.

10. See "Americana: Of Time and the Rebel," *Time*, 5 December 1960, 16-17; Dwight Macdonald, "Our Far-flung Correspondent: Massachusetts vs. Mailer," *New Yorker*, 8 October 1960, 154-66; and "The Boston Trial of *Naked Lunch*," *Evergreen Review* 9 (June 1965): 40-49, 87-88.

11. See Brock Brower, "In This Corner, Norman Mailer, Never the Champion, Always the Challenger," *Life*, 24 September 1965, 94-117 (hereafter cited in text); Joseph Roddy, "The Latest Model Mailer," *Look*, 27 May 1969, 22-28; and James Toback, "At Play in the Fields of the Bored," *Esquire*, December 1968, 150-55.

12. Richard Foster, *Norman Mailer* (Minneapolis: University of Minnesota Press, 1968), 42-43; hereafter cited in text.

13. See Richard Poirier, *Norman Mailer* (New York: Viking Press, 1972) (hereafter cited in text); Tony Tanner, "On the Parapet (Norman Mailer)," *City of Words: American Fiction, 1950-1970* (New York: Harper & Row, 1971), 344-71; Michael Cowan, "The Americanness of Norman Mailer," in *Norman Mailer: A Collection of Critical Essays*, ed. Leo Braudy (Englewood Cliffs, N.J.: Prentice Hall, 1972), 143-57 (revised and expanded as "The Quest for Empowering Roots: Mailer and the American Literary Tradition," in *Critical Essays on Norman Mailer*, ed. J. Michael Lennon [Boston: G. K. Hall, 1986], 156-74); Robert J. Begiebing, *Acts of Regeneration: Allegory and Archetype in the Works of Norman Mailer* (Columbia: University of Missouri Press, 1980) (hereafter cited in text); and Joseph Wenke, *Mailer's America* (Hanover, N.H.: University Press of New England, 1987) (hereafter cited in text).

14. See three essays by Robert F. Lucid: "Norman Mailer: The Artist as Fantasy Figure," *Massachusetts Review* 15 (Autumn 1974): 581-95; "Three Public Performances: Fitzgerald, Hemingway, and Mailer," *American Scholar* 43 (Summer 1974): 447-66; and "Prolegomenon to a Biography of Mailer," in *Critical Essays on Normon Mailer*, ed. Lennon, 174-84. See also three essays by J. Michael Lennon: "Mailer's Radical Bridge," *Journal of Narrative Technique* 7 (Fall 1977): 170-88; "Mailer's Sarcophagus: The Artist, the Media, and the 'Wad,'" *Modern Fiction Studies* 23 (Summer 1977): 179-87; and "Mailer's Cosmology," in *Critical Essays on Norman Mailer*, ed. Lennon, 145-56.

15. J. Michael Lennon, introduction to *Critical Essays on Norman Mailer*, ed. Lennon 2; hereafter cited in text as Lennon 1986a.

16. Richard Poirier, *The Performing Self* (New York: Oxford University Press, 1971), xv, 87.

17. *This Is My Best*, ed. Whit Burnett (Garden City, N.Y.: Doubleday, 1970), 99.

Chapter One

1. *The Armies of the Night* (New York: New American Library, 1968), 5-6; hereafter cited in text as *AOTN*.

2. *Current Biography* (New York: H. W. Wilson, 1948), 408; hereafter cited in text.

3. The second of these novels was finally published in a limited edition as *A Transit to Narcissus: A Facsimile of the Original Typescript* (New York: Howard Fertig, 1978). Mailer's introduction to this edition is much more interesting than the work itself.

4. "Rugged Times," *New Yorker*, 23 October 1948, 25; hereafter cited in text.

5. See "Norman Mailer," in *Brushfire*, ed. William Baines and Henry Nuwer (Reno: Associated Students of the University of Nevada, 1973), 19.

6. For an excellent book-length treatment of Mailer's shifting intellectual commitments, see Solotaroff, *Down Mailer's Way*. The best shorter treatment is Lennon's "Mailer's Cosmology."

7. *Deaths for the Ladies (and Other Disasters)* (New York: G. P. Putnam's Sons, 1962), n.p.

8. Mailer discusses his talk-show days in "Of a Small and Modest Malignancy, Wicked and Bristling with Dots," *Pieces* (Boston: Little, Brown, 1982), 13-81.

9. For more on Mailer's mayoralty campaign, see Joe Flaherty, *Managing Mailer* (New York: Coward-McGann, 1969), and Peter Manso, ed., *Running against the Machine* (Garden City, N.Y.: Doubleday, 1969).

10. The best account of Mailer's quarrel with women's liberation is his own *The Prisoner of Sex* (Boston: Little, Brown, 1971); hereafter cited in text as *POS*. See also Diana Trilling, "The Prisoner of Sex," in *Critical Essays on Norman Mailer*, ed. Lennon, 103-10, and Marcia Cohen, *The Sisterhood: The True Story of the Women Who Changed the World* (New York: Simon & Schuster, 1988), 288-306. For Mailer's endorsement of a Fifth Estate, see Patricia Bosworth, "Fifth Estate at the Four Seasons," *Saturday Review of the Arts*, March 1973, 5-7.

11. See Adams, "Existential Aesthetics," 212.

12. See Karen Jaehne, "Mailer's Minuet," *Film Comment*, July-August 1987, 11-12.

13. Among many interesting accounts of the conference, see Barbara Probst Solomon, "What Makes Writers Run," *Partisan Review* 53 (1986): 183-89, and Miriam Schneir, "The Prisoner of Sexism," *Ms.*, April 1986, 82-83. For Mailer's formal address to this convention, see Norman Mailer and Nadine Gordimer, "The Writer's Imagination and the Imagination of the State: Two Views," *New York Review of Books*, 13 February 1986, 23-25.

14. For a brief excerpt from this unpublished play, see "*Strawhead:* An Extract from Act One," *Vanity Fair,* April 1986, 62-67.

15. See, respectively, Norman Mailer, "Jackson Is a Friend of Life's Victims," *New York Times,* 18 April 1988, 23; Norman Mailer, "Fury, Fear, Philosophy," *Spin,* September 1988, 30-44, 78; and Walter Goodman, " 'No, the Pope Can't Join Our Club,' " *New York Times,* 17 May 1988, 20.

16. *Of Women and Their Elegance* (1980; New York: Pinnacle Books, 1981), 283.

17. See "A Piece of Harlot's Ghost," *Esquire,* July 1988, 80-82, 84-90, and "The Changing of the Guard," *Playboy,* December 1988, 87-88, 196-98.

18. For Mailer's credentials as a biographical critic, see chapter 7.

19. For a thoughtful review of Manso's book, see Anthony Burgess, "The Prisoner of Fame," *Atlantic Monthly,* June 1985, 100, 102-4.

20. For the excerpt, see Lucid, "Prolegomenon to a Biography of Mailer," in *Critical Essays on Norman Mailer,* ed. Lennon. Besides writing the essays on Mailer cited earlier, Lucid also edited *The Long Patrol* (New York: World, 1971), an anthology of Mailer's works, and *Norman Mailer: The Man and His Work* (Boston: Little, Brown, 1971), a collection of essays about Mailer.

Chapter Two

1. This short novel, "A Calculus at Heaven," is reprinted in *Advertisements for Myself,* 29-70.

2. See George Plimpton, ed., *Writers at Work: "The Paris Review" Interviews,* 3d series (New York: Viking Press, 1967), 260; hereafter cited in text.

3. The novel's popular success was such that it remained number one on the *New York Times* best-seller list for 11 weeks (22 June to 29 August).

4. Marvin Mudrick, "Mailer and Styron: Guests of the Establishment," *Hudson Review* 17 (August 1964): 347.

5. Ira Wolfert, "War Novelist," *Nation,* 26 June 1948, 723.

6. Norman Podhoretz, "Norman Mailer: The Embattled Vision," *Partisan Review* 26 (Summer 1959): 371; hereafter cited in text.

7. Harvey Breit, "Talk with Norman Mailer," *New York Times Book Review,* 3 June 1951, 20; hereafter cited in text.

8. *Cannibals and Christians* (New York: Dial Press, 1966), 112; hereafter cited in text as *CC.*

9. See, for example, Ihab Hassan, *Radical Innocence* (New York: Harper & Row, 1961), 141; Chester E. Eisinger, *Fiction of the Forties* (Chicago: University of Chicago Press, 1963), 37 (hereafter cited in text);

and Solotaroff, *Down Mailer's Way*, 14, 18. The phrase "young liberal" is Hassan's.

10. See especially Podhoretz, "Embattled Vision," 371-77; Solotaroff, *Down Mailer's Way*, 3-39; and Howard M. Harper, Jr., *Desperate Faith* (Chapel Hill: University of North Carolina Press, 1967), 96-103.

11. Barry Leeds, *The Structured Vision of Norman Mailer* (New York: New York University Press, 1969), 16-17; hereafter cited in text.

12. *The Naked and the Dead* (New York: Holt, Rinehart & Winston, 1948), 266-79; hereafter cited in text as *NATD*.

13. John M. Muste reaches the same conclusion in "Norman Mailer and John Dos Passos: The Question of Influence," *Modern Fiction Studies* 17 (Autumn 1971): 361-62.

14. John Aldridge, *After the Lost Generation* (New York: McGraw-Hill, 1951), 135 (hereafter cited in text). For Mailer's confirmation, see *Cannibals and Christians*, 112.

15. Randall Waldron, "The Naked, the Dead, and the Machine: A New Look at Norman Mailer's First Novel," *PMLA* 87 (March 1972): 273, 276.

16. See Podhoretz, "Embattled Vision," 373-77, and Aldridge, *After the Lost Generation*, 136-40.

17. Cummings's self-pity is revealed throughout the novel; see especially 78, 106, and 182. For hints more or less overt of his homosexuality, see 80, 83, 173, 322, 388, 408, and 425-26. Mailer subsequently regretted the homophobia of his first two novels; see "The Homosexual Villain," *Advertisements for Myself*, 222-23.

18. Part 3 of *The Naked and the Dead* is entitled "Plant and Phantom." The phrase comes from Nietzsche's *Thus Spake Zarathustra*.

19. Croft's sense of defeat would seem to contradict Raymond Wilson's claim that Croft "transcends" the social and existential pressures that have formed him. Wilson believes that *The Naked and the Dead* is far less pessimistic than critics like myself have supposed. See Raymond J. Wilson III, "Control and Freedom in *The Naked and the Dead*," *Texas Studies in Literature and Language* 28 (Summer 1986): 164-81, especially 174.

20. See Friedrich Nietzsche, *Thus Spake Zarathustra*, in *The Philosophy of Nietzsche*, ed. Willard Huntington Wright (New York: Modern Library, 1954), 6.

21. Mailer also dramatizes this division in his minor characters, especially Roth, Gallagher, Wilson, and Goldstein. My emphasis on the major characters somewhat distorts the value of these minor figures.

22. Croft's homosexuality is difficult to "prove" but seems to be hinted at throughout the book; see especially 145.

23. Mailer has confessed to a "secret admiration" for Croft; see *The Presidential Papers* (New York: G. P. Putnam's Sons, 1963), 136 (hereafter cited in text as *TPP*).

24. For evidence that Cummings does intend to execute Hearn when he assigns him to the I and R platoon, see 401 and 717.

25. Just before his death Hearn acknowledges the tawdriness of his motives and decides *not* to be like Cummings and Croft (584). He decides to turn in his commission but is murdered before he can make this last and most compelling gesture of rebellion.

26. The best recent critique of Mailer's first novel – and perhaps the best study early or late – is Donald Pizer's chapter in *Twentieth-Century American Literary Naturalism: An Interpretation* (Carbondale: Southern Illinois University Press, 1982), 90-114. Other recent essays of interest include Wilson's "Control and Freedom"; Bernard Horn's "Ahab and Ishmael at War: The Presence of *Moby-Dick* in *The Naked and the Dead*," *American Quarterly* 34 (Fall 1982): 379-95; Wenke's chapter on *The Naked and the Dead* in *Mailer's America*, 24-41; and Carol Schloss's chapter in *In Visible Light: Photography and the American Writer, 1840-1940* (New York: Oxford University Press, 1987), 233-49. Pizer stresses Mailer's links with the naturalistic tradition. Horn presents the most detailed study of Melville's influence on *The Naked and the Dead*. Like Wilson, Wenke reads the novel in light of Mailer's subsequent "existentialism," though Wenke acknowledges the many ways in which Mailer's first novel differs from his later works. Schloss argues that Mailer's experience in interpreting aerial photographs moved him toward a form of literary perspectivism.

Chapter Three

1. "History and Its Burdens: The Example of Norman Mailer," in *Uses of Literature,* ed. Monroe Engel (Cambridge, Mass.: Harvard University Press, 1973), 68.

2. See Jean Radford, *Norman Mailer: A Critical Study* (New York: Barnes & Noble, 1975), 17, 131-32 (hereafter cited in text), and Philip H. Bufithis, *Norman Mailer* (New York: Ungar, 1978), 32 (hereafter cited in text).

3. John Stark, *"Barbary Shore:* The Basis of Mailer's Best Work," *Modern Fiction Studies* 17 (Autumn 1971): 405-6.

4. In the first edition of this book I used the phrase "rigid allegory" to describe *Barbary Shore.* Begiebing rightly objects to this label. Elsewhere in his book, however, he says I fail to see that Mailer is an archetypal allegorist rather than a fabulist (Begiebing, *Acts of Regeneration,* 5, n. 8). I must admit that I still cannot see much in this distinction. I take allegory to be a branch of fabulation, and in any case most fabulators are allegorists, as Robert Scholes argues in the book cited in note 7 following.

5. "The Hazards and Sources of Writing," *Michigan Quarterly Review* 24 (Summer 1985): 400-401.

6. These essays are reprinted in *Advertisements for Myself,* 186-227.

7. For the best treatment of fabulation, see Robert Scholes, *The Fabulators* (New York: Oxford University Press, 1967), subsequently revised and expanded as *Fabulation and Metafiction* (Urbana: University of Illinois Press, 1979); hereafter cited in text.

8. For an extensive treatment of this problem in the later novels, see chapter 4.

9. See Irving Howe, "Some Political Novels," *Nation*, 16 June 1951, 568, and Solotaroff, *Down Mailer's Way*, 51-52.

10. *Barbary Shore* (New York: Rinehart, 1951), 9; hereafter cited in text as *BS*.

11. "Introduction," *The Short Fiction of Norman Mailer* (New York: Dell, 1967), 13.

12. James Rother, "Mailer's 'O'Shaugnessy Chronicle': A Speculative Autopsy," *Critique* 19 (1978): 21-39.

13. Sidney Alexander, "Not Even Good Pornography," *Reporter*, 20 October 1955, 46.

14. Not so strange, perhaps, if one thinks of the example of D. H. Lawrence. For Mailer's hatred of pornography, see especially *The Presidential Papers*, 12, and *Advertisements for Myself*, 181.

15. Michael Millgate, *American Social Fiction* (New York: Barnes & Noble, 1964), 162-63.

16. See, for example, Podhoretz, "Embattled Vision," 387; Donald L. Kaufmann, *Norman Mailer: The Countdown* (Carbondale: Southern Illinois University Press, 1969), 23-34 (hereafter cited in text); and Helen A. Weinberg, *The New Novel in America* (Ithaca, N.Y.: Cornell University Press, 1970), 112-24 (hereafter cited in text).

17. Richard Chase, "Novelist Going Places," *Commentary* 20 (December 1955): 582.

18. *The Deer Park* (New York: G. P. Putnam's Sons, 1955), 111; hereafter cited in text as *TDP*.

19. See Max F. Schulz, *Radical Sophistication* (Athens: Ohio University Press, 1969), 81-90.

20. This point is anticipated by Podhoretz, "Embattled Vision," 385-86.

21. Like Munshin, Sammy was once an office boy and more than a little "shameless." Moreover, his dealings with Julian Blumberg are such that Munshin might have come upon his "writing" methods in the pages of Budd Schulberg's *What Makes Sammy Run?* (New York: Random House, 1941).

22. Cf. Mailer's remark to James Baldwin: "I want to know how power works . . . how it really works in detail" (James Baldwin, "The Black Boy Looks at the White Boy," *Esquire*, May 1961, 105).

23. Perhaps I should say Mailer's one totally successful *fictional* character. The Marilyn Monroe of *Marilyn: A Biography* (New York: Grosset & Dunlap, 1974) (hereafter cited in text as *M*) and Nicole Baker of *The Executioner's Song* (Boston: Little, Brown, 1979) (hereafter cited in text as *ES*) are wonderful characters, whether or not they correspond to the "real" women on whom they are based.

24. Mailer plays on this resemblance in his dramatized version of *The Deer Park*. After Eitel outlines his script, Munshin remarks, "Parenthethically, I can say this is a snitch from *Miss Lonelyhearts*." Eitel replies, "It was an influence" (*The Deer Park: A Play* [New York: Dial Press, 1967], 112).

25. See Ernest Hemingway, introduction to *A Farewell to Arms* (New York: Charles Scribner's Sons, 1948), viii.

Chapter Four

1. See Sheldon Sacks, *Fiction and the Shape of Belief* (Berkeley: University of California Press, 1964), especially chapters 1 and 5; hereafter cited in text.

2. For a very different view of Mailer's revisions, see Hershel Parker, *Flawed Texts and Verbal Icons: Literary Authority in American Fiction* (Evanston, Ill.: Northwestern University Press, 1984), 181-212. Parker argues that the revisions are extensive and very much for the worse. I disagree on both counts, though I do not think the revisions improved the novel much.

3. Granville Hicks, "A Literary Hoax?" *Saturday Review,* 20 March 1965, 24; Philip Rahv, "Crime without Punishment," *New York Review of Books,* 25 March 1965, 4 (hereafter cited in text); and Elizabeth Hardwick, "Bad Boy," *Partisan Review* 32 (Spring 1965), 291.

4. See, for example, Tom Wolfe, "Son of Crime and Punishment; or, How to Go Eight Fast Rounds with the Heavyweight Champ – and Lose," *Book Week,* 14 March 1965, 1, 10, 12-13 (hereafter cited in text); Joseph Epstein, "Norman X: The Literary Man's Cassius Clay," *New Republic,* 17 April 1965, 22-25; and Hyman, "Yummy Rump," 16-17.

5. *An American Dream* (New York: Dial Press, 1965), 8; hereafter cited in text as *AAD*.

6. "Mr. Mailer Interviews Himself," *New York Times Book Review,* 17 September 1967, 40; hereafter cited in text.

7. See John William Corrington, "An American Dreamer," *Chicago Review* 18 (1965): 61; Kaufmann, *Countdown,* 41; Laura Adams, *Existential Battles: The Growth of Norman Mailer* (Athens: Ohio University Press, 1976), 78 (hereafter cited in text); Radford, *Critical Study,* 101; and Stanley T. Gutman, *Mankind in Barbary: The Individual and Society in the Novels*

of Norman Mailer (Hanover, N.H.: University Press of New England, 1975), 95 (hereafter cited in text).

8. See John W. Aldridge, "The New Energy of Success," in *Norman Mailer: A Collection of Critical Essays,* ed. Braudy, 118.

9. See Leo Bersani, "The Interpretation of Dreams," *Partisan Review* 32 (Fall 1965): 603-8 (hereafter cited in text), and Nathan A. Scott, Jr., *Three American Moralists: Mailer, Bellow, and Trilling* (Notre Dame, Ind.: Notre Dame University Press, 1973), 56-70.

10. Vincent Canby, "When Irish Eyes Are Smiling, It's Norman Mailer," *New York Times,* 27 October 1968, 15.

11. Quoted in Kaufmann, *Countdown,* 44-45.

12. "A Short Public Notice," *Partisan Review* 32 (Spring 1965): 181.

13. John W. Aldridge, "The Big Comeback of Norman Mailer," *Life,* 19 March 1965, 12.

14. See *The Presidential Papers,* 266; *The Armies of the Night,* 38, 87; and *Existential Errands,* 104.

15. Quoted in Kaufmann, *Countdown,* 44.

16. See Adams, "Existential Aesthetics," 198.

17. See *The Presidential Papers,* 151, 160, 192, 213-15, 245-47, 295, and *Cannibals and Christians,* 312-75, especially 325, 363.

18. Brom Weber, "A Fear of Dying: Norman Mailer's *An American Dream,*" *Hollins Critic* 2 (June 1965): 1-11.

19. See Adams, "Existential Aesthetics," 199-201.

20. Solotaroff's discussion anticipates my own in a number of ways, but he tends to concentrate more specifically on the mixture of realistic and unrealistic techniques in *An American Dream.* Also, he does not extend his reservations to *Why Are We in Vietnam?*

21. *Why Are We in Vietnam?* (New York: G. P. Putnam's Sons, 1967), 38; hereafter cited in text as *WAW.*

22. See especially Richard Pearce, "Norman Mailer's *Why Are We in Vietnam?:* A Radical Critique of Frontier Values," *Modern Fiction Studies* 17 (Autumn 1971): 413, and Rubin Rabinovitz, "Myth and Animism in *Why Are We in Vietnam?,*" *Twentieth Century Literature* 20 (October 1974): 303.

23. See Solotaroff, *Down Mailer's Way,* 199; Gutman, *Mankind in Barbary,* 137-38; Radford, *Critical Study,* 38; and Richard D. Finholt, " 'Otherwise How Explain?': Norman Mailer's New Cosmology," *Modern Fiction Studies* 17 (Autumn 1971): 378-79.

24. As D. J. elegantly says, "[Y]ou never know what vision has been humping you through the night" (208).

25. Robert Langbaum, "Mailer's New Style," *Novel* 2 (Fall 1968): 77. See also Roger Ramsey, "Current and Recurrent: The Vietnam Novel," *Modern Fiction Studies* 17 (Autumn 1971): 427.

26. Kenneth Burke, *Counter-Statement* (Los Altos, Calif.: Hermes Publications, 1953), 124.

27. For more recent treatments of *An American Dream*, see Begiebing, *Acts of Regeneration*, 58-88; Andrew Gordon, *An American Dreamer: A Psychoanalytic Study of the Fiction of Norman Mailer* (Rutherford, N.J.: Fairleigh Dickinson University Press), 129-71; Parker, *Flawed Texts*, 181-212; and Nigel Leigh, *Radical Fictions and the Novels of Norman Mailer* (New York: St. Martin's Press, 1990), 84-118 (hereafter cited in text). All are attractive for somewhat different reasons. Gordon's psychoanalytic reading is excessive but continuously interesting. Parker's study of the revisions is controversial but meticulous. Begiebing and Leigh offer extremely convincing thematic readings (though I do find their conclusions excessively positive).

Chapter Five

1. *Of a Fire on the Moon* (Boston: Little, Brown, 1970), 7; hereafter cited in text as *FOM*.

2. *Miami and the Siege of Chicago* (New York: New American Library, 1968), 56; hereafter cited in text as *MSC*.

3. Mailer's distaste for statistics is most obvious in his foreword to *The Idol and the Octopus* (New York: Dell, 1968) (hereafter cited in text as *IAO*), in which he recommends the "position papers" in his collection *because* they offer no statistics (11).

4. A. Alvarez, "Reflections in a Bloodshot Eye," *New Statesman*, 20 September 1968, 351.

5. Mailer's later collections, *Existential Errands* (1972), *Pieces* (1982), and *Pontifications* (ed. J. Michael Lennon [Boston: Little, Brown, 1985]) (hereafter cited in text as *P*), lack the running commentary that distinguishes the earlier miscellanies. I also think they include fewer first-rate selections.

6. Rolo, review of *Advertisements for Myself*, 168; "What Might Have Been," 127; and "The Crack-Up," *Time*, 2 November 1959, 90.

7. Laura Adams presents a similar argument but draws very different conclusions; see *Existential Battles*, 27-64.

8. Phoebe Adams, review of *The Presidential Papers*, *Atlantic Monthly*, December 1963, 168.

9. Richard Gilman, "Why Mailer Wants to Be President," *New Republic*, 8 February 1964, 24.

10. Mailer's earlier "poems" are collected in *Deaths for the Ladies (and Other Disasters)*. None of his books is less deserving of serious analysis.

11. See *The Armies of the Night*, 124, 180, and 185.

12. I have reluctantly decided against treating Mailer's literary pieces in this chapter. I do, though, discuss Mailer's literary criticism in chapters 4 and 7.

13. See *Advertisements for Myself*, 340-41, 348.

14. The early essays are almost never discussed in connection with Mailer's nonfictional persona. For the best characterization of the later persona, see Chris Anderson, "Norman Mailer: The Record of a War," *Style as Argument: Contemporary American Nonfiction* (Carbondale, Ill.: Southern Illinois University Press, 1987), 82-132; hereafter cited in text.

13. F. Scott Fitzgerald, *The Crack-Up*, ed. Edmund Wilson (New York: New Directions, 1956), 75.

Chapter Six

1. Book 1 of *The Armies of the Night* was first published in *Harper's*, March 1968. Book 2 was later published in *Commentary*, April 1968.

2. For a good discussion of how Hemingway structured his book along these lines, see Carlos Baker, *Hemingway: The Writer as Artist*, 3d ed. revised (Princeton, N.J.: Princeton University Press, 1963), 169-71.

3. George Plimpton, "The Story behind a Nonfiction Novel," *New York Times Book Review*, 16 January 1966, 41; hereafter cited in text.

4. David Galloway, "Why the Chickens Came Home to Roost in Holcomb, Kansas: Truman Capote's *In Cold Blood*," in *Truman Capote's "In Cold Blood": A Critical Handbook*, ed. Irving Malin (Belmont, Calif.: Wadsworth, 1968), 155-56.

5. Miller is almost certainly more "accurate" than Capote, for the simple reason that he usually writes about what he experienced firsthand, while Capote must often rely on witnesses who do not agree on points major and minor. For a revealing discussion of Capote's dilemma in choosing among conflicting sources, see Phillip K. Tompkins, "In Cold Fact," *Esquire*, June 1966, 125, 127, 166-71; hereafter cited in text.

6. Tompkins shows that Capote, in his portrait of Perry Smith, includes episodes and details that are at best unreliable; see Tompkins, "In Cold Blood," 127, 166-71.

7. Tony Tanner, "Death in Kansas," *Spectator*, 18 March 1966, 331.

8. See *The Armies of the Night*, 59-60, 120-21, 260-62, 272-76. Mailer also cites sources in order to refute them; see 3-4, 214-15.

9. See Truman Capote, *In Cold Blood* (New York: Random House, 1965), 298-302; hereafter cited in text.

10. Capote has described these pieces as just such a training ground for *In Cold Blood*; see Plimpton, "The Story," 2.

11. Tom Wolfe, *The Electric Kool-Aid Acid Test* (New York: Bantam Books, 1969), 371.

12. This distinction is a bit crude, for certain fictions are shaped by rhetorical ends; nonetheless, most novels are not so structured. My argument again relies on Sacks's *Fiction and the Shape of Belief*, especially chapter 1.

13. But see (a) Solotaroff's intelligent comparison of the two works in *Down Mailer's Way*, 219-22, and (b) Gordon O. Taylor's discussion of the two writers, "Of Adams and Aquarius," *American Literature* 46 (March 1974): 68-82.

14. D. W. Brogan, introduction to *The Education of Henry Adams*, by Henry Adams (Boston: Houghton Mifflin, 1961), v.

15. I suppose that time has come when notes must identify the once-familiar players. SDS stands for Students for a Democratic Society.

16. See Charles Reich, *The Greening of America* (New York: Random House, 1970), and John W. Aldridge, *In the Country of the Young* (New York: Harper's Magazine Press, 1970).

17. See Wayne Booth, "Metaphor as Rhetoric: The Problem of Evaluation," *Critical Inquiry* 5 (Autumn 1978): 58-69, and James Phelan, *Reading People, Reading Plots* (Chicago: University of Chicago Press, 1989), 197.

18. See J. Michael Lennon, "Norman Mailer," in *Contemporary Authors Bibliographical Series* (Detroit: Gale, 1986), 1:246; hereafter cited in text as Lennon 1986b.

Chapter Seven

1. See *The Faith of Graffiti* (New York: Praeger, 1974).

2. Warner Berthoff, "Witness and Testament: Two Contemporary Classics," in *Aspects of Narrative*, ed. J. Hillis Miller (New York: Columbia University Press, 1971), 196.

3. Jack Richardson, "The Aesthetics of Norman Mailer," in *Norman Mailer: The Man and His Work*, ed. Lucid, 199.

4. For examples of this oft-repeated claim, see *Advertisements for Myself*, 93, and *The Armies of the Night*, 25.

5. See Frank Kermode, *The Sense of an Ending: Studies in the Theory of Fiction* (New York: Oxford University Press, 1967).

6. *St. George and the Godfather* (New York: New American Library, 1972), 3.

7. See Richard Poirier, "The Ups and Downs of Mailer," *New Republic*, 23 January 1971, 23-26.

8. For a very different and more positive reading of this book, see Alvin B. Kernan, "The Taking of the Moon: The Struggle of the Poetic and Scientific Myths in Norman Mailer's *Of a Fire on the Moon*," *The Imaginary Library: An Essay on Literature and Society* (Princeton, N.J.: Princeton University Press, 1982), 130-61.

9. I do not mean to imply that Mailer was to abandon entirely the reporting of historical events. *St. George and the Godfather* and *The Fight* (Boston: Little, Brown, 1975) (hereafter cited in text as *TF*), though not Mailer's finest efforts, testify to his continuing attraction to this kind of reportage even as he was seeking other outlets for his method.

10. Brigid Brophy, "Meditations on Norman Mailer, by Norman Mailer, against the Day a Norman Mailest Comes Along," *New York Times Book Review*, 23 May 1971, 1.

11. For Millett's discussion of these writers, see *Sexual Politics* (New York: Equinox Books, 1971), 237-361.

12. For a more enthusiastic and thorough discussion of *The Prisoner of Sex*, see Peter Balbert, "From *Lady Chatterley's Lover* to *The Deer Park*: Lawrence, Mailer, and the Dialectic of Erotic Risk," *Studies in the Novel* 22 (Spring 1990): 67-81; hereafter cited in text.

13. As Laura Adams points out, Zolotow's complaint was that Mailer had quoted more passages than his publishers paid for, not that Mailer had "stolen" his work. Adams also remarks that Zolotow eventually apologized for the accusation; see Adams, *Existential Battles*, n. 181.

14. Ingrid Bengis, "Monroe According to Mailer: One Legend Feeds on Another," *Ms.*, 11 October 1973, 47.

15. *Genius and Lust: A Journey through the Major Writings of Henry Miller* (New York: Grove Press, 1976), x; hereafter cited in text as *GL*.

16. Mailer's first comments on Miller appeared in *Cannibals and Christians*, 198. More recently he published extended discussions of Miller in *The Prisoner of Sex*, 73-92, and in *American Review 24*, ed. Theodore Solotaroff (New York: Bantam, 1976), 1-40. Both discussions are incorporated into Mailer's commentary in *Genius and Lust*.

17. Mailer's more recent nonfiction has been a much more popular subject than his early nonfiction. Almost all general treatments address the books from *The Armies of the Night* to the present. Besides the essays by Berthoff, Kernan, and Anderson already cited, see especially the works by Mas'ud Zavarzadeh, John Hollowell, John Hellmann, and Ronald Weber that are listed in the Selected Bibliography.

Chapter Eight

1. I draw this conclusion from J. Michael Lennon's "A Ranking of Reviews of Mailer's Major Works," an unpublished guide to more than 300 reviews; hereafter cited in text.

2. Robert Begiebing, *Toward a New Synthesis: John Fowles, John Gardner, Norman Mailer* (Ann Arbor, Mich.: UMI Research Press, 1989), 120; hereafter cited in text.

3. J. Michael Lennon, ed., *Conversations with Norman Mailer* (Jackson: University Press of Mississippi, 1988), 139; hereafter cited in text.

4. "PW Interviews: Norman Mailer," *Publishers Weekly*, 8 October 1979, 8; hereafter cited in text.

5. For these facts, see Lennon, *Conversations with Norman Mailer*, 267; Peter Manso, *Mailer: His Life and Times* (New York: Simon & Schuster, 1985), 584; and Mailer's afterword to *The Executioner's Song*, 1024.

6. See John Hersey, "The Legend on the License," *Yale Review* 70 (October 1980): 1-25; hereafter cited in text.

7. Tom Wolfe and E. W. Johnson, eds., *The New Journalism* (New York: Harper & Row, 1973), 31-35.

8. See, respectively, Lennon, *Conversations with Norman Mailer*, 234, and Lawrence Grobel, ed. *Conversations with Capote* (New York: New American Library, 1985), 116 (hereafter cited in text).

9. For Capote's use of omniscient narration, see John Hellmann, *Fables of Fact* (Urbana: University of Illinois Press, 1981), 20 (hereafter cited in text), and Phyllis Frus McCord, "The Ideology of Form: The Nonfiction Novel," *Genre* 19 (Spring 1986): 71 (hereafter cited in text). For Capote's tendency to avoid entering his characters' minds, see Anderson, *Style as Argument*, 53.

10. See Tompkins, "In Cold Fact," 125, 127, 166-68, and 170-71; the quotation about Perry Smith is on 171.

11. See Jack De Bellis, "Visions and Revisions: Truman Capote's *In Cold Blood*," *Journal of Modern Literature* 7 (1979): 519-36.

12. Bell Gale Chevigny, "Twice-Told Tales and the Meaning of History: Testimonial Novels by Miguel Barnet and Norman Mailer," *Centennial Review* 30 (Spring 1986): 183; hereafter cited in text.

13. Steven G. Kellman, "Mailer's Strains of Fact," *Southwest Review* 68 (Spring 1983): 130.

14. Quoted in Ted Morgan, review of *The Executioner's Song*, *Saturday Review*, 10 November 1979, 57-58.

15. Earl Rovit, "True Life Story," *Nation*, 20 October 1979, 378.

16. The exception here is Hersey ("The Legend on the License"), who does question Mailer's accuracy. Others argue that everything in *The Executioner's Song* is fictive and that Mailer's primary point is precisely the fictionality of all so-called nonfiction. I address this more common reading in the concluding section of this chapter.

17. Richard Stern, "Missingeria and Literary Health," *Georgia Review* 34 (Summer 1980): 422-27.

18. Joan Didion, " 'I Want to Go Ahead and Do It,' " in *Critical Essays on Norman Mailer*, ed. Lennon, 82; hereafter cited in text.

19. Mailer's title has an interesting history. He first used it as the title of a poem published in a magazine called *Fuck You* in 1964; the poem was reprinted in *Cannibals and Christians*, 131-32; and in 1975 Mailer used the title again as the title for chapter 15 of *The Fight*. Though others have tried

to relate Mailer's meaning in these earlier works to *The Executioner's Song,*
I can see no significant connection. The title does work something like
Capote's does in *In Cold Blood,* for in each case the title refers both to the
killers who execute their victims and to the social order that in turn exe-
cutes the killers.

20. John Garvey, " 'The Executioner's Song,' " in *Modern Critical
Views: Norman Mailer,* ed. Harold Bloom (New York: Chelsea House,
1986), 140.

21. "Letters: Norman Mailer," *Hollywood Reporter,* 3 January 1980, 3.

22. For other brief but good discussions of Schiller, see Kellman,
"Strains of Fact," 132 and Wenke, *Mailer's America,* 211.

23. See especially 590, 677-78, and 762-63 of *The Executioner's Song.*

24. Mailer notes this point himself; see Lennon, *Conversations with
Norman Mailer,* 241.

25. Mark Edmundson makes this point in his forthcoming essay on *The
Executioner's Song,* "Romantic Self-Creations: Mailer and Gilmore in *The
Executioner's Song*"; see 1992 issues of *Contemporary Literature.* William
Buckley sees a similar bias in Gilmore's favor in the book's final sections;
see Lennon, *Conversations with Norman Mailer,* 229-30. For a contrary
view, see Begiebing, *Acts of Regeneration,* 191.

26. For the best discussion of Mailer's insistence on Gilmore's mysteri-
ousness, see Robert M. Arlett, "The Veiled Fist of a Master Executioner,"
Criticism 29 (Spring 1987): 215-31.

27. Robert L. McLaughlin, "History vs. Fiction: The Self-Destruction of
The Executioner's Song," *Clio* 17 (Spring 1988): 237.

28. Judith A. Scheffler, "The Prisoner as Creator in *The Executioner's
Song,*" in *Modern Critical Views: Norman Mailer,* ed. Bloom, 184.

29. Edmundson ("Romantic Self-Creations") includes an interesting
discussion of Gilmore as hipster.

30. See Wenke, *Mailer's America,* 201-2.

31. For good discussions of Mailer's affinities with the American roman-
tics, see Cowan, "Americanness," in *Critical Essays on Norman Mailer,* ed.
Lennon; "Mailer's Cosmology," in the same source; and Wenke, *Mailer's
America.*

Chapter Nine

1. At the end of *Ancient Evenings* (Boston: Little, Brown, 1983), 709
(hereafter cited in text as *AE*), Mailer dates the writing of the book from
1972 to 1982; occasionally he and others refer to its inception in 1971. In
Lennon, *Conversations with Norman Mailer,* 365, Mailer refers to writing
Tough Guys Don't Dance (New York: Random House, 1984) (hereafter
cited in text as *TGDD*) in two months. Unless otherwise noted, page references in this chapter are to this edition.

2. Harold Bloom, "Norman in Egypt: *Ancient Evenings,*" in *Modern Critical Views: Norman Mailer,* ed. Bloom, 195; hereafter cited in text.

3. Philip Kuberski, "The Metaphysics of Postmodern Death: Mailer's *Ancient Evenings* and Merrill's *The Changing Light at Sandover,*" *ELH* 56 (Spring 1989): 223; hereafter cited in text.

4. See Budge as quoted by Kuberski, "Metaphysics," 239.

5. "Unscientific" is Mailer's own word; see Lennon, *Conversations with Norman Mailer,* 326.

6. Richard Poirier, "In Pyramid and Palace," in *Critical Essays on Norman Mailer,* ed. Lennon, 82; hereafter cited in text.

7. See Lennon's introduction to *Critical Essays on Norman Mailer,* ed. Lennon, 18. Leigh, in *Radical Fictions,* sees these examples as "recklessly" expanding on Mailer's sources, 169.

8. See John T. Irwin, *American Hieroglyphics* (New Haven, Conn.: Yale University Press, 1980). At times, of course, such writers as Emerson, Poe, and Whitman seem to point beyond metaphoric resurrection to actual reincarnation. In this as in many other ways they anticipate Mailer.

9. See *Pontifications,* 22, 24.

10. For Mailer's confession of weakness with plot or story, see *Pontifications,* 174.

11. Judith Fetterley, *The Resisting Reader: A Feminist Approach to American Fiction* (Bloomington: Indiana University Press, 1978), 175-76.

12. See Plimpton, *Writers at Work,* 265, and Lennon, "Mailer's Radical Bridge," n. 186.

13. For more on the Melville-Mailer connection, see especially Lennon, "Mailer's Cosmology."

14. For Mailer's comments on the "risks" he took with this book, see Lennon, *Conversations with Norman Mailer,* 325.

15. See *Advertisements for Myself,* 512-32.

16. See *The Presidential Papers,* 81-98.

17. Lennon documents this hostile response in his "A Ranking of Reviews." The average "score" for *Tough Guys* is the lowest for any Mailer book.

18. For the writing of *The Armies of the Night,* see *Pontifications,* 152. For the writing of *Why Are We in Vietnam?,* see Lennon, *Conversations with Norman Mailer,* 106. Faulkner's motives for writing *As I Lay Dying* are discussed by Dianne L. Cox, introduction to *William Faulkner's "As I Lay Dying": A Critical Casebook,* ed. Dianne L. Cox (New York: Garland Press, 1985), xi-xv.

19. See John G. Cawelti, *Adventure, Mystery, and Romance* (Chicago: University of Chicago Press, 1976), 18; hereafter cited in text.

20. Raymond Chandler, "The Simple Art of Murder," in *The Art of the Mystery Story,* ed. Howard Haycraft (New York: Carroll & Graf, 1983), 225; hereafter cited in text.

21. Robert Frost, "Design," *Complete Poems of Robert Frost* (New York: Holt, Rinehart & Winston, 1949), 396.

22. Dorothy Sayers, "The Omnibus of Crime," in *Art of the Mystery Story,* ed. Haycraft, 72.

23. George Grella, "The Hard-boiled Detective Novel," in *Detective Fiction: A Collection of Critical Essays,* ed. Robin W. Winks (Woodstock, Vt.: Foul Play Press, 1988), 112; hereafter cited in text.

24. Raymond Chandler, introduction to *Trouble Is My Business* (New York: Ballantine Books, 1972), ix. Chandler wrote this introduction in 1950.

25. Paul Skenazy, *James M. Cain* (New York: Continuum, 1989), 30.

26. For this point, see Jon Tuska, *Dark Cinema: American Film Noir in Cultural Perspective* (Westport, Conn.: Greenwood Press, 1984), xxi; hereafter cited in text.

27. Alfred Appel, Jr., *Nabokov's Dark Cinema* (New York: Oxford University Press, 1974), 196.

28. Robert G. Porfirio, "No Way Out: Existential Motifs in the Film Noir," *Sight and Sound* 45 (1974): 217.

29. J. P. Telotte, *Voices in the Dark: The Narrative Patterns of Film Noir* (Urbana: University of Illinois Press, 1989), 53; hereafter cited in text.

30. Mailer cites *The Asphalt Jungle* as a "very good" film in *Maidstone: A Mystery* (New York: New American Library, 1971), 144; hereafter cited in text as *MAM.* He goes on to praise Huston's *The Maltese Falcon* (1941) as well; see *Maidstone,* 145.

31. See especially Wenke, *Mailer's America,* 235-36.

Selected Bibliography

PRIMARY SOURCES

Fiction

An American Dream. New York: Dial Press, 1965.
Ancient Evenings. Boston: Little, Brown, 1983.
Barbary Shore. New York: Holt, Rinehart & Winston, 1951.
The Deer Park. New York: G. P. Putnam's Sons, 1955.
Harlot's Ghost. New York: Random House, 1991.
The Naked and the Dead. New York: Holt, Rinehart & Winston, 1948.
The Short Fiction of Norman Mailer. New York: Dell, 1967.
Tough Guys Don't Dance. New York: Random House, 1984.
A Transit to Narcissus. New York: Howard Fertig, 1978.
Why Are We in Vietnam? New York: G. P. Putnam's Sons, 1967.

Nonfiction

The Armies of the Night: History as a Novel/The Novel as History. New York: New American Library, 1968.
The Executioner's Song. Boston: Little, Brown, 1979.
The Faith of Graffiti. New York: Praeger, 1974.
The Fight. Boston: Little, Brown, 1975.
Of a Fire on the Moon. Boston: Little, Brown, 1970.
Genius and Lust: A Journey through the Major Writings of Henry Miller. New York: Grove Press, 1976.
King of the Hill. New York: New American Library, 1971.
Marilyn: A Biography. New York: Grosset & Dunlap, 1973.
Miami and the Siege of Chicago. New York: New American Library, 1968.
The Prisoner of Sex. Boston: Little, Brown, 1971.
St. George and the Godfather. New York: New American Library, 1972.
Some Honorable Men: Political Conventions, 1960-1972. Boston: Little, Brown, 1976.
The White Negro: Superficial Reflections on the Hipster. San Francisco: City Lights Books, 1957.
Of Women and Their Elegance. New York: Simon & Schuster, 1980.

231

Miscellanies

Advertisements for Myself. New York: G. P. Putnam's Sons, 1959.

Cannibals and Christians. New York: Dial Press, 1966.

Existential Errands. Boston: Little, Brown, 1972.

Pieces. Boston: Little, Brown, 1985.

Pontifications. Ed. J. Michael Lennon. Boston: Little, Brown, 1985.

The Presidential Papers. New York: G. P. Putnam's Sons, 1963.

Other Writings

The Bullfight: A Photographic Narrative with Text by Norman Mailer. New York: CBS Legacy Collection Book, 1967.

Deaths for the Ladies (and Other Disasters). New York: G. P. Putnam's Sons, 1962.

The Deer Park: A Play. New York: Dial Press, 1967.

The Idol and the Octopus: Political Writings by Norman Mailer on the Kennedy and Johnson Administrations. New York: New American Library, 1968.

Maidstone: A Mystery. New York: New American Library, 1971.

SECONDARY SOURCES

The literature on Mailer is extensive, and so I have had to be quite selective. I have included all books published on Mailer and those essays I think most useful for the study of his works. The most complete bibliography (through the early 1970s) is Laura Adams's *Norman Mailer: A Comprehensive Bibliography* (Metuchen, N.J.: Scarecrow Press, 1974). The best recent guide is J. Michael Lennon, "Norman Mailer," in *Contemporary Authors Bibliographical Series* (Detroit: Gale, 1986), 1:219-60.

Books

Adams, Laura. *Existential Battles: The Growth of Norman Mailer.* Athens: Ohio University Press, 1976. Concerned with the evolution of Mailer's thought in relation to his art. An informed study but less useful than Solotaroff's earlier book on the subject.

_____, Ed. *Will the Real Norman Mailer Please Stand Up?* Port Washington, N.Y.: Kennikat Press, 1974. A good collection that includes several previously unpublished essays.

Bailey, Jennifer. *Norman Mailer: Quick-Change Artist.* New York: Barnes & Noble, 1979. An intelligent book that seems to offer no real thesis about Mailer's career.

Begiebing, Robert J. *Acts of Regeneration: Allegory and Archetype in the Works of Norman Mailer.* Columbia: University of Missouri Press, 1980. The best reading of Mailer's novels as relatively subtle allegories. A formal study that complements Solotaroff's analysis of Mailer's philosophy.

Bloom, Harold, ed. *Modern Critical Views: Norman Mailer.* New Haven, Conn.: Chelsea House, 1986. A good sample of criticism early and late. Bloom's "Norman in Egypt: *Ancient Evening,*" 193-200, is an extremely suggestive review of *Ancient Evenings.* Unreliable on a few textual details, but very good on Mailer's relationship to his ancient Egyptian materials. Robert Merrill, in "The Armies of the Night," 127-37, contributes a formal analysis stressing the ways in which books 1 and 2 are related.

Braudy, Leo, ed. *Norman Mailer: A Collection of Critical Essays.* Englewood Cliffs, N.J.: Prentice Hall, 1972. Perhaps the best collection of essays on Mailer. Includes two excellent essays published here for the first time: Michael Cowan's "The Americanness of Norman Mailer" and Leo Braudy's "Norman Mailer: The Pride of Vulnerability."

Bufithis, Philip H. *Norman Mailer.* New York: Ungar, 1978. An extremely well-written general introduction. Almost always sensitive to Mailer's intentions and achievement.

Cohen, Sandy. *Norman Mailer's Novels.* Amsterdam: Rodopi, 1979. A brief and not terribly original survey of the novels.

Ehrlich, Robert. *Norman Mailer: The Radical as Hipster.* Metuchen, N.J.: Scarecrow Press, 1978. An interesting study that sees all of Mailer's works as offshoots of "The White Negro." The complexity of Mailer's development is underestimated here.

Flaherty, Joe. *Managing Mailer.* New York: Coward-McCann, 1969. An amusing account of Mailer's mayoralty race in 1969.

Foster, Richard. *Norman Mailer.* Minneapolis: University of Minnesota Press, 1968. This pamphlet is probably the best short introduction to Mailer's career through 1967.

Gordon, Andrew. *An American Dreamer: A Psychoanalytic Study of the Fiction of Norman Mailer.* Rutherford, N.J.: Fairleigh Dickinson Press, 1980. An intelligent, thoroughgoing psychoanalytic reading of the novels. Interesting but narrow.

Gutman, Stanley T. *Mankind in Barbary: The Individual and Society in the Novels of Norman Mailer.* Hanover, N.H.: University Press of New England, 1975. Another attempt to explain Mailer's thematic development that merely confirms Solotaroff's insights.

Kaufmann, Donald L. *Norman Mailer: The Countdown.* Carbondale: Southern Illinois University Press, 1969. The most uneven full-length study of Mailer. Weak on the novels but pioneering on Mailer's social and political ideas.

Leeds, Barry H. *The Structured Vision of Norman Mailer.* New York: New York University Press, 1969. Develops the unconvincing thesis that

Mailer's canon reveals a consistent evolution from "pessimistic" to "positive" themes.

Leigh, Nigel. *Radical Fictions and the Novels of Norman Mailer.* New York: St. Martin's Press, 1990. A fascinating if somewhat abstract review of the political implications of Mailer's novels through *Ancient Evenings.*

Lennon, J. Michael, ed. *Conversations with Norman Mailer.* Jackson: University Press of Mississippi, 1988. An indispensable collection of 34 major interviews in which Mailer discusses virtually all of his works.

_____, ed. *Critical Essays on Norman Mailer.* Boston: G. K. Hall, 1986. The most recent and the most useful collection of criticism. Lennon's introduction, 1-39, is comprehensive and authoritative, and his "Mailer's Cosmology," 145-56, is an excellent review of Mailer's philosophical commitments. Joan Didion's " 'I Want to Go Ahead and Do It,' "78-82, is perhaps the most sympathetic early response to *The Executioner's Song* and is especially good on the book's women. Robert F. Lucid's "Prolegomenon to a Biography of Mailer," 174-84, is a provocative overview of Mailer's career from a biographical point of view, soon to be embodied in the authorized biography. "In Pyramid and Palace," 82-89, by Richard Poirier, is an excellent, seminal review of *Ancient Evenings.*

Lucid, Robert F., ed. *Norman Mailer: The Man and His Work.* Boston: Little, Brown, 1971. A very useful collection of essays and reviews that first appeared in the 1960s.

Manso, Peter. *Mailer: His Life and Times.* New York: Simon & Schuster, 1985. This "oral biography" includes a wealth of interesting information in the form of unassimilated interviews. A collection of such interviews rather than a biography.

Middlebrook, Jonathan. *Mailer and the Times of His Time.* San Francisco: Bay Books, 1976. An unpersuasive defense of the notion that Mailer is a latter-day transcendentalist.

Mills, Hilary. *Mailer: A Biography.* New York: Empire Books, 1982. A sympathetic but disappointing study informed by no thesis or even point of view about Mailer's career.

Poirier, Richard. *Norman Mailer.* New York: Viking Press, 1972. A difficult study arguing that Mailer's virtues are those of a stylist and "performer," not those of a literary craftsman. A first-rate discussion despite its dubious thesis.

Radford, Jean. *Norman Mailer: A Critical Study.* New York: Harper & Row, 1975. Yet another study of Mailer's intellectual development. Intelligent but insufficiently original.

Solotaroff, Robert. *Down Mailer's Way.* Urbana: University of Illinois Press, 1974. The most thorough treatment of Mailer's intellectual growth.

The best book on Mailer and one of the better books on any contemporary American writer.

Weatherby, W. J. *Squaring Off: Mailer vs. Baldwin.* New York: Mason/Charter, 1977. Traces Mailer's personal and literary relations with James Baldwin. Interesting for its biographical, not its literary, implications.

Wenke, Joseph. *Mailer's America.* Hanover, N.H.: University Press of New England, 1987. An engaging, informed discussion of Mailer's preoccupation with America. Includes shrewd assessments of the later novels.

Book Chapters and Articles

Anderson, Chris. "Norman Mailer: The Record of a War." In *Style as Argument: Contemporary American Nonfiction*, 82-132. Carbondale: Southern Illinois University Press, 1987. The most extensive – and persuasive – treatment of Mailer's style.

Arlett, Robert M. "The Veiled Fist of a Master Executioner." *Criticism* 29 (Spring 1987): 215-31. The best discussion of how Mailer handles Gary Gilmore in *The Executioner's Song.*

Balbert, Peter. "From *Lady Chatterley's Lover* to *The Deer Park*: Lawrence, Mailer, and the Dialectic of Erotic Risk." *Studies in the Novel* 22 (Spring 1990): 67-81. An excellent analysis of Mailer's affinities with Lawrence.

Begiebing, Robert J. "Norman Mailer: The Magician as Tragic Hero." In *Toward a New Synthesis: John Fowles, John Gardner, Norman Mailer.* Ann Arbor, Mich.: UMI Research Press, 1989, 87-125. Easily the most detailed and reliable reading of *Ancient Evenings.*

Berthoff, Warner. "Witness and Testament: Two Contemporary Classics." In *Aspects of Narrative*, ed. J. Hillis Miller, 173-98. New York: Columbia University Press, 1971. The second half of this essay offers the best published discussion of *The Armies of the Night.*

Dickstein, Morris. *Gates of Eden: American Culture in the Sixties.* New York: Basic Books, 1977. Includes several discussions of Mailer's works. Especially good on the nonfiction.

Fetterley, Judith. "An American Dream: 'Hula, Hula,' Said the Witches." In *The Resisting Reader: A Feminist Approach to American Fiction*, 154-89. Bloomington: Indiana University Press, 1978. An extensive attack on *An American Dream.* Perverse but forcefully formulated.

Foster, Richard. "Mailer and the Fitzgerald Tradition." *Novel* 1 (Spring 1968): 219-30. An impressive attempt to define the nature of Mailer's romanticism.

Hellmann, John. "Journalism as Nonfiction: Norman Mailer's Strategy for Mimesis and Interpretation." In *Fables of Fact: The New Journalism as*

New Fiction, 35-65. Athens: Ohio University Press, 1980. Perhaps the best treatment of Mailer as a so-called New Journalist.

Hersey, John. "The Legend on the License." *Yale Review* 70 (October 1980): 1-25. Includes a fascinating (if literal-minded) attack on the "veracity" of *The Executioner's Song*.

Hollowell, John. "Mailer's Vision: History as a Novel, the Novel as History." In *Fact and Fiction: The New Journalism and the Nonfiction Novel*, 87-125. Chapel Hill: University of North Carolina Press, 1977. A very reliable account of Mailer's nonfiction in the late 1960s and early 1970s.

Horn, Bernard. "Ahab and Ishmael at War: The Presence of *Moby-Dick* in *The Naked and the Dead*." *American Quarterly* 34 (Fall 1982): 379-95. The most thorough treatment of Melville's influence on Mailer's first novel.

Kaufmann, Donald L. "The Long Happy Life of Norman Mailer." *Modern Fiction Studies* 17 (Autumn 1971): 347-59. A first-rate discussion of Mailer and Hemingway that emphasizes the differences between these often-associated writers.

Kernan, Alvin B. "The Taking of the Moon: The Struggle of the Poetic and Scientific Myths in Norman Mailer's *Of a Fire on the Moon*." In *The Imaginary Library: An Essay on Literature and Society*, 130-61. Princeton, N.J.: Princeton University Press, 1982. The best and most extensive discussion of this text.

Kuberski, Philip. "The Metaphysics of Postmodern Death: Mailer's *Ancient Evenings* and Merrill's *The Changing Light at Sandover*." *ELH* 56 (Spring 1989): 229-54. Very good in describing Mailer's attraction to an "unscientific" worldview. A bit too unconcerned with the book's specific structure.

Langbaum, Robert. "Mailer's New Style." *Novel* 2 (Fall 1968): 69-78. One of the first and more impressive attempts to argue that *An American Dream* and *Why Are We in Vietnam?* represent a viable new "style" for Mailer's fiction.

Lennon, J. Michael. "Mailer's Radical Bridge." *Journal of Narrative Technique* 7 (Fall 1977): 170-88. A good discussion of point of view in Mailer, especially as it relates to his thought.

_____. "Mailer's Sarcophagus: The Artist, the Media and the 'Wad.'" *Modern Fiction Studies* 23 (Summer 1977): 179-87. A shrewd review of Mailer's conception of his audience as it helps to shape his work.

Lucid, Robert F. "Norman Mailer: The Artist as Fantasy Figure." *Massachusetts Review* 15 (Autumn 1974): 581-95. One of the best studies of Mailer's conception of the artist.

_____. "Three Public Performances: Fitzgerald, Hemingway, Mailer." *American Scholar* 43 (Summer 1974): 447-66. An extremely well-written essay that examines the nature of Mailer's public "legend."

McCord, Phyllis Frus. "The Ideology of Form: The Nonfiction Novel." *Genre* 19 (Spring 1986): 59-79. An interesting essay that stresses – perhaps excessively – the fictionality of *The Executioner's Song*.

Merrill, Robert. "Mailer's Sad Comedy: *The Executioner's Song*." *Texas Studies in Literature and Language* 34 (Spring 1992): 129-48. A general reassessment of *The Executioner's Song*.

_____. "Mailer's *Tough Guys Don't Dance* and the Detective Traditions." Forthcoming in *Critique*. An extended critical discussion in which *Tough Guys* is placed within several detective traditions.

_____. "Norman Mailer's Early Nonfiction: The Art of Self-Revelation." *Western Humanities Review* 28 (Winter 1974): 1-12. A study of Mailer's emerging persona in the essays preceding *The Armies of the Night*.

Miller, James E, Jr. "The Creation of Women: Confessions of a Shaken Liberal." *Centennial Review* 18 (Summer 1974): 231-47. Includes an unsympathetic discussion of Mailer's quarrel with Kate Millett.

Muste, John M. "Norman Mailer and John Dos Passos: The Question of Influence." *Modern Fiction Studies* 17 (Autumn 1971): 361-74. A perceptive analysis of *The Naked and the Dead* that radically qualifies the common view that Dos Passos was a major influence on Mailer's book.

Olster, Stacey. "The Transition to Post-Modernism: Norman Mailer and a New Frontier in Fiction." In *Reminiscence and Re-creation in Contemporary American Fiction*, 36-71. New York: Cambridge University Press, 1989. A very perceptive thematic reading that sees Mailer replacing a millenial with an existential perspective.

Parker, Hershel. "Norman Mailer's Revision of the *Esquire* Version of *An American Dream* and the Aesthetic Problem of 'Built-in Intentionality.' " In *Flawed Texts and Verbal Icons: Literary Authority in American Fiction*, 181-212. Evanston, Ill.: Northwestern University Press, 1984. An exquisitely detailed study of Mailer's revisions of *An American Dream*. Argues that the revisions effectively disfigured a major novel – a very difficult conclusion to accept.

Pizer, Donald. "Norman Mailer: *The Naked and the Dead*." In *Twentieth Century American Literary Naturalism: An Interpretation*, 90-114. Carbondale: Southern Illinois University Press, 1982. Perhaps the best single study of Mailer's first novel. Emphasizes Mailer's complex connections with the naturalistic tradition.

Podhoretz, Norman. "Norman Mailer: The Embattled Vision." *Partisan Review* 26 (Summer 1959): 371-91. The first general essay on Mailer and still one of the better assessments.

Rother, James, "Mailer's 'O'Shaugnessy Chronicle': A Speculative Autopsy."
     Critique 19 (1978): 21-39. An interesting if unpersuasive attempt to
     trace Mailer's failure to continue the saga of Sergius O'Shaugnessy to
     his reading of Lawrence Durrell's *Alexandria Quartet*.

Schloss, Carol. "Norman Mailer and Combat Photography: Exposure under
     Fire." In *In Visible Light: Photography and the American Writer, 1840-
     1940*, 233-49. New York: Oxford University Press, 1987. An engaging
     attempt to see Mailer's experience in interpreting aerial photographs
     as pushing him toward literary perspectivism. Suggestive but finally
     unpersuasive.

Schrader, George A. "Norman Mailer and the Despair of Defiance." *Yale
     Review* 51 (December 1961): 267-80. A rigorous attack on the philo-
     sophical assumptions underlying Mailer's hipsterism.

Tanner, Tony. "On the Parapet (Norman Mailer)." In *City of Words: Ameri-
     can Fiction, 1950-1970*, 344-71. New York: Harper & Row, 1971. The
     best single essay on Mailer's novels. Devoted mainly to Mailer's evolv-
     ing themes.

Taylor, Gordon O. "Of Adams and Aquarius." *American Literature* 46
     (March 1974): 68-82. A fine study of *The Education of Henry Adams*
     and *Of a Fire on the Moon*. Traces remarkable parallels between the
     two books.

Trilling, Diana. "The Radical Moralism of Norman Mailer." In *Claremont
     Essays*, 175-202. New York: Harcourt Brace Jovanovich, 1962. Like
     Podhoretz's essay, an early study of enduring value. Focuses on Mailer's
     passionate commitment to ideas.

Waldron, Randall H. "The Naked, the Dead, and the Machine: A New Look
     at Norman Mailer's First Novel." *PMLA* 87 (March 1972): 271-77. An
     interesting reassessment of *The Naked and the Dead*. Marred by its
     insistence that Mailer's intentions were those of a conventional liberal.

Weber, Ronald. *The Literature of Fact: Literary Nonfiction in American
     Writing*. Athens: Ohio University Press, 1980. Includes many brief dis-
     cussions of Mailer's nonfiction. Somewhat introductory but very reli-
     able.

Wilson, Raymond J., III. "Control and Freedom in *The Naked and the
     Dead*." *Texas Studies in Literature and Language* 28 (Summer 1986):
     164-81. A revisionary piece that stresses the "existential" elements in
     Mailer's first novel. Concludes that *The Naked and the Dead* is much
     less pessimistic than is usually assumed.

Zavarzadeh, Mas'ud. *The Mythopoeic Reality: The Postwar American Non-
     fiction Novel*. Urbana: University of Illinois Press, 1976. *The Armies of
     the Night* is used throughout as an example of a nonfiction novel in
     which authorial interpretation is consciously eschewed. A very strange
     thesis but argued with great energy.

Index

Abbott, Jack Henry, 8
Adams, Henry, 116
Adams, Laura, 211-12, 232
Aesop, 80
Alexander, Sidney, 38
Aldridge, John, 17, 18, 64-65, 67, 70
Allingham, Margery, 193
Alvarez, A., 84
"American Scholar, The" (Ralph Waldo Emerson), 177
Anderson, Chris, 155, 160, 235
Arlett, Robert M., 235
Arnold, Matthew, 124
As I Lay Dying (William Faulkner), 191
Asphalt Jungle, The (film), 202
Auden, W. H., ix
Austen, Jane, 17, 67

Bailey, Jennifer, 232
Balbert, Peter, 204, 235
Baldwin, James, 84, 92, 130
Barth, John, 81
Beckett, Samuel, ix
Begiebing, Robert J., xii, 33, 151, 172, 183, 184, 186, 188, 190, 218n4, 221-22n27, 232-33, 235
Behan, Brendan, 6
Bellow, Saul, 43, 212
Bersani, Leo, 63
Berthoff, Warner, 235
Big Sleep, The (Raymond Chandler), 199-200

Bloom, Harold, 179, 180, 183, 184, 185, 186, 187, 189, 190, 233
Bobby (*The Deer Park*), 49, 56, 57
Body Heat (film), 202
Booth, Wayne, 126-27
Braudy, Leo, 233
Brossard, Chandler, 146
Brown, Harry, 12
Budge, E. A. Wallis, 181
Bufithis, Philip H., 32-33, 233
Burke, Edmund, 92
Burke, Kenneth, 81

Cain, James, 200-203
Candide (Voltaire), 67
Capote, Truman, 106, 107, 108-11, 113, 115, 154-56, 158, 160
Carr, John Dickson, 192
Catch-22 (Joseph Heller), 12
Cawelti, John G., 191, 193, 196, 197, 198, 199
Chandler, Raymond, 180, 192, 196-97, 198, 199, 200, 201, 206
Chase, Richard, 39
Chaucer, 63
Cherry (*An American Dream*), 62, 63, 69, 70, 73, 204
Christie, Agatha, 192, 193, 194
Conrad, Joseph, 75
Cowan, Michael, xii
Crack-Up, The (F. Scott Fitzgerald), 87

Croft (*The Naked and the Dead*), 18-28, 217n22

Cummings (*The Naked and the Dead*), 11, 13, 15, 18-28, 195, 217n17, 217n24

Dalleson (*The Naked and the Dead*), 24

Dante, 63, 66, 67, 68, 69

Dickens, Charles, 17, 68, 81

Dickstein, Morris, 235

Didion, Joan, 93, 151, 164, 165, 166, 175, 176, 234

Disenchanted, The (Budd Schulberg), 38

Divine Comedy, The (Dante), 66, 67

D.O.A. (film), 202

Doctorow, E. L., 152, 153, 158

D. J. (*Why Are We in Vietnam?*), 74-80, 195

Dos Passos, John, 13, 15, 16, 17, 19

Double Indemnity (film), 202

Double Indemnity (James Cain), 201, 203

"Dover Beach" (Matthew Arnold), 124

Dreiser, Theodore, 164

Education of Henry Adams, The (Henry Adams), 116

Ehrlich, Robert, 233

Eisinger, Chester, 20

Eitel, Charley (*The Deer Park*), 4, 34, 36, 37, 39, 40, 41, 42, 43-46, 47, 48, 49, 50-60

Electric Kool-Aid Acid Test, The (Tom Wolfe), 113

Ellman, Richard, 10, 148

Emerson, Ralph Waldo, 164, 177

Esposito, Elena (*The Deer Park*), 4, 36, 39, 41, 43, 44, 45, 49, 50-60

Falco, Madeleine (*Tough Guys Don't Dance*), 193, 194, 200, 201, 202, 203, 204, 207

Farewell, My Lovely (Raymond Chandler), 197

Farewell to Arms, A (Ernest Hemingway), 58

Farrell, James, 13, 15

Faulkner, William, 17, 75, 80, 147, 191

Faye, Marion (*The Deer Park*), 39, 43, 45, 46-50, 57, 58, 59, 175

Fellinka, Luke (*Why Are We in Vietnam?*), 74, 75

Fetterley, Judith, 189, 235

Fielding, Henry, 17

Fitzgerald, F. Scott, 42, 87, 103, 147, 188

Flaherty, Joe, 233

Forman, Milos, 8, 209

Forster, E. M., 28

Foster, Richard, xii, 51, 83, 233, 235

Fuller, Edmund, xi

Gallagher (*The Naked and the Dead*), 16-17

Gallery, The (John Horne Burns), 12

Galloway, David, 109

Genet, Jean, 79, 140

Gide, André, 169

Gilman, Richard, 90

Godard, Jean Luc, 9

Goodman, Mitchell, 117

Gordon, Andrew, 221-22n27, 233

Great Expectations (Charles Dickens), 66, 67

Great Gatsby, The (F. Scott Fitzgerald), 42

Green Hills of Africa (Ernest
      Hemingway), 107-8, 109,
      110, 115, 159
Grella, George, 197
Guinevere (*Barbary Shore*), 32,
      33, 34
Gutman, Stanley, 70, 233

Hammett, Dashiell, 196, 197,
      198, 199, 200, 201, 206
Hardwick, Elizabeth, 62, 63, 64
Hearn (*The Naked and the
      Dead*), 15, 18-28, 218n25
Hellmann, John, 160, 235-36
Hemingway, Ernest, 42, 58, 80,
      107-8, 109, 110, 111, 112,
      115, 147, 201
Hersey, John, 12, 153, 163, 236
Hicks, Granville, 62
Hoffman, Frederick J., xi
Hollingsworth (*Barbary Shore*),
      33, 34
Hollowell, John, 236
Horn, Bernard, 218n26, 236
Howe, Irving, 34
Huston, John, 202
Huxley, Aldous, 33
Hyde, Tex (*Why Are We in
      Vietnam?*), 74, 78, 79

In Cold Blood (Truman Capote),
      107, 108-11, 115, 154-56,
      157, 158, 159, 160
In the Belly of the Beast (Jack
      Henry Abbott), 8
Into the Valley (John Hersey), 12
Irwin, John T., 183

Jethroe, Rusty (*Why Are We in
      Vietnam?*), 74, 75, 76, 77
Johnson, Samuel, 63, 67, 81
Jones, James, 12, 14-15, 146
Joyce, James, 35, 156

Kasdan, Lawrence, 202
Kaufmann, Donald L., 85,
      233, 236
Kelly, Barney Oswald, 63, 69, 73
Kermode, Frank, 138
Kernan, Alvin B., 236
Kerouac, Jack, x
Kesy, Ken, 113
King Lear (William
      Shakespeare), 9
Kuberski, Philip, 236

Langbaum, Robert, 79, 236
Lareine, Patty (*Tough Guys Don't
      Dance*), 192, 194, 196,
      199, 200, 203
Last Tycoon, The (F. Scott
      Fitzgerald), 38
Lawrence, D. H., 140, 146,
      183-84
Le Carré, John, 206
Leeds, Barry, 16, 85, 233-34
Leeds, Barry, 16, 85, 233-34
Leigh, Nigel, 221-22n27, 234
Lennon, J. Michael, xii, 127, 156,
      181, 182, 184, 234, 236
Litvak, Anatole, 202
Long Goodbye, The (Raymond
      Chandler), 200
Lowell, Robert, 118, 212
Lucid, Robert, xii, 10, 216n30,
      234, 236-37

McCord, Phyllis Frus, 174, 237
Macdonald, Ross, 206
McLeod (*Barbary Shore*), 33, 34
Madden, Dougy (*Tough Guys
      Don't Dance*), 194, 195,
      202, 205, 206, 210
Madden, Tim (*Tough Guys Don't
      Dance*), 9, 192-96, 198-99,
      200-207, 210-11
Madison, Lannie (*Barbary
      Shore*), 33, 34

Mailer, Norman

Films
Beyond the Law, 7, 209
Executioner's Song, The, ix, 8,
    167, 209-10
Maidstone, 7, 153, 209
Tough Guys Don't Dance, ix, 9,
    209, 210-11, 212
Wild 90, 7, 209

Writings
"Advertisements for Myself on
    the Way Out," 37, 87, 191
Advertisements for Myself, 3, 4,
    5, 15, 35, 37, 59, 80, 84, 85-
    88, 91, 92, 93, 94, 95, 103,
    105, 129
American Dream, An, ix, xiv, 6,
    9, 17, 34, 61, 62-74, 75, 77,
    79, 80, 129, 183, 185, 192,
    195, 201, 203, 204-7, 209
Ancient Evenings, x, xiv, 9, 17,
    72, 86, 179, 180-90, 191,
    195, 212
Armies of the Night, The, ix, x,
    1-2, 5, 7, 84, 101, 103, 104,
    105-27, 129, 130, 132, 134,
    151, 152, 153, 157, 159,
    170, 174, 191, 211, 212
Barbary Shore, xiv, 31-35, 37,
    61, 129, 185, 187, 189
"Calculus at Heaven, A," 15
Cannibals and Christians, 6,
    71, 84, 90-92, 116, 167
"David Riesman
    Reconsidered," 94
"Dead Gook, The," 35
*Deaths for the Ladies (and
    Other Disasters),* 6
Deer Park, The, xiv, 3, 4, 5,
    31-60, 106, 129, 169, 187,
    211, 212
"Dynamic of American Letters,
    The," 146

"Evaluations – Quick and
    Expensive Comments
    on the Talent in the
    Room," 146
"Evening with Jackie Kennedy,
    An," 100, 101, 103
Executioner's Song, The, ix, x,
    xiv, 8, 9, 10, 105, 130, 151-
    78, 182, 185, 195, 210-11,
    212
Existential Errands, 129, 151
Fight, The, 84, 129, 156,
    157, 179
"First Day's Interview,
    The," 90
Genius and Lust, 8, 146-49
Harlot's Ghost, 9
"Homosexual Villain, The," 94
Idol and the Octopus, The,
    38, 129
"In the Red Light," 98-99, 100,
    103, 121, 131, 134, 140
"Interview with Jackie
    Kennedy, An," 191
King of the Hill, 129
"Language of Men, The," 35
"Man Who Studied Yoga,
    The," 35-37
Marilyn: A Biography, 8, 84,
    130, 139, 142-45, 212
"Meaning of Western Defense,
    The," 94
"Metaphysics of the Belly,
    The," 94
*Miami and the Siege of
    Chicago,* 7, 84, 112-13,
    129, 130-37, 138, 139,
    145, 156
Naked and the Dead, The, xi,
    2, 5, 10, 11-29, 31, 61, 151,
    156, 180, 195, 209, 211,
    212
"Notebook, The," 35

Of a Fire on the Moon, x, 8, 84, 129, 130-34, 137-39, 145, 156, 176, 191

Of Women and Their Elegance, 9

"Paper House, The," 35

"Political Economy of Time, The," 90

Presidential Papers, The, 6, 10, 71, 84, 88-90, 92

Prisoner of Sex, The, 8, 79, 84, 130, 139-42, 145, 184

St. George and the Godfather, 84, 131, 138

"Some Children of the Goddess," 146

Some Honorable Men, 129

"Speech at Berkeley on Vietnam Day, A," 76-77

Strawhead, 9

"Superman Comes to the Supermarket," 66, 83, 89, 90, 96-97, 103, 111, 131, 142

"Ten Thousand Words a Minute," 90, 100-103, 129, 135, 138, 140, 142, 153

"Time of Her Time, The," 35, 37, 87

Tough Guys Don't Dance, xiv, 9, 10, 179, 180, 191-207, 212

Transit to Narcissus, A, 215n3

"White Negro, The," 3, 4, 5, 7, 46-48, 87, 93, 94-95, 122, 175

Why Are We in Vietnam? xiv, 6, 17, 34, 61, 62, 189, 191, 195, 212

Mailer: His Life and Times (Peter Manso), 10

Making It (Norman Podhoretz), 146

Malaquais, Jean, 32, 95

Malraux, André, ix

Manso, Peter, 10, 234

Marlowe, Christopher, 147

Marquez, Gabriel Garcia, 180

Martin, Shago (*An American Dream*), 63, 69, 205

Martinez (*The Naked and the Dead*), 16

Maté, Rudolph, 202

Melville, Herman, 2, 147, 190

Menenhetet I (*Ancient Evenings*), 182, 183, 186, 187-89, 190, 195

Menenhetet II (*Ancient Evenings*), 182, 187, 188, 189, 190

Merrill, Robert, 233, 237

Meyers, Lulu (*The Deer Park*), 42, 44, 45, 46, 52, 53, 57

Middlebrook, Jonathan, 234

Miller, Henry, 109, 110, 140, 146-49

Miller, James E., Jr., 237

Millett, Kate, 140-41

Millgate, Michael, 38, 39, 52

Mills, Hilary, 10, 234

Misfits, The (film), 144

Miss Lonelyhearts (Nathanael West), 55

Moby-Dick (Herman Melville), 13-14

Morris, Willie, 139

Mudrick, Marvin, 15

Munshin, Collie (*The Deer Park*), 39, 41, 42, 46, 52, 55, 56, 57

Muses Are Heard, The (Truman Capote), 111

Nabokov, Vladimir, 81

Nevins, Nelson (*The Deer Park*), 55

Nietzsche, Frederick, 24

Nissen, Spider (*Tough Guys Don't Dance*), 196, 197, 199, 200, 205

O'Faye, Dorothea (*The Deer Park*), 45, 56
Olster, Stacey, 237
Orwell, George, 33
O'Shaugnessy, Cassius ("The Man Who Studied Yoga"), 37
O'Shaugnessy, Sergius (*The Deer Park*), 35, 37, 39, 41, 43-46, 47, 48, 50, 52, 53, 58, 59

Paretsky, Sara, 197
Parker, Hershel, 220n2, 221-22n27, 237
Parker, Robert, 197
Performing Self, The (Richard Poirer), xiii
Phelan, James, 126
Pilgrim's Progress, The (John Bunyan), 67
Pizer, Donald, 218n26, 237
Podhoretz, Norman, 18, 25, 41, 131, 146, 237
Poirer, Richard, xii, xiii, xiv, 76, 79, 81, 186, 187, 212, 234
Polack (*The Naked and the Dead*), 17
Pond, Jessica (*Tough Guys Don't Dance*), 192, 194, 196, 200
Pope, Alexander, 63
Postman Always Rings Twice, The (James Cain), 201

Queen, Ellery, 192

Radford, Jean, 32-33, 141, 234
Ragtime (film), 8, 209
Rahv, Philip, 62, 63, 64, 67
Raleigh, John Henry, 32
Ramses II (*Ancient Evenings*), 187, 189

Rasselas (Samuel Johnson), 67
Red Harvest (Dashiell Hammett), 197
Regency, Alvin (*Tough Guys Don't Dance*), 191, 193, 194, 196, 197, 200, 201, 204, 205, 206
Richardson, Jack, 17, 133-34
Riesman, David, 174
Robbins, Harold, 38
Rojack, Stephen (*An American Dream*), 9, 62-74, 78, 195, 201, 203, 205-7
Rosy Crucifixion, The (Henry Miller), 147
Rother, James, 37, 238
Rymer, Thomas, 63

Sacks, Sheldon, 62, 66-67, 68, 74, 81
Salinger, J. D., 146
Sartre, John Paul, 79
Sayers, Dorothy, 196
Schloss, Carol, 218n26, 238
Scholes, Robert, 80
Schrader, George A., xi, 238
Sexual Politics (Kate Millett), 140
Shakespeare, William, 147
Skenazy, Paul, 201
Slovada, Eleanor ("The Man Who Studied Yoga"), 36-37
Slovada, Sam ("The Man Who Studied Yoga"), 35-37
Solotaroff, Robert, xii, xiv, 34, 57, 64, 65, 66, 67, 71, 126-27, 133, 134, 213n7, 221n20, 234-35
Sorry, Wrong Number (film), 202
Stark, John, 33
Stern, Richard, 160
Sun Also Rises, The (Ernest Hemingway), 42, 201
Swados, Harvey, xi

Tanner, Tony, xii, 111, 238
Taylor, Gordon O., 238
Telotte, J. P., 202
Teppis, Herman (*The Deer Park*),
  38, 39, 41, 42, 46, 52, 56
Thin Red Line, The (James Jones),
  12, 14-15
Thoreau, Henry David, 127, 177
Tolstoy, Leo, 164
Tom Jones (Henry Fielding), 66
Tompkins, Phillip K., 155,
  223n5,n6
Trilling, Diana, xi, 238
Tropic of Cancer (Henry Miller),
  110, 148

U.S.A. (John Dos Passos), 17

Valsen, Red (*The Naked and the
  Dead*), 18-28
Ventura, Michael, 204
Voltaire, 67, 139

Walden (Henry David
  Thoreau), 177
Waldron, Randall H., 18, 238
Walk in the Sun, A (Harry
  Brown), 12
Wallace, Irving, 38
Wardley (*Tough Guys Don't
  Dance*), 192, 194, 197,
  199, 200, 206, 207
Weatherby, W. J., 235
Welles, Orson, 105, 202
Wenke, Joseph, xii, 171, 176,
  192, 199, 204, 218n26, 235
Wilder, Billy, 202
Wilson, Raymond J., III,
  217n19, 238
Wolfe, Tom, 113, 154, 200
Wolfert, Ira, 13, 15

Yeats, William Butler, 183

Zavarzadeh, Mas'ud, 238
Zola, Emile, 35
Zolotow, Maurice, 142

The Author

Robert Merrill received his bachelor's degree from the University of Utah in 1966. He then began graduate work at the University of Chicago, where he received his M.A. in 1967 and his Ph.D. in 1971. Since 1971 he has taught at the University of Nevada, Reno, where he is currently a University Foundation Professor of English. He is the author of the first edition of *Norman Mailer* (1978) and of *Joseph Heller* (1987), also in Twayne's United States Authors Series. In 1989 he edited *Critical Essays on Kurt Vonnegut.* His essays on Shakespeare, the American romance, Norman Mailer, and many other American novelists have appeared in such journals as *Modern Language Quarterly, Modern Philology, American Literature, Modern Fiction Studies, Texas Studies in Literature and Language, Studies in American Fiction, Critique, Centennial Review,* and *New Orleans Review.* He is currently working on a book-length study of modern detective fiction. He lives in Reno with his wife, Dotson, and two cats, Angel and Pike.